BUDDHIST AND FREUDIAN PSYCHOLOGY

BUDDHIST AND FREUDIAN PSYCHOLOGY

Fourth Edition

PADMASIRI DE SILVA

Centre for Studies in Religion
School of Historical Studies
Monash University, Victoria, Australia

Foreword by
ROBERT H. THOULESS, Sc. D. (Cambridge)
Fellow of Corpus Christi College, Cambridge

SHOGAM
PUBLICATIONS

EU RP (for authorities only)
eucomply OÜ
Pärnu mnt 139b-14
11317 Tallinn, Estonia
hello@eucompliancepartner.com +3375690241

Shoga
Carlton North, Victoria, 3054
www.shogam.org

First Edition 1973
Second Edition 1978
Third Edition 1992
Fourth Edition 2010

National Library of Australia Cataloguing-in-Publication data:
de Silva, Padmasiri, 1933– .
Buddhist and Freudian Psychology / Padmasiri de Silva
New ed.
ISBN 978-0-9805022-1-3 (pbk.)
Interim CIP record.
Includes Index.
Bibliography.
1. Freud, Sigmund, 1856-1939. 2. Psychoanalysis and religion.
3. Buddhism—Psychology.
150.195

Cover design by Mila Nikko © IDEE
Cover photography *Bay of Islands* by Mike Leonard, www.lenscape.com.au
Buddha Statue by Alinta T. Giuca, www.alitangi.com

TO

Kalyani Maneesh, Adeesh and Chandeesh

Author's other works:

An Introduction to Buddhist Psychology, 4th edition, Macmillan-Palgrave, Hampshire & New York, 2005
Buddhist & Freudian Psychology, NUS Press, Singapore, 1992
Buddhism, Ethics & Society, Monash University, 1992
Twin Peaks: Compassion & Insight, Singapore Research Society, 1992
Explorers of Inner Space, Sarvodaya Vishvalekha, 2007
An Introduction to Mindfulness-Based Counselling, Sarvodaya Vishvalekha, 2008.

CONTENTS

	Abbreviations	ix
	Foreword	xi
	Preface to the First Edition	xv
	Preface to the Third Edition	xvii
	Preface to the Fourth Edition	xviii
	PRELUDE	xxiii
	The contemporary dialogue	xxiv
	New perspectives on the unconscious	xxxi
I	THE CONCEPT OF MAN	
	Humanism in early Buddhism and Freud	1
	The contemporary spiritual crisis in the West	3
II	THE CONCEPT OF MIND IN EARLY BUDDHISM AND FREUD	5
	Approaches to the study of mind	5
	Mind as a psychophysical complex	6
	The fourfold analysis of mind	9
	The concept of mind in Freud	22
	Relationship of early Buddhist and Freudian psychology	28
III	THE UNCONSCIOUS	34
	The unconscious in Freud	34
	The unconscious in early Buddhism	49
	Early Buddhist concept of unconscious in light of Freud	71

IV MOTIVATION 76
Motivation in Freud and Buddhism 76
The libido 82
Kāma-taṇhā 95
The libido and the concept of kama-taṇhā 107
The ego 110
Bhava-taṇhā 119
The ego instincts and bhava-taṇhā 127
The death instinct and bhava-taṇhā 133
Vibhava-taṇhā 140
The death instinct and vibhava-taṇhā 149
Conclusion 151

V THE THERAPEUTIC BASIS OF EARLY BUDDHIST PSYCHOLOGY 154
The roots of morality and religion 154
The moral sense according to Buddha 158
The origin of guilt according to Freud 160
Buddhist meditation and psychotherapy 163

VI THE FREUDIAN SEARCH FOR THE IDEAL THERAPEUTIC MODEL 173
A Buddhist perspective 173
Analysis, terminable and interminable 178
The dilemmas of ego psychology 183

Appendix I 187
Appendix II 204
Footnotes 219
Bibliography 238
Index 244
About the author 246

ABBREVIATIONS

A	*Anguttara-Nikāya* (Gradual Sayings), Vols. I, II and V, Translated by Woodward; Vols. III, IV, Translated by Hare, P.T.S., London, 1932-1936.
D	*Dīgha-Nikāya* (Dialogues of the Buddha), Part I, Translated by T. W. Rhys Davids; Part II, III, Translated by T. W. and Mrs. Rhys Davids, P.T.S., London, 1956-1957.
E.R.E	*Encyclopaedia of Religion and Ethics*, editor, James Hastings, N. York and Edinburgh, 1910-27.
M	*Majjhima-Nikāya* (Middle Length Sayings), Vols. I, II and III, Translated by I.B. Horner, P.T.S., London, 1954-1959.
S	*Samyutta-Nikāya* (Kindred Sayings), Part I and II, Translated by Mrs. Rhys Davids; Parts III, IV, V, Translated by Woodward.
SE	*The Standard Edition of the Complete Psychological Works of Sigmund Freud*, Translated from German under the general editorship of James Strachey, Hogarth Press, London, 1953.

FOREWORD

When, in 1940, I was invited to give the Riddell Memorial Lectures at Durham University, one of the topics I dealt with was the parallelism between the point of view of Freud and that of early Buddhism.[1] My interest in this matter gives me special reason for welcoming Dr. de Silva's much more thorough treatment of the subject made with a much better knowledge than I had of Buddhist thought. I am encouraged to find that my preliminary suggestions seem to have been on right lines and I am glad to find the matter more fully elucidated by the present work.

The parallelism between the thought of Freud and the teachings of Buddhism does not necessarily imply that Freud had any direct knowledge of Buddhist writings. There is certainly a possibility of indirect influence. Freud knew the writings of Hartmann who was much influenced by Schopenhauer who was himself influenced by Buddhism. Such indirect influence may have been present although I do not know of any evidence of it from Freud's own writings. Whether there was such indirect influence or not, I do not think it is the main factor in such parallelism as may be found between the thought of Freud and the teaching of the Buddha. More important, I think, is the fact that both were dealing with the same sort of problem from a somewhat similar (but not identical) point of view.

Freud's point of view was that of scientific medicine. Scientific medicine had one obvious characteristic in common with Buddhism: that it was concerned with the salvation of men from suffering. In this respect it diverged from the Jewish-Christian tradition of accepting salvation from sin as the central purpose of its system.

A second respect (originally pointed out by Mrs. Rhys Davids) in which medical science shared the point of view of Buddhism rather than that of the surrounding Christian culture was in its acceptance of the principle of cause and effect even with respect to the results of human actions. This would seem to be essentially the same as the Buddhist principle of dependent origination and it led to similar implications for behaviour. The surgeon who pricked himself accidentally with a septic scalpel did not deal with the situation by repenting of his action; he dealt with it by applying antiseptics to the wound or dosing himself with antibiotics. One might say that, in this situation, he was behaving more as a Buddhist than as a Christian. In the wider application of this principle of scientific causation, the aim of medical science was to discover the nature of the various diseases, their causes, the methods of their cure, and the remedies that led to their cure. This, in the restricted field of organic illnesses, is a programme closely parallel to the Buddha's four noble truths concerning suffering.

The orthodox medical science of the nineteenth century differed, however, from the Buddhist tradition in the fact that it recognised as causes of illness only physical causes, such as the presence of pathogenic organisms in the blood stream, or the injury or malfunctioning of some physical organ such as the heart or liver. In the face of such diseases as hysteria, where there appeared to be no physical cause, the medical science of that period could offer no understanding that could lead to cure. Freud's great contribution to medical science was that he recognised and studied the mental causation of such disorders and introduced mental methods of treating them. If free-association on a psychoanalyst's couch is a somewhat different process from the Buddhist meditation practice, it can be regarded as being directed towards the same end: that of getting rid of the mental causes of suffering.

There is, of course, a marked difference between the radicalism of the treatment in the two cases. Freud was content with an aim that was considerably less than 'the destruction, in which no passion remains, of this very thirst; the laying aside of, the getting rid of, the being free from, the harbouring no longer of this thirst'.[2] This difference is expressed by Dr. de Silva when he says that all that Freud could do was to translate 'hysterical misery into common unhappiness'. One can speculate on the possibility of a future development of the therapy based on psychoanalysis to do more than this, to produce a radical mental reorientation that led to the complete disappearance of internal sources of unhappiness. If such a development of psycho-therapy did take place, one can predict that it is likely to demand more time and energy than those of the few hours per week taken up by psychoanalysis. It is more likely to be a life-long activity as is that of those striving for the final achievement of the Buddhist saint.

Victorian scientists had also deviated from traditional Christian ways of thought in their evaluation of sin and of the sense of guilt. Whereas the sense of sin had been highly valued (particularly in the Puritan tradition of Christianity) the Victorian scientists tended to regard it as unimportant. Freud carried this change further by treating the sense of guilt as something pathological, and regarding it as the duty of the psychotherapist to relieve his patients of it if they suffered from such guilt feeling. H. G. Wells expressed the new attitude towards sin when he said: 'The modern man is not worrying about his sins'.[3] The men of Wells's time had not, of course, ceased to worry, but their worries were about other things than their sins, and these other worries included their internal sources of unhappiness. The end result of such dissatisfactions was to drive them to the consulting room of the psychoanalyst or other psychotherapist, where, if they had a sense of guilt, the psychotherapist would try to relieve them of it.

There were, of course, differences between the point of view of the Buddha and that of Freud. One of the most striking of these was that Freud was concerned only with giving his patients sufficient peace and inner harmony to enable them to carry on the business of the present life; the Buddha aimed at relieving his disciples from the burden of suffering for both the present life and future lives.

The aim of Freud was necessarily confined to the present life since the idea of future lives was altogether alien to the tradition of scientific medicine which he inherited. The tradition rejected not only the idea of a continuing soul which was, of course, also denied by the Buddha. It also rejected the idea of any kind of existence after bodily death, either of immortality or of reincarnation. The second of these ideas would be even more alien to Freud's thought than the first. Immortality was an element of the Christian tradition which was very commonly denied by men of science, whereas the idea of reincarnation was not even a live issue since it was neither a part of the western religious tradition nor of its scientific tradition. Reincarnation has not been regarded as a possible subject of study by western science until very recent times when it began to be studied by Dr. Ian Stevenson.[4]

If it is not generally accepted in the European and American culture system; it has ceased to be a dead issue. This however, had not happened at the time of Freud's death; when he wrote, the incarnation hypothesis would not have been considered a serious possibility by a European scientist. Yet, as Dr. de Silva suggests, Freud's idea of the collective unconscious plays something of the same part in explaining present mental dispositions as does the karmic after-effect of past lives in Buddhist psychology.

There are clearly both parallelisms and divergences between the teachings of Freud and those of the Buddha. In the present book, Dr. de Silva has discussed these with much more exact knowledge of the Buddhist teachings than I have. It gives me pleasure to commend his work to those interested in this subject.

Cambridge, September 19th, 1972
Robert H. Thouless

PREFACE TO THE FIRST EDITION

Some students of philosophy are occasionally struck by the apparent aridity of the philosophical puzzles that baffle professional philosophers. It was in such a mood that I dipped a little into the fresh pastures that lie at the outer periphery of the philosophical world. This is a factor that brought me into contact with the work of Sigmund Freud—the fascinating explorer of the underworld of human impulses and human behaviour in general. As I became acquainted with Freud's work, I discovered to my satisfaction, that a number of philosophers had at that time already examined the conceptual framework of Freudian theory.

This project for a comparative study of Buddhist and Freudian psychology could never have been worked out in this manner but for the encouragement, guidance and assistance I received at the Department of Philosophy, University of Hawaii, where I pursued my research for three years.

I should like to express my thanks to the East-West Centre for granting me a scholarship that enabled me to pursue this work as a graduate student. The fundamental aim of the Centre is to 'foster understanding and mutual respect among people from differing cultures working together in seeking solutions to common problems'. The programme in comparative philosophy which I followed in Hawaii touches the ideological base of such intercultural issues. I earnestly hope that this little book will remain as a tangible expression of the kind of vision envisaged in the basic aims of the East-West Centre.

This book is a revised and reconstructed development of the theses that were submitted in partial fulfilment of the degrees of M.A. and Ph.D. in philosophy. It is my pleasant duty to thank the following who served in the committees that examined these theses: Prof. Winfield Nagley, Prof. Harold McCarthy, Prof. S. K. Saksena, Prof. Kenneth K. Inada and Prof. R. P. Haynes (Department of Philosophy), Prof. John M. Digman and Prof. Collin J. Herrick (Department of Psychology) and Prof.

Walter H. Maurer (Department of Languages). I also owe a great deal to fellow-students who participated in some lively and stimulating seminars on philosophical psychology.

It is with a deep sense of gratitude that I acknowledge the many valuable suggestions and comments made by the late Prof. K. N. Jayatilleke, of the University of Ceylon, who evinced a very keen interest in this project.

It is not possible to name the wide array of authors whose writings helped me to clarify my own ideas on the subject. Out of them, two works need special mention: *Psychoanalysis and Zen Buddhism*, ed. Erich Fromm and others, and *Buddhist Psychology of Perception*, E. R. Sarachchandra. While Fromm's writings became an inspiring source for my thinking, I must say that in spite of the rather critical stance I have adopted towards Sarachchandra's work, it did stimulate me to work on the psychological aspects of motivational theory in early Buddhism.

A special word of appreciation is due to Prof. R. H. Thouless who patiently read the manuscript and wrote a very timely foreword to this book. Mr. G. J. Yorke, Literary Advisor at George Allen & Unwin, made some valuable comments in the revision of an early draft of this work.

I am thankful to the University of Ceylon (Peradeniya Campus) Research Committee for granting me a sum of Rs. 400/- to cover the expenses incurred in typing the manuscript. Mr. Doreswamy did an excellent job in typing this work, and Mr. Godwin Samararatne ungrudgingly helped me by reading the proofs and making some useful comments.

The publication of this work would have been indefinitely postponed but for the personal interest taken by Mr Nissanka Wijeyeratne, Secretary, Ministry of Cultural Affairs, and the other officials of the Department for the financial assistance granted towards this publication.

I must also thank Mr H. Amarasinghe and Mr G. M. B. Herat of Lake House Investments Ltd. who took a very keen interest in the publication of this work.

M. W. P. de Silva
Department of Philosophy
University of Ceylon Peradeniya, Ceylon

PREFACE TO THE THIRD EDITION

Buddhist and Freudian Psychology has already gone through two editions and it is gratifying to discover there is again a need for another edition. In fact, today I find an even richer intellectual climate to place the new edition before the readers. First, there has been among the psychologists during recent times an emerging interest in the spiritual and philosophical traditions of the East which contain psychological reflections and insights. This interest is quite evident from a number of conferences held during recent times on psychology East and West as well as a few good anthologies in this area.

Secondly, due to these interests, the course content of studies undertaken in departments of philosophy, religion, psychology and sociology and cross-cultural and comparative psychologies do show various attempts to integrate these emerging concerns to regular teaching. Thirdly, in certain clinical settings, the interest in Buddhist meditation techniques and related doctrinal concepts has been quite evident. Perhaps in the near future, a process of cross-fertilisation across the cultural and philosophical concerns of East and West will generate more interest in the psychologies of the East. Finally, for the student of Buddhism, the psychological orientation of Buddhism will be a central concern. A companion to this work is my *Introduction to Buddhist Psychology*, which has also been released in a new edition by the Macmillan Press. Together, *Buddhist and Freudian Psychology*, and this introduction to Buddhist psychology offer to the reader the central psychological concerns of a rich ancient tradition.

I am very happy to help the publishers to bring out a new edition, with an additional new chapter. I am also glad that the book will be available for interested readers again.

PREFACE TO THE FOURTH EDITION

The first two editions of this work were published in Sri Lanka and the third in Singapore. I am delighted that Kagyu E-Vam Buddhist Institute and Shogam Publications are publishing a fourth edition of *Buddhist and Freudian Psychology* in Australia and I thank them for their interest. Australia has been my second home, having left Sri Lanka many years ago, and I have profited from the dialogues and conferences on the relevance of developing a Buddhist counselling program held in Australia.

Though *Buddhist and Freudian Psychology* emerged out of my research in Buddhist philosophy and psychology, the work has interested many therapists over the years. And after receiving the qualifications and training as a counsellor during recent times, I felt a renewed interest in the present book and in relating it to the new dialogues on Buddhism and psychotherapy. Also, though today the practitioners of cognitive behaviour therapy have greatly increased, many practitioners of multifaceted therapies do still use the psychodynamic model, and the work of Sigmund Freud is certainly a remarkable and fascinating chapter in the history of therapy.

However, there is an emerging dialogue between Buddhism and psychotherapy, greatly articulated in the book *Buddhism and Psychotherapy: Across Cultures, a collection of essays on theories and practices* (Mark Unno (ed.) 2006, Wisdom Publishers, Boston). Buddhism and psychoanalysis are 'beginning to intersect in remarkable ways', and this dialogue has generated to 'new depths and subtleties'. I have located the present edition of *Buddhist and Freudian Psychology* within the context of this emerging dialogue by adding a new introduction to the present book.

There is also additional material on the new perspectives of the nature of the subliminal/unconscious in Buddhism, as well as a fascinating reference to a Sutta on 'Defence Mechanisms' in Buddhist thought.

I am also grateful to Jack Engler for the celebrated phrase, 'You first need to become somebody before you become nobody', an aphorism that generated a dialogue for years. Last, but not least, being introduced to the writings of Mark Epstein during my training in the Buddhist psychotherapy program of Sophia College, Perth and having read a number of his books over the years, I was amazed at how he has brought back the insights of Freud and the dialogue with Buddhism with a remarkable freshness.

I am greatly indebted to Traleg Kyabgon Rinpoche for introducing me to this new dialogue within the course of the Buddhism and Psychotherapy conference recently held in Healesville, Australia. I also wish to thank the Shogam publishers for undertaking to bring out this new edition. This work has gone out of print, and perhaps there is a new generation of therapists and general readers who may enjoy reading the book for both its insights on Buddhist psychology and therapy.

Padmasiri de Silva
Faculty of Historical Studies
and the Centre for Religion & Theology
Monash University, Victoria, Australia
pdesilva@alphalink.com.au

Post-script: I have supplemented the original bibliography with a number of new titles for this edition. As the new chapter has a central focus on issues pertaining to the 'self' in Buddhism and psychotherapy, I have included some coverage on issues pertaining to the self with which I have got immersed over the years. Also, the work on philosophical analysis and Freud cited in this new bibliography (*The Analytic Freud*, ed. Michael P. Levine) offers new horizons for 'demonstrating the fertility of Freud's thought in several key topics in the philosophy of mind and moral philosophy' (John Cuttingham). There is a perennial interest in the thought of the Buddha and Freud and this revival of interest in Freud, and also in Buddhism and psychotherapy present us with number of reasons to offer a new edition of *Buddhist and Freudian Psychology*.

NOTES OF OPTIMISM AND PESSIMISM

'Looking back, then, over the patchwork of my life's labours, I can say that I have made many beginnings and thrown out many suggestions. Something will come of them in the future, though I cannot myself tell whether it will be much or little. I can, however, express a hope that I have opened up a pathway for an important advance in our knowledge.'
—Freud

'I have not the courage to rise up before my fellow men as a prophet, and bow to the reproach that I can offer them no consolation: for at bottom that is what they are all demanding—the wildest revolutionaries no less passionately than the most virtuous believers.' —Freud

PRELUDE

THE CURRENT DIALOGUE BETWEEN BUDDHISM AND PSYCHOTHERAPY

Many decades back, as I entered the precincts of the University of Hawaii to embark on a comparative study of Buddhist and Freudian psychology, the area of Buddhist psychology and therapy were relatively new. The only study that gave me some idea in this field was *Zen and Psychoanalysis*, with writings from Erich Fromm, D.T. Suzuki and R. de Martino (Fromm, 1960). My work was a labour of love exploring the material in the Buddhist Sutta literature and the complete works of Sigmund Freud. The final publication of *Buddhist and Freudian Psychology* was well received both within and outside Sri Lanka.

While the excitement of this project lasted for some time, and I added several new chapters to the second and third editions (published by NUS, Singapore, 1992), it was during the period that I completed the Sophia College examinations for counselling and Buddhist psychotherapy that I encountered a veritable mine of ideas in the work of Mark Epstein: *Thoughts without A Thinker*, (Epstein, 1992), *Going to Pieces Without Falling Apart* (Epstein, 1998), *Going on Being* (Epstein, 2001), and more recently *Psychotherapy Without a Self: A Buddhist Perspective* (Epstein, 2007). Another important document was a posthumous publication of Erich Fromm, *The Art of Listening*.

During a number of years before his death, Erich Fromm was in regular correspondence with the Buddhist monk Venerable Nyanaponika, and his influence on Fromm is cited in this book.[1] Fromm often felt that divested of the issues pertaining to sexuality and libido, Freud's paper 'On Narcissism' had profound insights, as does the controversial work, 'Beyond the Pleasure Principle', and it is for these reasons and the revival of interest in psychotherapy and cross-cultural issues that I felt a new edition of *Buddhist and Freudian Psychology* would be useful.

Though in my clinical practice I have more often used the mindfulness-based cognitive therapy approach (de Silva, 2008), psychodynamic theory (which was part of the Sophia College training) comes in useful at the most unexpected moments in therapy and life, and in the book on counselling, I have many references to Freud.

THE CONTEMPORARY DIALOGUE BETWEEN PSYCHOTHERAPY AND BUDDHISM

There has been a recent revival of interest in the cross-cultural interaction between Buddhism and psychotherapy (Unno, 2006).

> Both Buddhism and psychotherapy are cultural institutions that originally developed as expressions of the values and the complex tensions and contradictions within their cultures of origins. Both are systems of healing that have evolved over time as culture has evolved, as the configurations of the self have evolved, and as new cultures have. Both have transformed the cultures in which they evolved, as the configurations of the self have evolved, and as new cultures have assimilated them.[2]

Discussing the tensions and apparent contradictions in this dialogue, Jack Engler makes ten interesting points, out of which I shall discuss the most central ones. Engler raises a preliminary question in terms of a query made by Harvey Aronson, 'Why is it that meditation, in the absence of psychotherapy or personal work, does not prevent or reduce mental anguish for some people?'[3]

Engler also observes that personal work in one area of life does not automatically transfer into other areas in life. However, Mark Epstein presents a somewhat different perspective. From my own background, I would say that practising counselling, having a commitment to a Buddhist lifestyle and being a meditator are facets of my life that enrich each other. I have experiential grounds for this position and I have carried over these ideas to my teaching of Buddhist ethics and psychology and when conducting workshops for Buddhists.

During the time of the Buddha, therapy was not a live profession, though the Buddha's advice contains rich material for therapy from a contemporary perspective. I do not think it is possible to adjudicate upon the relative roles of meditation and therapy. Even in western cultures, especially Australia with its rich multicultural community, the experiences of therapists, clients and meditators vary and specific contexts are crucial in this discussion.

Jack Engler, examining both the perils and the promises of the spiritual path in the context of the practice of psychotherapy, observes that our practice and that of our clients 'is not immune from our personal history, our character, our inner conflicts, and our defensive styles.'[4] In detailed instructions on how to engage in Buddhist meditation practice, the teacher advises the student to 'focus on the present'. It is also expected that the student leave the past with its little dramas and personal history aside and not project too much onto the future. Jack Engler and a number of others using Buddhist techniques in psychotherapy have raised a number of issues to which I am attempting to make a response from my own background, both as a teacher of Buddhist philosophy and psychology and as a practising meditator and counsellor.

PROMISES AND PERILS OF THE SPIRITUAL PATH

1) According to Engler, the quest for perfection and invulnerability is a western narcissistic ideal. Mark Epstein, following the celebrated saying by Engler, 'You have to be somebody before you can be nobody', and discussing Engler's claim that western students of eastern spiritual traditions who 'jumped into meditation with little preparation sometimes experienced emotional distress', makes some significant deviations from Engler.[5] Engler's view was that psychotherapy may be seen as a prelude to spiritual work. While Engler did later question himself about this stand (Engler, 2003), Epstein, in offering another perspective, thinks his experience is different:

> Meditation helped me to come to grips with various narcissistic issues before I had any real therapy, helping me to become somebody.[6]

He was initially immersed in Buddhist meditation and then pursued the career of a psychotherapist. By the time he had shifted to psychotherapy, he had perhaps developed a very mature outlook on identity issues. Some psychotherapists feel that it is an anomaly in western culture that individuals with narcissistic vulnerabilities tend to gravitate towards spiritual disciplines. But this need not be true of only western cultures. A very balanced view on these issues, acceptable to both Engler and Epstein, may be that a prerequisite level of personality organisation is necessary for meditation/therapy. But if you look at the subtleties of the inroads of conceit on the Buddhist path to liberation, we may agree with Epstein that:

> Just as this narcissistic residue reverberates throughout the life circle, affecting goals, aspirations and interpersonal relationships, so it can be seen to reverberate throughout the meditative path, where psychic structures derived from this infantile experience must be, at various times, gratified, confronted or abandoned.[7]

He also says that the Buddhist ideal of perfection (*arahat*), representing the fruition of meditative practice, provides a means by which the narcissistic remnants that inevitably persist are seized and redirected.[8] I think it is necessary to contextualise the many sided aspects of this debate. One of the living arahats, Achariya Mahabowa in Thailand, says that in the final state of being an arahat, he feels at one with all other humans, and a sense of humility and oneness with others pervades.

Looking at my personal experience, first as a philosopher and then as a therapist, for me the Buddhist liberation quest was my primary concern. But during a crisis period, a short encounter with therapy gave me the confidence that I could take charge of my life, and it is the regular practice of meditation and mindfulness in daily life that gave me a firm footing of confidence. Secondly, the way I understood the essence of the moral basis (*sīla*) of our lives was important, not as legalistic precepts but in understanding the positive ideals of compassion, in respecting what belongs to others and having appreciative joy about the success of others, in contentment, in a sane and balanced lifestyle with a strong footing in the family, in transparency to one's self in word, thought and deed, and, as far as possible while enjoying cooking and a good meal, in avoiding food and drinks that disturb the practice of mindfulness.

This was the royal road to sanity, but the practice of therapy, and especially four years of free counselling for people with problems, opened up vistas of compassion, empathy, generosity and a sense of attunement with the world and one's self. I think the practice of counselling has enriched my understanding of Buddhism and my reflections and research on Buddhist psychology have enriched my practice of counselling. Thus there are many and varied answers to the questions raised by Engler and due contextualisation may help to see each issue in its proper setting. Though I have lived in Australia as a migrant from Sri Lanka for fifteen years, the family, Sri Lankan community and the Buddhist temple contributed to the attunement and connectedness within me to the world. This is the message I take to the Parliament of World Religions taking place in Melbourne and to the panel I am participating in, 'Strangers in a Strange Land'.

2) A fear of individuation, for taking responsibility and being assertive and competent, may be avoided through a defensive pursuit of the ideal 'selflessness'. At the doctrinal level, there need not be a problem about 'individuation' (*attabhāva*) which is often glossed over due to the spelling of the doctrine of *anattā*. The psychological wholeness and coherence of each person as distinct from the state of being split and fragmented may vary. The idea of not-self does not deny that each person has an individual character. The Buddhist concept of individuation leaves room for the diversity of character. The Buddha respected this point in prescribing certain forms of meditation that suit the individual.

As my meditation teacher Venerable Uda Eriyagama Dhammajiva says, the recommended meditation exercises were 'not obtainable over the counter' but depended on the prescription of the Buddha. In looking at the five hindrances, the Buddha realised that the domination of each of these varies from person to person, and he even presented a picture of personalities located in the different roots of greed, hatred and delusion. There is also great variety in the personalities of those who attained the state of perfection.

3) Avoidance of responsibility and accountability. According to Engler, the goal of freeing oneself from egocentric desires may result in the avoidance of anxiety producing situations, taking responsibility and

being in charge of one's life. In doctrinal Buddhism, freedom, karmic correlation and 'serial individuality' give meaning and direction to the notion of responsibility and the focus on mindfulness in daily life is important. In my own work—mindfulness based counselling often using the framework of cognitive-behaviour therapy—mindfulness in daily life is crucial in getting people to manage their problems with clarity and perspective, and especially in dealing with issues like addictions and making the client first 'take charge of his or her life'. There is a great deal of misunderstanding on this issue and Rubin, for instance, says, 'in throwing out the bath water of egocentricity, Buddhism eliminates the baby of human agency'.[9]

Rubin has missed the distinction about the 'conventional self' which helps to accept the idea of agency and the self in a more ultimate sense, accepting the full implications of the *anattā* doctrine.

Aronson has located a number of tension points between western practice and Buddhist therapeutic advocacy. Among them is the emphasis on individuality in the west and the Asian emphasis on interdependence. These tension points are important in looking at both the theory and the practice of Buddhist psychotherapy, and culture-specific issues have to be duly contextualised (Aronson, 2004).

4) The stance of 'non-attachment' can rationalise fear and anxieties associated with intimacy, feelings of being exposed, estrangement and loneliness. This becomes a difficult issue if we do not have the right balance between meditating in solitude and developing mature relations like that of the '*kalyāṇa mitta*' (friendship in the spiritual context) or if we do not participate in Buddhist community gatherings including social work or if, as lay people, we do not follow the ideals of family life laid down in the *Sigālovāda Sutta.* The meditation teacher would always be open to communication and discussion. The practice of loving-kindness, compassion, appreciative joy and equanimity emphasises the interconnectedness of beings. Buddhist migrants in Australia who come for therapy always find the family gives them great strength and confidence.

5 In the case of grief and mourning, Engler says that mindfulness practice may dissociate a person from feelings of real loss, confusion and sadness or acknowledge them from a safe distance. I wish to cite the observations of two therapists who have worked on grief from a Buddhist perspective, and thirdly cite my personal contribution to understanding

and managing grief. Sameet Kumar from a study of grieving mindfully makes the following observations:

> By being aware of grief rather than ignoring or denying it, and by working to understand what drives this pain, you can release yourself into the person you are and the person you want to be. In other words, with mindfulness-awareness of grief, you can move closer to the people in your life who matter most, and change habits or ideas that have been keeping you from living fully. Full awareness, especially in your grief… can take you from living with misery and discontent to living with openness and passion.[10]

Ladner in his book, *The Lost Art of Compassion*, says that when dealing with grief and love, we need to move away from the exclusive focus on pathology in the west that has dominated western psychology; we try to repair the damage rather than aim at positive health.[11] I have written a personal narrative on how I used the four divine states of loving-kindness, compassion, altruistic joy and equanimity as methods that helped me to transform the experience of grief into a transforming and liberating experience. Equanimity is the balancing factor. Dedication through gratitude very much rooted in the Thai and Sri Lankan traditions is a Buddhist pathway for responding to grief.[12] In Australia, both Sri Lankan and other migrant communities have developed techniques to deal with grief and even the grief counselling offered by those with a more western orientation presents a diversity of approaches, as was evident to me in participating in a C.A.P.A.V group session on grief management.

Certain cultures provide culturally positive ways of dealing with grief. Catherine Lutz's study of the emotions of grief, sadness and compassion in the Ifaluk atoll in the Pacific explains how they used this culture specific concept of *fago*, which is a 'thick' concept that at the same time covers compassion, love and sadness. In this culture, there is an automatic and durable link between the suffering of one person and nurturing by others.[13]

6) Avoidance of feeling. Engler cites examples of clients who had problems with anger management. Whether it is west or east, this is one of the most important concerns that emerges in both therapy and medita-

tion practice. As Engler says:

> The labelling of aversive emotions as 'defilements' or as 'unwholesome' in Buddhist practice can lead to thinking that the goal is not to feel any disturbing emotion, and then feel guilty if you do.[14]

While it is easy to deal with this kind of issue in therapy using 'the non-judgemental and acceptance of feelings approach', teachers of meditation have to be very clear about this issue. My own approach is to accept that anger and related emotions like *kodha, kopa, dosa* and ill-will (*vyāpadā*) are hindrances, and *patigha* (*anusaya*) are unwholesome at the level of *sīla* (morality), but in the meditation setting—especially perhaps more so in insight meditation—one 'changes gears' so that the anger is neither good nor bad, yours nor mine, and it is a process which emerges, stays for a while and passes away.

In *dhammanupassanā*, the meditator makes the anger an object of meditation; in *cittanupassanā*, like in mindfulness-based cognitive therapy the meditator becomes aware of the thought components and the auto-pilot process that feeds anger; in *vedanānupassanā*, one 'puts on the brakes' at the initial emergence of disagreeable feelings (*dukkha vedanā*) and does not let it develop into anger. In tranquillity meditation, the development of a state of bodily and mental calm may temporarily push the anger aside, but it may not radically deal with its roots. In *kāyanupassanā*, which is focused on the body and is the preliminary meditation in the Buddhist fourfold scheme (*satipaṭṭhana*), we develop attention towards a very central ingredient of negative emotions and body-reactivity.

In this context, tranquillity meditation too can be effective. In the last analysis, it is necessary to have in mind that Buddhism has no generic term for emotion, and it is an initial feeling (*vedanā*) that becomes an emotion. And as such, an emotion is a construction composed of an initial bodily/mental feeling which is pleasurable/painful/neutral and which, by the addition of thoughts, appraisals, desires/craving, grasping and physiological arousal gets converted to an emotion. In my *viveka* program for healing emotions, I used all these different facets of an emotion to direct mindfulness/reflection in the client as meditator.

I think the issues raised by Engler are important and he has selected certain crucial issues for reflection, especially for those who practise therapy, whether it is the west or the east. Out of the ten issues cited by him, I have selected the most important issues for comments and reflection. This response reflects my own background and training.

There is one more point I would like to raise before I complete this prelude. Independent of whether we are therapists, meditators or both, there is a strange dialectic about these paradoxes of identity. While it is necessary to have some sense of personality organisation, the paradoxes and apparent contradictions about the self provide a good setting for the practice of insight meditation.

NEW PERSPECTIVES ON THE UNCONSCIOUS IN FREUD AND BUDDHISM

While I still value all the concepts and comparative perspectives that appeared in my work *Buddhist and Freudian Psychology*, throughout the long period from its first appearance to its third edition, there has been one important change in the way I have used the notion of the unconscious, partly from my practice of counselling that has been greatly influenced by mindfulness-based cognitive therapy and partly from a new reading of certain relevant Sutta passages.

THE ARCHAEOLOGICAL METAPHOR

As Oatley says:

> The archaeological metaphor was one of Freud's favourites. Once one had brought one's disowned intentions to consciousness, it would be possible to take responsibility for them, and in that movement we could be free of their tyranny over us.[15]

Oatley also says that Tim Beck, who started working as a psychoanalytic therapist and then moved into cognitive behaviour therapy, shifted his stance to consider that these thoughts, 'hovered at a threshold between the conscious and the unconscious' and not at the very deep levels of the Freudian unconscious, and thus, to find the instigators of anxieties, depression and bad moods, one does not have to excavate long-buried conflicts, but rather look at the auto-pilot within us, the incessant thoughts from moment to movement: thus look at them and consider whether they are logical, arbitrary inferences, selective abstractions, magnifying a selected incident, personalising and polarised thinking into black and white categories. While this is the road that cognitive therapy took, gradually MBCT (mindfulness-based cognitive therapy) was born. Mindfulness-based cognitive approaches focus on changing one's relationship to cognitions and attention rather than changing the contents of the thoughts themselves. Similar perspectives have also entered the stream of psychoanalytic thought, especially that of Mark Epstein:

> Yet in Buddhism—and even in more recent psychoanalytic schools—there has emerged a different model, one that is less about digging and more about opening. At the root of this difference lies an alternative view of the unconscious.[16]

Epstein cites an interesting Tibetan story that captures in a beautiful way the new perspectives on the unconscious. A woman named Manibhadra, who was engaged in advanced meditation, was carrying water from the village to her home and one day dropped the pitcher so that the water gushed out onto the ground. The broken pitcher served as a powerful model for meditation for her and she was suddenly liberated:

> This jarring loose, or breaking free—this going to pieces without falling apart—is what Buddhism acknowledges as one of the self's secret needs to be released from a belief in absolute reality.[17]

The metaphor of opening up rather than digging in, apart from generating awareness and acceptance of any emotions labelled as negative emotions or defilements, also opens up a more creative dimension for the untapped reservoirs of life:

> Most people live, whether physically, intellectually or mor-

ally, in a very restricted circle of their potential being. They make use of a very small portion of their possible consciousness. We all have reservoirs in life to draw upon, of which we do not dream.[18]

SUBLIMINAL PROCLIVITIES (ANUSAYA)

In writing this chapter, I have charted out a new line of describing the levels of the architecture of the mind which I described as 'unconscious' in the text *Buddhist and Freudian Psychology* (1992), partly due to my fascination with the Freudian model. But all the valuable material I have presented in this book on mind and motivation are not greatly affected by this innovation. The proclivities towards lust, anger and conceit are more like 'sleeping passions' that may wake up due to certain triggers and invade us in a quick impulsive manner.

Recent studies by Joseph Ledoux (Ledoux, 1996) on the emotion of fear, indicate such a context. A man walking on a lonely forest track tramples on dry twigs and is subject to the flight or fight response, where he is about to run, thinking it is a rattlesnake. In such contexts, the central nervous system has been hijacked by the amygdala, and then impulsive action follows. In normal circumstances, the CNS processes the information and this provides the basis for action. Such tendencies to fear or anger may lie at a subliminal/dormant level (*anusaya bhūmi*); they may emerge as thought processes (*pariyuṭṭhāna-bhūmi*) or they may become fierce and ungovernable and result in impulsive actions (*vītikkama-bhūmi*).

DEFENCE MECHANISMS IN FREUD AND BUDDHISM

Erich Fromm rediscovered the importance of Freud's paper 'On Narcissism' and observed, 'Perhaps this principle is nowhere expressed more radically than in Buddhism'.[19] J.C. Flugel recognised Freud's 'Beyond the Pleasure Principle' and described it as a, 'short but immensely pregnant work'.[20] In the same way, Freud's daughter Anna Freud felt her father's writings on defence mechanisms are important. These reflections are found in her *The Ego and the Mechanisms of Defence*.

Joseph Goldstein, in reflecting on the 'mindful awareness' of emotions, says that very often we are not aware as to 'what emotion is present before us', partly because they have no clear boundaries and partly as they often come in constellations (Goldstein, 1993). Also, there is no constant awareness of what is wholesome or unwholesome. Thus it is necessary to recognise each emotion as it arises. But people also try to cover up what is painful or unflattering, to repress it, avoid and deny it, or let it emerge in a distorted and disguised manner.

Sigmund Freud made a detailed analysis of these distortions and escape routes and called them 'defence mechanisms': repression, aggression, projection, regression, compensation, denial, isolation, rationalisation and reaction formation, while sublimation may be healthy. Some of these mechanisms are cited in relation to the religious life in the discourses of the Buddha, though this is going back twenty-six centuries in time. Analogically, it is like a soldier using a shield as defence, or using a mask, or techniques of camouflage. While the Buddha's analysis is directly addressed to the monks, it may be easily extended to laymen.

1 *Repression*: When monks reprove a fellow monk for committing an offence, the reproved monk pleads forgetfulness, 'I don't remember'.
2 *Aggression*: When monks reprove a fellow monk for committing an offence, the reproved monk gets angry and says, 'What right have you to talk, you stupid fool'?
3 *Projection*: When monks reprove a fellow monk for an offence, the reproved monk says, 'It is you that committed the offence'.
4 *Regression*: When monks reprove a fellow monk for an offence, the reproved monk when reproved evades the question and reverts to childlike disorganised behaviour.
5 *Compensation*: When monks reprove a fellow monk for an offence, the reproved monk tries to drown out this talk; he talks with a lot of gesticulation in the assembly and tries to cut a figure.
6. *Isolation*: When monks reprove a fellow monk for an offence, the reproved monk tries to disregard it and isolates himself from the problem.
7 *Denial*: When monks reprove a fellow monk for an offence, the reproved monk says that he is not guilty and not concerned about it at all.

8 *Physical isolation*: When monks reprove a fellow monk for an offence, the reproved monk says they need not worry about him at all and gives up being a monk.

While I am indebted to the late Rune Johanson, the Danish psychologist, for this reference to the suttas (Johanson, 1983), I have mentioned two other additional ones in my writings.[21] The Buddha rejected the way of extreme asceticism as an alternative to the way of sensuality, and offered the middle path, as this move towards self-mortification is a reaction-formation. Wholesome sublimation is the only technique that may be recommended as it is the redirection of energy into a different goal. Self-centered desires may be eliminated by a desire to end desire (*taṇhām nidsaya taṇhām pahātabbam*). It is a higher order desire. One of the differences with Freud is that for the Buddhist these mechanisms function close to ordinary life at the subliminal rather than at the level of the deeper Freudian unconscious.

I

THE CONCEPT OF MAN

HUMANISM IN EARLY BUDDHISM AND FREUD

The analysis of motivational theory presented here has to be viewed against the background of the spirit of 'humanism' found both in the Pāli texts of early Buddhism and also the works of Sigmund Freud. It is the deep sense of humanism in these works that gives meaning and purpose to a comparative study. The Buddha did not claim any special authority derived from an omnipotent being or any external power. The attainment of Buddhahood was for him the finest flower of the potentialities within man. It is human energy and human effort that helped him to discover a solution for the ills of man. There is no divine being that man has to serve. He is limited by the law of moral causation, but that merely means that he is not the creature of blind chance or of strict determinism.

The Buddhist theory of causation avoids the two extremes of indeterminism and strict determinism. According to strict determinism the present and the future are dependent on the past and therefore unalterable, for every event is predetermined by the will of a personal god. The Buddhist theory holds the doctrine of dependent origination: whenever A occurs B occurs, and whenever A does not occur B does not occur; thus, A and B are causally related. Such a theory of causality is compatible with free will. 'Free will' in this context means the ability of a person to control the dynamic forces of the past and present and make the future different from what it would otherwise have been. This ability to control the forces at work within the framework of the law of dependent origination makes him the master of his fate. No one is condemned to sin and any criminal has the potentiality to turn a new leaf. There is the classic instance of the criminal Angulimāla who, after having injured hundreds, attained the holy state (*arahat*) in that very same life. Buddhism says that, in the last analysis, the potentiality for good and bad is within one's own power and one is the master of his own destiny.

The Buddha also exhorts each person to use his reason without blindly following the dictates of authority. The *Kālāma Sutta,* which embodies this idea, is sometimes referred to as the Buddha's 'Charter of Free Inquiry'.[1] It is said that we should not accept anything that is a mere rumour, because it is a traditional belief, because it is the opinion of the majority, because it is found in the scriptures, because it is a product of mere logic or inference, because of the prestige of the teacher, etcetera. It is this spirit of free inquiry and healthy criticism which again marks Buddhism as a humanistic rather than an authoritarian creed. This aspect of humanism has roused the attention of psychologists like Erich Fromm:

> One of the best examples of humanistic religions is early Buddhism. The Buddha is a great teacher, he is the 'awakened one' who recognises the truth about human existence. He does not speak in the name of a supernatural power but in the name of reason. He calls upon every man to make use of his own reason and to see the truth which he was only the first to find.[2]

Apart from the factor of moral responsibility, the potentiality for spiritual transformation and the power of reason common to all humanity, there is another factor which brings men together. All men are impelled by the basic desires of sensuality, self-preservation and aggression. These desires, when they emerge in the form of the desire for power and self-love, certainly bring about antagonisms between man and man. When this aspect of man takes an excessive turn, it paves the way for mutual destruction, the kind of phenomenon so well presented in Freud's *Civilization and Its Discontents.*[3] But, in a paradoxical way, these aspects of inhumanity display the common humanity of man, the 'universal neurosis of man'. It is the same point which is summed up in the axiom *sabbe sattā ummattakā* (all worldlings are deranged). Furthermore, all men, whatever race or country they come from, are subject to suffering (*dukkha*), i.e. disease, decay, death and anguish in various forms. Because there is such a universal malady common to all humanity, the Buddha advocated a remedy obtainable by all humanity without distinction.

Apart from the fact that Freud is the founder of psychoanalysis, he must also be considered a great humanist who brought forth solace for the ills of his age. He was a man who grappled persistently with the problem of human suffering. It is stated in Freud's autobiography that his original interest was in 'human concerns' and that is how, in spite of his scientific career, he found in psychoanalysis the way of giving expression to the deep desire within him.[4] Fromm says:

> Freud expressed his humanism primarily in his concept of the unconscious. He assumed that all men share the same unconscious strivings and hence, that they can understand each other once they dare to delve into the underworld of the unconscious.[5]

Freud's method of therapy is based on the assumption man can acquire the means to cope with his problems rationally. MacIntyre says:

> Freud is so often presented as undermining the rationalist conception of man as a self-sufficient, self-aware, self-controlled being, that we are apt to forget that, although he may have abandoned such a conception as an account of what man is, he never retreated from it as an account of what man ought to be.[6]

Freud does not describe the unconscious side of man out of curiosity, but because he wants us to control it and be aware of it. MacIntyre also says that although Freud denied any moralistic purpose in his work, the ideal of conscious rationality gives to his writings a moral fervour and prescriptive flavour.

THE CONTEMPORARY SPIRITUAL CRISIS IN THE WEST: FREUD AND THE BUDDHA AS PHYSICIANS

Apart from the basic humanism found in the two systems, there is yet a deeper reason which prompted this comparison of two great philosophies separated by such a vast expanse of time. Both the Buddha and Freud are physicians of the soul. The condition of man today gives a sense of timeliness to our underlying theme: the image of man as a patient, society as sick and the Buddha and Freud as physicians. A detailed analysis of the two therapeutic systems is found in chapter five, so here it is only necessary to note briefly their significance for man's spiritual crisis.

According to Fromm, 'Psychoanalysis is a characteristic expression of western man's spiritual crisis, and an attempt to find a solution.' This is explicitly so in the more recent developments of psychoanalysis, in 'humanist' or 'existentialist' analysis.[7] The term 'spiritual crisis' sums up very briefly the sense of despair, alienation and allied themes vividly presented in works like W.H. Auden's *The Age of Anxiety,*[8] T.S. Eliot's *Wasteland,*[9] Freud's *Civilization and Its Discontents*[10] and Jean-Paul Sartre's *Nausea.*[11] This particular predicament of man has been given a philosophical formulation by the existentialist philosophers. In spite of the variety of schools within existentialism and the somewhat obscure terminology used by many of them, it is a symptom of a deep spiritual anguish within modern man. But apart from depicting and displaying the malady, they do very little in the way of offering a solution.[12] The Buddha's solution to such an atmosphere of spiritual anguish is presented in chapter five, where the therapeutic systems of early Buddhism and Freud are compared.

Fromm has charted out a useful line of thought in his essay on *Psychoanalysis and Zen Buddhism.*[13] Though he restricts his analysis to Zen Buddhism, his work has helped us to throw into sharper relief the analogies between Freudian and early Buddhist views on man, mind, motivation and therapy.

II

THE CONCEPT OF MIND IN EARLY BUDDHISM AND FREUD

APPROACHES TO THE STUDY OF MIND

The analysis of mind is a more complex and intricate process than the study of matter and material phenomena and hence it is not surprising that the analysis of mind and mental phenomena has been viewed from a number of vantage points in Buddhist psychology. Thus, we see that the approach to the study of mental phenomena in the *Sutta Piṭaka* differs from that in the *Abhidhamma Piṭaka*. It is not that one is opposed to the other, but that for purposes of emphasis and exegesis different kinds of analysie have been adopted.

In one sense, the Abhidhamma analysis of mental phenomena supplements the analysis of the *Sutta Piṭaka*. Firstly, there is what may be called the *nāma-rūpa* analysis. Here the approach is analytic, aspects of mind like perception, feeling and volition, being brought out with their differentiating characteristics. In the second place, there is the *paṭicca-samuppāda* analysis. This is a more synthetic approach, showing the dependence and the interdependence of all phenomena. The difference in these two approaches will be treated later when the role of *viññāṇa* (consciousness) as one of the five groups and as a link in the wheel of dependent origination is discussed.[1] The dependent origination analysis is cast in the wider dimensions of the great cycle of endless births (the 'samsaric' wheel).

In the Abhidhamma, that is, in the later systematisation of Buddhist psychology, a more self-conscious attempt to synthesise the study of mind is discernible. This approach combines analysis and synthesis and works out all the possible permutations and combinations of mental phenomena. The most valuable analysis in the Abhidhamma is that contained in the work called *Paṭṭhāna*.[2] Herein are outlined twenty-four possible correlations between cause and effect. It brings out the condition, the circumstances and relations that determine the emergence of phenomena. This is a very valuable analysis, and we will later treat in detail the first of these correlations called the 'root-condition' (*hetu-paccaya*).

Elsewhere in the Abhidhamma, we find an even more comprehensive and extensive analysis of eighty-nine forms of thought (*citta*) and fifty-two mental factors (*cetasika*). These eighty-nine forms of thought are in turn divided into four groups: the sense-plane (*kāmaloka*), the form-plane (*rūpaloka*), the formless plane (*arūpaloka*), and the supramundane plane (*lokuttara*). The fifty-two mental factors are also divided into four groups: the universal mental factors, the particular factors, the moral factors and the immoral factors. A detailed analysis of this system is given in the *Abhidhammattha-Saṅgaha*.[3] In summation then, the approaches that form the basis of Buddhist psychology are:

1. The *nāma-rūpa* analysis
2. The *paṭicca-samuppāda* analysis
3. The *Paṭṭhāna* analysis
4. The Abhidhamma classification of *citta* (thought) and *cetasika* (mental factors).

These are all different standpoints that help our understanding of the psychology of mind and motivation in Buddhism. In the Freudian analysis of mental personality too are found a number of vantage points from which Freud examined the concept of mental personality. These were referred to by Freud as the dynamic, the economic, the topographic and structural, and the genetic points of view.

MIND AS A PSYCHOPHYSICAL COMPLEX

The Buddha denies the existence of any permanent mental or physical entity. He considers the mind as a psychophysical complex or *nāma-rūpa*, to use the Pāli term. *Nāma* and *rūpa* are together referred to as the five 'aggregates' or 'groups' (*pañcakkhanda*). *Nāma* is used generally to refer to the four non-material 'groups' (*khandas*): 1) feeling (*vedanā*), 2) perception (*saññā*), 3) disposition (*saṅkhāra*), and 4) consciousness (*viññāna*). *Rūpa*, the fifth aggregate, is the material shape derived from extension, cohesion, heat and mobility.

It is an interesting fact that the Buddhist analysis of the mind has been compared to the tripartite division of mind into cognition, conation and affection so common in western psychology. Of course, contemporary western psychologists consider this an artificial and over-simplified analysis. But, as Flugel says:

> Some such classification is probably necessary if we are to attain any kind of ordered understanding of the rich facts of mental experience...[4]

Thus, we can use this classification as a way of understanding the mind, without of course, putting absolute value on it. Accordingly we can say that feeling (*vedanā*) refers to the category of affection, disposition or volition (*saṅkhāra*) to conation and perception (*saññā*) and consciousness (*viññāna*) to cognition. This resemblance has been pointed out by a number of writers on Buddhist psychology.[5]

The Buddhist concept of mind, considered as a psychophysical complex, has a number of significant logical features. The Buddha maintained that all things, including both mind and body, are subject to change, transitory (*anicca*). He described the universe in terms of the arising, decay and dissolution of all things. By this rejection of any eternally abiding substance it follows that he also rejected an eternally abiding pure ego (*attā*). According to the Buddha, then, neither inside nor outside of mental and physical phenomena is there any permanent substance. The mind is often compared to a flame, whose existence depends upon a number of conditions, i.e. the wick, oil, etcetera. The Buddha maintained there is no substance but a continuous flux of material and mental processes arising from their particular conditions. That is why it has been remarked that Buddhism had to begin very early in the history of humanity, to 'psychologise without a soul.'[6] The mind as a dynamic process is also compared to a stream (*sota*) in the Pāli Suttas.[7]

Another very significant feature of the early Buddhist concept of mind is the mutual dependency of the body on the mind and the mind on the body. This is clearly brought out by the law of dependent origination (*paṭicca-samuppāda*). According to one usage, as we have seen, mind and body (*nāma-rūpa*) are the twofold division of the five groups of existence. But according to another usage *nāma-rūpa* is the fourth link in the formula of dependent origination. The Buddhist scriptures bring out the dependency of mind and body thus:

> Sound is not a thing that dwells inside the conch-shell and comes out from time to time, but due to both, the conch-shell and the man that blows it, sound comes to arise. Just so, due to the presence of vitality, heat and consciousness, this body may execute the acts of going, standing, sitting and lying down, and the five sense organs and the mind may perform their various functions.[8]

Both the mind and body have a conditioned existence and it is possible to conceive of a variety of relations between the mind and the body. Early Buddhism was not embarrassed by any kind of Cartesian dualism. The Buddhist concept of mind as a dynamic continuum is not limited to one span of life. The mind is always in flux and extends to a number of births. This is a very significant fact and will be of crucial importance in our comparison of the Freudian and Buddhist concepts of mind. The concept of the unconscious in early Buddhism is closely connected with the Buddhist doctrine of rebirth. It has been pointed out by K. N. Jayatilleke, that in early Buddhism, man is considered:

> ... a psychophysical unit whose 'psyche' is not a changeless soul but a dynamic continuum composed of a conscious mind as well as an unconscious in which is stored the residue of emotionally charged memories going back to childhood as well as into past lives.[9]

The mind, viewed in this way, is continuously subjected to pressure by threefold desire, viz. sense-gratification (*kāma-taṇhā*), self-preservation (*bhava-taṇhā*) and self-annihilation (*vibhava-taṇhā*). Jayatilleke concludes:

> Except for the belief in rebirth, this conception of mind sounds very modern, and one cannot fail to observe the parallel between the threefold desires of Buddhism and the Freudian conceptions of the eros, libido and thanatos.[10]

It will be our chief objective to bring out some remarkable points of similarity between motivational theory in early Buddhism and Freud. Apart from the very striking similarity between the threefold desires of Buddhism and their counterpart in Freud mentioned above, an attempt will be made to show that in early Buddhism there existed a concept of the unconscious, although not systematically worked out as such.

To sum up, we have mentioned a number of significant features of the early Buddhist concept of the mind, viz. the rejection of the concept that the mind is a substance, but rather that it is a psychophysical complex and a dynamic process in continuous flux, and the mutual dependency of the mind and body as a result of their conditioned nature. It was also mentioned that early Buddhist psychology considers the mind to be a dynamic continuum composed of both a conscious and an unconscious aspect. Thus it is not surprising that early Buddhist motivational theory should offer some striking resemblance to the dynamic psychology of Freud. But before dealing with motivational theory, it will be necessary to examine the concept of mind in Buddhism and Freud in greater detail.

FOURFOLD ANALYSIS OF MIND

1 VIÑÑĀṆA (CONSCIOUSNESS)

There has been a great controversy regarding the exact meaning of the word *viññāṇa*. There are four strands of meaning attributed by various scholars to the word: 1) cognitive consciousness, 2) survival factor, 3) the medium in which *jhānic* or spiritual progress takes place, and 4) a sort of anoetic sentience. However, before considering these different views, we should notice two distinct contexts in which *viññāṇa* is used. The first is what may be called consciousness as a 'short range' concept when it refers to one of the five *khandas* (groups). The second is a 'long range' concept when it refers to consciousness as a link in the chain of causation (*paṭicca-samuppāda*).

Obscurity about the meaning of *viññāṇa* arises because in certain contexts it is said that *nāma-rūpa* depends on *viññāṇa* and *viññāṇa* on *nāma-rūpa*,[11] and in certain other contexts *viññāṇa* is included in the definition of *nāmā-rūpa*.[12] Sarachchandra considers this a contradiction and the usage of *viññāṇa* as a transmigrating entity to be a later intrusion.[13]

The very contradictions inherent in the explanation show it up as a later intrusion. It is said that if *viññāṇa* did not descend into the mother's womb, the growth of *nāma-rūpa* would be prevented. If *nāma-rūpa* here stands for the whole individual composed of mental and physical factors we should have to regard *viññāṇa* as something over and above *nāma-rūpa*, a position which is not consistent with the rest of the Buddhist teaching. *Nāma-rūpa*, wherever it stood for the individual, always included *viññāṇa* as well.[14]

It seems, however, that there need be no contradiction between the two usages of *viññāṇa*. In fact, later we will see how the term *saṅkhāra* (disposition) also has a similar usage. The two terms *saṅkhāra* and *viññāṇa* are used in the analysis of the five aggregates in the narrow sense of those dispositions and acts of consciousness which manifest themselves only so long as the body and mind are together. In this sense, mind and body form a configurational complex based on conditions. But they also have a deeper sense in the formula of dependent origination. There has loomed round this usage a large controversy. Does *viññāṇa* pass over from one body to another? There are some who feel that this concept goes against the empiricist view of the mind found in the canon.[15]

Yet O. H. de A. Wijesekera has made a good case for the usage of *viññāṇa* in a deeper sense as a link in the samsaric wheel. He says that apart from biological evolution, there is samsaric evolution.[16]

It is said in the Pāli canon, that if *viññāṇa* does not descend into the mother's womb, if it were to become extinct, name and form (*nāma-rūpa*) would not become constituted therein or if *viññāṇa* having descended into the mother's womb, were to become extinct, name and form would not come into existence. Again it is said were *viññāṇa* to be extirpated from a youth or maiden, name and form would not attain to growth, development and expansion.[17] Thus in this sense *viññāṇa* is the basis of name and form. Thus the question arises as to how *viññāṇa* is dependent on name and form, for the sequence is *viññāṇapaccayā nāmarūpaṃ* and *nāmarūpapaccayā viññānaṃ*.[18] In elucidating this point the Pāli canon says that if *viññāṇa* were to gain no foothold in name and form, it would not manifest itself in that concatenation of birth, death and the origin of pain.[19] Thus name and form will be together with *viññāṇa*, so far as there is a process of birth, growth, decay, death and rebirth. This is a very crucial usage of the word *viññāṇa* and it is not possible to accept Sarachchandra's contention that it is a later intrusion into Buddhist thought. In fact, a special term *saṃvattanika viññāṇa* is used to refer to consciousness as a surviving factor in the individual. As he says:

> At the breaking up of the body after dying, this situation exists, that the evolving consciousness (*saṃvattanika viññāṇa*) may accordingly reach imperturbability.[20]

Horner thus translates the term *saṃvattanika viññāṇa* as 'evolving consciousness.' This is what Wijesekera refers to as the survival factor. In fact, it is difficult to find an equivalent for this in western terminology. The closest seems to be what C. D. Broad calls the 'psychic factor' in his comments regarding evidence for human survival.[21] He says 'instead of a single mind which animates a successive series of organisms we should have a single psychic factor which combines with such a series of organisms to form a successive series of minds.' This type of concept has the advantage of dealing with the 'origin' of the mind at conception as well as some kind of 'end' at death.

Some critics find this type of interpretation unsatisfactory because they wrongly believe that by this we consider consciousness a permanent entity or a substance which transmigrates. The Buddha certainly rejected the conception of consciousness as a permanent entity. In the suttas, it is said that consciousness is one of the four substances (*āhāra*) for the maintenance of beings that have come to birth.[22]

The Buddha says that if someone raises the question, 'Who now is it, lord, who feeds on the consciousness?' it is not a proper question, but if someone were to ask 'Of what, lord, is the consciousness a sustenance?' that is a proper question.[23] The answer is that the consciousness sustenance is the cause of renewed becoming, of rebirth in the future. Consciousness is the influx conditioned by a causal pattern and it is a dynamic continuum. It is also referred to as a 'stream of consciousness' (*viññāṇasota*) and also a stream of becoming (*bhavasota*).[24] The evolving consciousness which continues after death maintains its dynamism because it is nourished by the manifestations of craving. There is a residuum derived from the psychological part of the individual. This dynamism makes possible the continuation of the phenomenal existence and the continuation of individuality (*nāma-rūpa*).

The Buddha admitted the existence of a life beyond. But this is not a theory based on pure reason (*takka*), but it is based on supernormal powers attained by the Buddha[25] and his disciples.[26] It is possible to acquire the power of recollecting past births (*pubbenivāsānussati*) and also to observe the death and survival of beings by clairvoyance (*dibbacakkhu*).[27] It is also noteworthy that the evidence for rebirth has been brought under experimental investigations by psychologists today.[28] It is time that the psychoanalyst worked out the clinical implications of the hypothesis of rebirth. The comparative significance of this point will be discussed in the section on Freud.

So far we have referred to a very significant use of the word *viññāṇa*, viz. the survival factor in the individual. There seem to be three more strands of meaning to the word *viññāṇa*: 1) cognitive consciousness, 2) the 'medium' in which *jhānic* or spiritual progress takes place, and 3) a sort of anoetic sentience.

Let us take usages 1 and 3 first, as they refer to *viññāṇa* as the fifth of the five *khandas* (groups). The *Mahāhatthipadopama Sutta*[29] describes the condition of perception thus: *Ajjhatikañ ce āvuso cakkhuṃ aparibhinnaṃ hoti bāhirā ca rūpā na āpāthaṃ āgacchanti no ca tajjo samannāhāro hoti, n'eva tāva tajjassa viññāṇabhāgassa phātubhāvo hoti*. Horner renders this passage to mean:

> ... even if the eye that is internal is intact, but external material shapes do not come within its range and there is no appropriate impact, then there is no appearance of the appropriate section of consciousness.[30]

What this passage describes is the conditions of cognition: 1) the eye as the organ of sight, 2) external form coming within the field of vision, 3) *tajjo samannāhāro hoti*, which Horner renders as an 'appropriate impact,' but which could be rendered as an 'act of attention.'

Now the crucial word here is *viññāṇabhāgassa* which Horner renders as 'section of consciousness', Sarachchandra as 'resulting sensation' and Jayatilleke as 'perception.' This divergence shows the ambiguity in the word *viññāṇa* in describing cognitive consciousness. Sarachchandra considers *viññāṇa* a kind of 'anoetic consciousness' or 'bare sentience' in this context. This seems to be his basic theme in the attempt to connect *viññāṇa* and his theory of *bhavaṅga*. He says:

> We shall attempt here to analyse the various meanings of *viññāṇa*, and to show that, though it stood in the early texts as a general term for sense-consciousness, when it came to be applied to the psychology of perception, it meant not full cognition but bare sensation, a sort of anoetic sentience that occurs before the object is completely apprehended. In this sense, we shall perhaps find the later Abhidhamma meaning of this word was consistent with the earliest tradition.[31]

Thus Sarachchandra considers the usage of *viññāṇa* in the psychology of perception as a sort of anoetic sentience and goes on to say that *viññāṇa* in the earliest texts was synonymous with *saññā*.

Though the idea that *viññāṇa* as anoetic sentience is connected with the *bhavaṅga* theory has a certain structural neatness, it is not true to the spirit of the Pāli sources. For one thing, as will be noted in a later chapter, the concept of *bhavaṅga* is not of such focal significance to early Buddhist psychology as Sarachchandra maintains. Secondly, *viññāṇa* in these contexts has a cognitive import, and we should not lose sight of this fact. When it is used in the context of the process of perception, *viññāṇa* is rather a general term for cognition or cognitive consciousness than any kind of anoetic sentience. Six kinds of consciousness are described:

1 Visual consciousness through the eye and material shapes
2 Auditory consciousness through the ear and sounds
3 Olfactory consciousness through the nose and smells
4 Gustatory consciousness through the tongue and tastes
5 Bodily consciousness through the body and touches
6 Mental consciousness through the mind and mental states.[32]

The sense-organs are referred to as 'internal sense fields' (*ajjhattikāyatana*). Sense objects are referred to as 'external sense fields' (*bāhirāyātana*).

Now let us analyse the use of *viññāṇa* in the sense of the 'medium' in which the course of meditation progress takes place. Later, when we analyse the concept of *ālayavijñāṇa*, we shall examine the role of this usage in the development of the idealist tradition. For the present, the fact that interests us is that the stages of spiritual development (*samāpatti*) are called the 'footholds' or 'abiding places of *viññāṇa*' (*viññāṇatthiti*).

Regarding the usage of the word *viññāṇatthiti*, Wijesekera says that throughout all these states of spiritual development, the stream of consciousness (*viññāṇasota*) appears to abide in a certain plane of existence for some duration.[33] In the first *jhānic* state, *viññāṇa* manifests as 'reasoning and investigation' (*vitakkavicāra*), *vitakka* is 'thinking with concepts', and *vicāra* is 'discursive thinking'. In the second *jhānic* state, there is a subsiding of reasoning and investigation, followed by tranquillity and oneness of mind. It is born of concentration (*samādhi*), filled with rapture (*pīti*) and joy (*sukha*), but yet is a state of consciousness.

Even up to the sixth stage, or the second of the higher stages, consciousness is present. The sixth stage is called 'the infinity of *viññāṇa*', a stage that may be described as 'unbounded consciousness'. Beyond this is the 'stage of nothingness'. Both these states are called *viññāṇatthiti*. Then the final abiding place of *viññāṇa* is the sphere of neither *saññā* nor *asaññā* (*nevasaññā-nāsaññāyatana*). This shows that although this is not a 'conceptual' state, it is some form of experience. However, even this does not imply the attainment of *nibbāna*. *Viññāṇa* ceases to manifest only in the final state of cessation of conceptual and empirical experience.

Now it is clear that there are a number of strands of meaning in the word *viññāṇa* that we have attempted to disentangle. From our point of view, what is going to be of great significance for the study of motivational theory is the use of *viññāṇa* as the factor of survival and the relationship of *viññāṇa* to craving and clinging, which provides a residuum (*upādhi*) for the further dynamism of *viññāṇa*.

This peculiar quality of *viññāṇa* is due to its position in the wheel of dependent origination, but it seems that it retains at least a part of this connection as one of the five *khandas*. This is very clearly apparent from the following passage.[34] (A person) thinks, 'Such was my vision in the distant past, such were material shapes,' and his consciousness (*viññāṇam*) is bound fast there by desire and attachment (*tattha candarāgapatibaddhaṃ hoti*). The commentary to the *Majjhima Nikāya* refers to this type of consciousness by the term *nikanti viññāṇa*, which is a 'consciousness that is characterised by desire, craving and longing'.[35]

There is another context in which it is said that 'consciousness is tied by lust to the material element' (*rūpadhāturāgavinibaddhaṃ*). In the same way, it is said that consciousness is tied by lust to *saññā*, *vedanā* and *saṅkhāra*.[36] It is difficult to disassociate consciousness from its connection with the body and sense-organs as then it has craving as its base.[37]

2. SAṄKHĀRA (DIRECTED DISPOSITION)

Saṅkhāra is an extremely difficult word to render into English. This is likewise true of many concepts in the Pāli canon, which do not have equivalents within the conceptual framework of western philosophical systems. The problem is made even more difficult by the fact that within the Pāli canon itself the term has different shades of meaning in different contexts.

There are four basic shades of meaning of this word in the Buddhist scriptures.[38] As a link in the wheel of dependent origination (*paṭicca-samuppāda*) *saṅkhāra* has an active aspect of 'forming' and signifies karma, i.e. wholesome or unwholesome volitional activity of body, speech or mind. Horner renders *saṅkhāra* in this sense by 'karmic formations,'[39] the same terminology as suggested by Nyanatiloka Thera.[40]

As a suffix to *kāya*, *vacī*, *citta* or *mano* it is rendered by Horner as a function, impulse or activity.[41] *Saṅkhāra* occurs also as the fourth of the five *khandas*. Horner renders *saṅkhāra* in this usage as 'habitual tendencies.' It also occurs in the sense of anything formed and conditioned and so often refers to phenomenal existence in general as it is conditioned. In the phrase 'all formations are impermanent' (*sabbe saṅkhāra aniccā*) this meaning is found. It is because of these varying shades of meaning that *The Pāli Text Society Dictionary* says, 'We can only convey an idea of its import by representing several of its applications, without attempting to give a 'word' as a definite translation'.[42]

Horner states that there may be some inner bond of reference that so far escapes interpreters of Buddhism.[43] Horner, to support this claim, refers to an analysis in the *Majjhima Nikāya* and its commentary, where the *saṅkhāras* are referred to as sixty-nine types of body, speech and mind.[44]

However, this kind of unity of reference is not very helpful in getting at the role of *saṅkhāra* in motivational theory. It has been pointed out by some that the concept of will is central to the meaning of *saṅkhāra*.[45] While it is not wise to simplify the complex strands of meanings woven into this difficult word, it seems safe to say that *saṅkhāra* refers to the conative aspect of behaviour. But what kind of evidence tends to strengthen this conclusion?

Reference has already been made to the threefold classification of mental processes into the categories of cognition, affection and conation popular in western psychological literature, on the basis of which it could be said that *viññāṇa* and *saññā* refer to the category of cognition, *vedanā* to the category of affection and *saṅkhāra* to the category of conation.

In the *Sutta Piṭaka*, *cetanā* and *saṅkhāra* are used synonymously. In the Abhidhamma, *cetanā* is used instead of *saṅkhāra* in the sense of volitional activity. In the *Saṃyutta Nikāya* the question, 'What is *saṅkhāra*?' is raised, and it is said that the *saṅkhāras* are the six seats of will (*sañcetanā*).[46]

There are terms like *abhisaṅkhāra* and *sasaṅkhāra* which shed light on this usage. The Pāli Text Society Dictionary says the term *abhisaṅkhāra* implies 'purposive intellection.'[47] In the *Dīgha Nikāya*, (III, 217) and the *Saṃyutta Nikāya* (II, 82) the term *abhisaṅkhāra* is brought under a threefold classification: 1) *puññ abhisaṅkhāra,* 2) *apuññ abhisaṅkhāra,* and 3) *aneñj abhisaṅkhāra*. These refer to the meritorious, demeritorious and the imperturbable karma formations.[48] The term 'karma formation' in this context is suggested by Nyanatiloka Thera. *Abhisaṅkhāra* in the *Dīgha Nikāya* is rendered by Rhys Davids by 'complexes'[49] and in similar context in the *Saṃyutta* by Mrs. Rhys Davids and F. L. Woodward by 'planning.'[50] This difference in terminology again shows how many interpretations of *abhisaṅkhāra* are possible.

The idea of a complex or a compound is not quite a central implication of *saṅkhara* or *abhisaṅkhāra* in the *Sutta Piṭaka*. It is found in the latter Abhidhamma classification. As Zan Aung points out, in the Abhidhamma classification, *saṅkhāra* is a collective name given to the fifty mental properties (*cetasikas*) which go to make up *citta* (consciousness).[51] 'They are named *saṅkhāras* because, as concomitants, they perform their respective functions in combination as a whole, of act, speech or thought.[52] Aung says that since *phassa* (contact), *vedanā* (feeling) or *saññā* (perception) were not pre-eminently active elements the only other representative property was chosen to be the namesake of the other forty-nine namely, that volitional activity which we understand by both *cetanā* and *saṅkhāra*.[53]

Rendering *abhisaṅkhāra* as 'karma formation' can be accepted but we must visualise the nature of a karma formation as such. This is well brought out with a graphic image in the *Aṅguttara Nikāya*: 'The wheel kept rolling so long as the impulse that set it moving lasted (*abhisaṅkhārassa gati)*, then it circled round and round and fell to the ground.'[54] Here *abhisaṅkhāra* refers to some kind of momentum. It is because of this momentum and dynamism that some consider the usage of *saṅkhāra* in the *paṭicca-samuppāda* as a synonym of the developed *cetanā* (karma).[55]

The terms *sasaṅkhāra* and *asaṅkhāra* form the defining character of two types of consciousness, the latter referring to thought that is spontaneous and effortless in an act of will, and the former referring to an act done with deliberation. According to the *Atthasālinī*, the following explanation of *sasaṅkhāra* is given:

> For instance, a bhikshu dwelling in the neighbourhood of a vihāra is inclined when duty calls him to sweep the terrace round the sthūpa, wait on the elders, or listen to the Dhamma, to find the way too far and shirk attendance. Second thoughts, as to the impropriety of not going, induce him to go. These are prompted either by his own conscience (*attano vā payogena*), or by the exhortation of another who, showing the disadvantage in shirking, and the profit in attending, says, 'Come, do it!' And the 'good thought,' i.e. of course, the resolve to go, is said 'to have arisen by way of a concomitant motive, by way of the taking hold of a cause.[56]

This illustrates the idea of deliberation or planning associated with the word *saṅkhāra*. It seems, then, that through the diversity of meanings associated with the word *saṅkhāra* there run two basic threads of meaning: 1) the idea of deliberation, planning, making a choice, persistence in an effort, aspects suggested by volition and conation, 2) dynamism, disposition, habit, in which sense it is often associated with karma. For instance, the dynamic *saṅkhāras* in one's own person which have the potentiality of bringing about the next birth are called *ponobhaviko bhavasaṅkhāra*.[57] Thus *saṅkhāra* is associated with some kind of momentum, like the wheel that moves as long as the impulse that set it rolling lasts. The term 'directed dispositions' may do justice to both these elements and hence this is here suggested as a translation of *saṅkhāra*.

The fusing of concepts like that of deliberation and habit behaviour into one concept is not foreign to western psychology. For instance, Flugel cites the case of the concept of orexis which cuts through both conation and affection. He says:

> It is true that the distinction between affection and conation has proved in many cases more difficult than that between either of these and cognition, hence the increasing use in recent years, at least among British psychologists, of the term 'orexis' to cover both affection and conation as distinguished from cognition.[58]

3. VEDANĀ (FEELING TONE)

Commenting on the meaning of *vedanā*, Mrs. Rhys Davids says:

> *Vedanā* is a term of very great import, meaning sentience or reaction, bodily or mental, on contact or impression. Sensation is scarcely so loyal a rendering as feeling, for though *vedanā* is often qualified as 'born of the contact' in sense-activity, it is always defined generally as consisting of the three species-pleasure (happiness), pain (ill) and neutral feeling—a hedonistic aspect to which the term 'feeling' is alone adequate.[59]

In accordance with this observation, *vedanā* can be rendered 'hedonistic tone'. The role of pleasure and the threefold manifestations of craving become quite meaningful if feeling is understood in this manner. The commentary to the *Dhammasaṅgani* describes the nature of feeling with a very apt metaphor. It says:

> As regards enjoying the taste of an object, the remaining associated states enjoy it only partially. Of contact there is (the function of) mere touching, of perception the mere noting or perceiving, of volition the mere coordinating (the associated states of exerting or being active), of consciousness the mere cognising. But feeling alone, through governance, proficiency, mastery, enjoys the taste of an object. For feeling is like the king, the remaining states are like the cook.[60]

Feeling has thus been described in the analogy of taste and the function of feeling becomes the experience of flavour. As is evident from the *Bahuvedanīya Sutta*, feeling can be classified in various ways:

> Ananda, two feelings are spoken of by me according to (one) classification, and three feelings are spoken of by me according to (one) classification, and five feelings... six feelings... eighteen feelings and thirty-six feelings... and one hundred and eight feelings are spoken of by me according to (one) classification. Thus, Ananda, Dhamma is taught by me according to classification.[61]

The twofold classification is a reference to bodily and mental feelings; the threefold to pleasant, painful and neutral feelings; the fivefold to feelings based on the five sense organs; the six-fold to those based on the sensory impingements by way of the sense doors; the eighteenfold refers to the six ways of attending to material shapes based on happiness, six founded on grief and six on equanimity; the thirty-six-fold refers to the six forms of happiness connected with the household life, the six connected with renunciation, six forms of misery connected with the household life, six with renunciation, the six indifferences of a householder and the six indifferences of renunciation; the hundred-and-eightfold refers to the thirty-six feelings as manifest in the past, present and future.[62]

Feelings are also analysed on an ethico-psychological basis into a threefold manifestation: wholesome (*kusala*), unwholesome (*akusala*) and indeterminate (*avyakata*). This is a very significant classification which brings in an ethical dimension to the study of feelings which is foreign to a psychology like that of Freud. Pleasant feeling induces an attachment (*upādāna*) to a pleasant object. There is a potency in pleasant feelings to arouse latent sensuous greed (*rāgānusaya*), in painful feelings to arouse latent anger and hatred (*patighānusaya*).[63]

It is also said in the Pāli canon that greed emerges due to unwise reflection (*ayonisa manasikāra*) on an attractive object and hate through unwise reflection on a repulsive object. Greed (*lobha* or *rāga*) comprises all degrees of 'attractedness' towards an object from the faintest trace of personal desire up to gross egoism, whilst hatred (*dosa*) comprises all degrees of 'repulsion' from the faintest trace of ill-humour to the highest pitch of hate and wrath.[64]

Unwholesome feelings rest on these twofold roots of greed and hatred as well as on a third root *moha*, usually translated 'delusion.' These three moral roots make feelings wholesome and the three immoral roots make feelings unwholesome. The psychology of feelings in early Buddhism can never be grasped without an understanding of these roots of human motivation. In general, though feelings are directly conditioned by contact (*phassa*), their nature depends on a number of factors. Flugel, making an analysis of the basis of feeling, says:

> The visual perception of a bowl of choice fruit or of a lovely girl may in their different ways pleasantly stir the imagination even when the desire for eating or for sexual intimacy is absent owing to satiation or to other causes.[65]

This strengthens the Buddhist claim that even though desires can be temporarily satisfied at a purely physiological level, their psychological roots are strong. Human desires continually emerge to the level of consciousness and find temporary satisfaction (*tatratatrābhinandinī*), but they ever remain unsatisfied and thus provide fuel for the continuation of the individual. Hence, we should not lose sight of the ethical dimensions in which the pleasure-pain polarity is analysed in Buddhism.

Buddhism does not insist that with any feeling there emerges craving; rather it says that, if there is craving, then feeling is a condition by way of decisive support (*upanissaya*). The *Visuddhimagga* describes the position thus:

> The Greatest Sage announced the law
> 'With feeling as condition, craving.'
> Since all three feelings thus can be
> Conditions for all kinds of craving.
> Though feeling is condition, still
> Without inherent-tendency (*anusaya*)
> No craving can arise... [66]

Thus the relationship of *anusaya* to *vedanā* is very significant for an understanding of the role of craving (*taṇhā*). The *Nettippakarana* makes out a grouping of persons based on motivational roots and feelings. It is said that 1) a person of lusting temperament (*rāgacarita*) liberates himself by abandoning greed as a root of that which is unprofitable and by not approaching contact felt as pleasant; 2) a person of hating temperament (*dosacarita*) liberates himself by abandoning hate as a root of that which is unprofitable and by not approaching contact felt as painful; 3) a person of deluded temperament (*mohacarita*) liberates himself by abandoning delusion as a root of that which is unprofitable and by not approaching contact felt as neither painful nor pleasant.[67] This analysis illustrates the deep-rooted nature of feeling.

4. SAÑÑĀ (PERCEPTION)

As one of the groups subsumed under *nāma-*, *saññā* is generally rendered 'perception'. Mrs Rhys Davids considers it as a relatively simple form of intellection or cognition which consists in the discernment, recognition and assimilation of sensations.[68] The role of *saññā* seems to fall between pure sentience or awareness and a sophisticated judgment.

There is a very interesting analogy mentioned by Jayasuriya which throws light on the nature of *saññā*.[69] He states that the relationships among *saññā*, *viññāna* and *paññā* are clarified by an analogy. A gold coin is given to a child, a villager and a goldsmith. Each one conceives it differently: the child knows it as a coloured object; the villager knows it as something capable of procuring many things he needs; the goldsmith knows a great many things about it, such as its nature, impurities, tests and purification.

Likewise *saññā* is translated as 'noting' by Jayasuriya, because it makes a note of the object as being of such a colour, of such a shape and size, etcetera so as to identify it subsequently. Wisdom (*paññā*) understands that object as having a real unchanging nature, as being impermanent, etcetera. Cognition (*viññāna*) is the medium which assists the diversification of thinking by the mental factors. This analysis is based on the Abhidhamma tradition, But it also shows the role of *saññā* as discernment or recognition, as found for instance in the *Majjhima Nikāya* (*Mahāvedalla Sutta*).[70]

Saññā is sometimes divided into two kinds: *patigha-saññā* and *adi-*

vacana-saññā. *Saññā* that arises out of contact with the sense organs is described as *patigha-saññā*. *Adivacana-saññā* is of a nominal character and includes sense images and concepts. As perception it is of six kinds: visual forms, sounds, smells, tastes, bodily sensations and images.

In a more popular sense, *saññā* denotes a 'sign' or 'mark'. The basis of this usage seems to be the underlying element of recognition in a sign or mark. As the *Atthasālinī* says, 'We may see this procedure when the carpenter recognizes a piece of wood which he has marked by special knowledge,'[71] or when 'we recognise a man by his sectarian mark on the forehead.'[72] There are some other contexts in which it is used. Sometimes it stands for consciousness in its entirety (*nevasaññā-nāsaññāyatana*), the realm of neither perception nor non-perception.[73] It also refers to ideas which are objects of meditation like impermanence (*anicca*), non-soul (*anattā*), impurity (*asubha*), etcetera.

Though *saññā* is used in different contexts, its dominant role is as the third of the five groups. Compared with *saṅkhāra* or *viññāna* it does not involve so much subtlety and complexity. However, it has been translated by a number of terms which are practically synonyms, for example: discernment, recognition, noting, concept, idea, notion, sign, mark, all of which emphasise aspects of perceptual activity. But as was mentioned earlier, *saññā* seems to fall between 'pure sentience' and 'sophisticated cognition'. There are some scholars who render *viññāna* as 'cognition' and *saññā* as 'recognition.'

THE CONCEPT OF MIND IN FREUD

MODELS AND VANTAGE POINTS

In charting the nature of mental personality Freud introduced a number of conceptual models. There are various approaches and vantage points that Freud took to plot out the complex psychological phenomena. He introduced two basic conceptual models to delineate the nature of mental personality: 1) the conscious, preconscious and unconscious, and 2) the ego, id and super-ego.[74] He viewed his two conceptual models from various angles, viz. the dynamic, the economic, the genetic, the topographic and structural.

The Freudian concept of mind can also be examined under the threefold category of cognition, affection and conation. As was pointed out earlier, though this threefold division is somewhat artificial, it is very useful for evaluating theories of motivation.[75]

The value of the Freudian system lies in elucidating the complicated nature of the affective processes. According to the topographic viewpoint the psychic apparatus is threefold, consisting of the conscious, the preconscious and the unconscious. Freud says that consciousness is not a necessary attribute of the psychical. He considers consciousness the sensory organ of the mind. As the eye sees the object in the outer world, so the function of consciousness is to discern endo-psychic processes.

The 'eye' of consciousness is somewhat similar to the *manodvāra* (mind-door) in Buddhism. The preconscious contains memory traces which can be recalled without much effort. The term 'preconscious' refers to latent ideas which are accessible to consciousness under ordinary conditions. In the case of the unconscious, it is not accessible without a special procedure, such as hypnosis or free association.

This topographic model had to be revised in the light of new findings and this revised model is referred to as the structural model. According to this revision we get the division of personality into the id, ego and the super-ego. The id represents the archaic impulses and the ego the seat of reason and sanity. The super-ego is the voice of conscience, morality, prohibitions and demands.

The dynamic represents the mind as an interaction of forces. The upsurge of desires and wishes, their interplay and conflict can be designated as the psycho-dynamic point of view. As Hartmann points out, in the early beginning (even after the significance of unconscious processes had been discovered), Freud upheld the theory of associationism.[76] It is only when he found conflict to be a primary motivating force that he built up a dynamic psychology:

> The consideration of mental processes from this angle of synergistic or antagonistic motivating forces is what has since been known as the dynamic aspect of psychoanalysis. The systematic and objective study of conflict has remained one of its essential aspects and has proved a necessary and fruitful avenue to the explanation of human behaviour.[77]

Connected with the dynamic avenue is another approach called the 'economic'. This deals with the measurement or the quantitative analysis of these conflicting forces. The forces are described in terms of energy. The basic instinctual drives like sex, self-preservation and aggression are the main sources of energy. These various approaches to the study of mind are called 'meta-psychology' by Freud. This term may offer some similarity to the Abhidhamma (literally the 'Further Dhamma') of Buddhism. Hartmann says that the prefix meta- here points to a theory 'beyond' the investigation of conscious phenomena, adding that meta-psychology is really nothing but a term for the highest level of abstraction in analytic psychology.[78] A variety of approaches to the study of mental personality has now been presented. It was noted that there are two basic conceptual models introduced by Freud, the one involving conscious, preconscious and unconscious; and the one involving the id, ego and super-ego. The id and ego will now be treated in detail and the concept of unconscious motivation will be taken up later.

THE ID AND ITS STRUCTURE

One of Freud's greatest discoveries was that hysterical paralysis was caused by purely psychological factors. He traced these causative factors to early infancy, to certain traumatic factors buried in the past. Freud considered the unconscious as the area of repressed memories. Later he realised that the unconscious was not only the area of repressed memories, but was the receptacle of deep instinctual desires, which try to find expression in socially recognised ways. Thus Freud came to realise that a part of the ego was unconscious. Then he introduced the concept of the id. The id gave a broader basis to his psychology than the unconscious in the sense of 'repressed.' Freud says:

> To the oldest of these psychical provinces or agencies we give the name of id. It contains everything that is *inherited, that is present at birth, that is laid down in the constitution*— above all, therefore, the instincts, which originate from the somatic organization and which find a first psychical expression here (in the id) in forms unknown to us.[79]

A note on this says: 'The oldest portion of the psychical apparatus remains the most important throughout life; moreover, the investigations of psychoanalysis started with it.'[80] The italicised words suggest a parallel between the id and the *āsavas* of the Buddhist scriptures, the dark affective bases inherited through countless births. According to Freud:

> There is nothing in the id that corresponds to the idea of time; there is no recognition of the passage of time, and—a thing that is most remarkable and awaits consideration in philosophical thought—no alteration in its mental processes is produced by the passage of time. Wishful impulses which have never passed beyond the id, but impressions, too, which have been sunk into the id by repression, are virtually immortal; after the passage of decades they behave as though they had just occurred.[81]

Freud felt that this offered an approach to 'some profound truths', but that he himself did not make much progress in that direction. At this point he came up with the notion of the collective unconscious and of the archaic heritage of man. But these speculations led to no significant progress, nor did Jung's enthusiastic preoccupation with the problem lead to a clarification of the real psychological issues involved. An attempt to work out the clinical implications of the concept of rebirth and the basis of the archaic unconscious could be really rewarding.

The id is the obscure, inaccessible part of our personality. The little that has been learned about it is based on the study of dreams and the formation of neurotic symptoms. We can come nearer to the id with the aid of analogies and call it a chaos, a cauldron full of seething excitations.[82] It is supposed that it is somewhere in direct contact with the somatic processes and takes over from them instinctual needs and gives them mental expression, but it cannot be discovered in what substratum this contact is made.

These instincts fill it with energy, but it has no organisation and no will; it has only an impulse to obtain satisfaction for instinctual needs in accordance with the pleasure principle. It is irrational. Laws of logic, for instance, that of contradiction, do not hold for processes of the id; contradictory impulses exist side by side without neutralising one another. At most they combine in compromise formations under the overpowering pressure to discharge their energy. In the id there are no negatives, only contents cathected with greater or lesser strength. There is also no recognition of the passage of time. The energy of these instinctual impulses is extremely mobile and fluid and within the id the organic instincts operate in the form of the pleasure principle and the death instinct. The one and only endeavour of these instincts is to obtain satisfaction.

An immediate satisfaction of instinct would lead to perilous conflict with the external world. But the id functions in a world of its own. The processes (primary process) which take place in the id differ largely from those familiar to us by conscious perception. For the id, which is cut off from the external world, has its own world of perception. As the ego is governed by the reality principle, the id is governed by the pleasure principle.

On the other hand, this does not mean that the id is completely cut off from consciousness. The id is always alive and dynamic. It has a dominant impact and continuous influence on the secondary processes of the ego. The id remains the 'affective base of the personality'. This is a very important concept as the novelty of the Freudian revolt lies in demonstrating the impact of the affective base on the conative and cognitive aspects of personality.

Perception, thinking, reasoning, willing and other aspects of cognition and conation are under the influence of this affective base in the personality. This is very clearly brought out in Freud's *Ego and the Id*.[83] In the analysis of his concept of the unconscious, and especially in what he later called the id, the tremendous dynamism of the affective processes is evident. Freud has, however, been criticised for adopting a kind of psychic determinism. If the affective bases predominate in the unconscious and influence the functions of the ego and super-ego, does man use his will freely and act rationally?

In the same way that the id represents the affective processes, the ego represents what we call reason and sanity in contrast to the id which contains the passions. To decide whether Freud does justice to conation and will it is necessary to understand Freud's conception of the ego.

There is a very interesting hypothesis put forward by R. S. Peters in *The Concept of Motivation*.[84] He says that when Freud speaks in the language of cause and effect, he introduces a causal model, the primary process of the id. When Freud speaks in the language of purpose, he introduces the purposive model, the secondary process of the ego. This hypothesis has a basis in Freud's own work, and the distinction between primary and secondary processes is clearly brought out in his 'Formulations Regarding the Two Principles in Mental Functioning.'[85]

In the psychology that is founded on psychoanalysis, our starting point is the unconscious mental processes. These seem to be the older primary processes, the residues of a phase of development in which they were the only mental processes. These processes obey the pleasure-pain principle. Satisfaction is at the level of hallucination, fantasy and dreams. But these mental processes have to form a conception of the real circumstance in the outer world. Thus, what is conceived of is no longer pleasant but that which is real, even if it should be unpleasant. With the introduction of the reality principle one mode of thought activity was split off; it was kept free from 'reality-testing' and remained subordinate to the pleasure principle alone. This is the act of fantasy-making, which begins even in the games of children and is later continued in daydreaming where it abandons its dependence on real objects.

This is not merely limited to the phenomena of dreams as such. These primary processes dominate in our ideational processes. These processes which basically ignore reality are referred to by Freud as 'autistic.' They are controlled by wishes and desires, not by external reality. When Freud wants to describe goings-on of which it is appropriate to say that a man is acting, that he has a reason for what he does and so on, he talks about the ego; when on the other hand, he wants to say that a person suffers something, or is made or driven to do something, he speaks of the id.[86]

Freud used the model of the ego and the id to show that sometimes we take account of facts, act deliberately, plan means to ends, and impose rules of procedure on our conduct, while other times we take no account of facts, act impulsively and are driven and obsessed.

EGO, THE SEAT OF COGNITION AND CONATION

Those who criticise Freud for having introduced a morbid theory of psychic determinism are not quite justified. Freud quite clearly associated with the ego the function of controlling and organising the instincts. The ego has to observe the external world and preserve a true picture of it in the memory traces left by its perceptions and by means of the reality-test. It has to eliminate any element in this picture of the external world which emerges as an internal source of excitation of the id. The ego controls the paths of access to motility, but it interpolates between desire and action the procrastinating factor of thought during which it makes use of the residues of experience stored up in memory. In this way it dethrones the pleasure principle which exerts undisputed sway over the processes in the id and substitutes for it the reality principle. However, the characteristic which marks the ego in contradistinction to the id is a tendency to synthesise its contents, to bring together and unify its mental processes. It is this alone that produces that high degree of organisation which the ego needs for its highest achievements. The ego advances from the function of perceiving instincts to that of controlling them.

The question of determinism has also been discussed by A. C. Maclntyre.[87] He discusses the problem in a different setting, comparing the neurotic and the successfully analysed patient. The sharpest distinction in Freud's clinical practice is presumably that between the suffering neurotic and the successfully analysed patient. The former goes through compulsive rituals, is harassed by delusive beliefs, cannot understand his own behaviour and cannot control it; the latter is characterised by what Freud calls, 'self-knowledge and greater self-control'.[88] Even if Freud's theory of human behaviour as it is, sounds deterministic, the ideal that he sets before the patient is self-knowledge and self-control. The Freudian message is summarised in the statement, 'Where id was, there ego shall be.'[89]

THE RELATIONSHIP OF EARLY BUDDHIST AND FREUDIAN PSYCHOLOGY

Freud is so often portrayed as the champion of a materialistic creed and a pan-sexual theory of man that it needs some persuasive argument to prove that this viewpoint is superficial. However, the work done by scholars like Erich Fromm and Philip Rieff gives us a more sympathetic and penetrating analysis of Freudian Psychology. Fromm has pointed out that Freudian psychology is certainly not antagonistic to humanistic religions like early Buddhism. However, inasmuch as the Freudian concept of man was dealt with in chapter one, it need not be taken up again here, and so we may proceed to discuss some points of similarity between the two systems.

1) Buddhist psychology does not belong to the tradition of pure scientific psychology. It is not a theoretical enterprise without any practical aim in view. On the other hand, it has been often called an ethico-psychology. A very important work on Buddhist psychology, a translation of the *Dhamma-saṅgani*, is referred to as a work on 'psychological ethics.'[90] The Buddha pursued theoretical questions only insofar as it helped him to diagnose the condition of suffering man and advocates a way out of this tragic dilemma.

The Buddha was interested in the fundamental tragedy of man: the suffering individual. Thus it was an ethico-psychology with a therapeutic basis. Buddhism as a therapeutic system is based on a study of human psychology. But though it is a psychological theory, it has a practical aim. The Buddha makes a psychological analysis of mind and its state with a moral purpose, the purging of the mind of unwholesome states (*kilesas*). In its attempt to find therapeutic principles for this purpose, the Buddhist scriptures give us an insight into the instinctual and emotional forces that obstruct moral development. This accounts for the ethico-psychological scaffolding of motivational theory in Buddhism.[91]

A celebrated work, the *Visuddhimagga*, has a neatly laid ethico-psychological basis, being divided into three sections: 1) virtue (*sīla*), 2) concentration (*samādhi*) and 3) understanding (*paññā*). The realm of morality, by which one can refrain from actual transgression, is treated under the first of these. But defilements temporarily put away by morality can crop up again and can be potent, at least at the ideational level. Of course, stimuli at the ideational level can impel a man to action when he loses his sense of restraint. The second section, then, dealing with concentration and mental involvement attempts to get at the evil thought processes. However, this process really only pushes the defilements into the background for some time. The defilements are entirely rooted out by means of understanding (*paññā*). It is only at the third level that there is insight into the nature of one's motives. Without such an understanding no release is possible.[92]

Another interesting feature in Buddhist psychology is that the springs of human action are described as wholesome roots (*kusala mūla*) and unwholesome roots (*akusala mūla*). The word *kusala* is sometimes translated as 'good', 'skilful' or 'wholesome'. The unwholesome states are rooted in greed (*lobha*), hatred (*dosa*) and delusion (*avijjā*); the wholesome states are rooted in their opposites, charity (*cāga*), compassionate love (*mettā*) and knowledge (*vijjā*). The word *kusala*, apart from referring to the ethically good (as against the bad), also implies the idea of skill and also health. This ethico-psychological nature of terms like greed and hatred is an instance of a feature peculiar to all the concepts, words and terms used in Buddhist motivational theory.

Freud apparently tries to use his concepts with a semblance of neutrality, for example by using technical terms like libido without calling it sensuous greed. However, there is a natural tendency to consider motives as character assessments, and the logic of this usage is embedded in some types of motivational psychology. Even if this is denied regarding Freud, Freudian psychology was cast in a certain therapeutic framework, and this practical aspect is found in Buddhism too.

2) Another aspect of early Buddhism that should attract the Freudian is its interest in dynamic and motivational psychology. What is called 'dynamic psychology' is often considered as the psychology of motivation. A recent psychologist defines the term dynamic psychology thus:

> Dynamic psychology is concerned with the various psychological and related factors which drive, steer, integrate and sometimes disintegrate the mental life. Dynamic psychology aims to explain mental life causally; to find laws that control mental life.'[93]

Dynamic psychology implies the complex interplay of forces both at the conscious and the unconscious level.

Jayasuriya has made a significant analysis of some aspects of dynamic psychology in Buddhism. Though he bases his analysis mostly on the later tradition as found in the Abhidhamma, the results of his analysis concerning the distinction between structural and dynamic approaches to mental phenomena are true generally of Buddhist psychology. Introducing a chapter entitled 'Dynamic Psychology', he says:

So far the approach to the study of material and mental phe-

> nomena has been a static one, in that the taxonomic interest or the interest in the structure of things was predominant. Yet we have had occasion to consider dynamic questions such as how the body lives, grows and perishes, or how mind acts on the body. Here, we take the dynamic question in greater detail, to describe how the mind works, i.e. thinks, reflects, imagines, dreams, rests, understands others, and laughs, or how the individual gets both the mind and the body to do the things it wishes; how the continuity of life and mind is maintained from life to life, and how the mind gets tainted or is purified.[94]

Our analysis of motivational theory in early Buddhism seeks to present Buddhism as a dynamic psychology. Freudian psychology was a pioneer in the field of dynamic psychology and its similarity to early Buddhism in this respect cannot be overlooked too easily.

3) Now may be taken up the question as to whether Freudian psychology is abnormal psychology and Buddhist psychology is otherwise. Though Freud was primarily interested in the mentally sick, his psychology had a broader basis.[95] Rieff points out that Freud's dictum that 'we are all somewhat hysterical' and the Freudian claim that the difference between so-called 'normality' and 'neurosis' is only a matter of degree is a key statement.[96] This position resembles the Buddhist axiom: 'All worldlings are deranged' (*sabbe puthajjanā unmattakā*).[97]

Diseases have been classified into bodily disease (*kāyiko rogo*) and mental disease (*cetasiko rogo*). A person suffers from bodily diseases from time to time, but psychological ailments continue until the final state of sainthood is attained.[98] Fromm says that it is only at a superficial level that Freud appears as a creator of a new therapy for mental illness. He says that Freud's own system transcended the traditional concept of illness and cure, and thus he was concerned, 'with the "salvation" of man, rather than only with a therapy for mentally sick patients.'[99]

4) What can be said of the personality of the founders of these systems of psychology? In the case of the Buddha, it is hardly necessary to emphasise that his preaching and practice harmonised perfectly: 'As he spoke, thus he acted' (*yathāvādi tathākāri*). Freud too, does not belong to that class of philosophers or psychologists who dwell academically

on the profundities of life, but leave them severely alone in their private lives. He was deeply involved and immersed in everything he wrote and he himself underwent a vigorous process of self-analysis before he worked out his final psychoanalytic theories. This vigour and inner seriousness are manifest in his relationship with his patients. He was averse to moralising and preaching to his patients, but he was prepared to analyse a patient for a prolonged period of time. As Fromm says:

> Freud considered the emancipation, the well-being and the enlightenment of even one individual a matter of concern in the final analysis. He did not measure his results in terms of money and time.[100]

Commenting on the personality of Freud, Jones says:

> An overpowering need to come at the truth at all costs was probably the deepest and strongest motive force in Freud's personality, one to which everything else—ease, success, happiness—must be sacrificed. And, in the profound words of his beloved Goethe, 'The first and last thing required of his genius is love of truth'.[101]

This love of truth implies that Freud considered honesty to be of great value. According to Rieff:

> Secrecy is the category of moral illness, for it provides a hiding place for false motives. It is our secrets, hidden from ourselves, that fester and infect action. Thus, the entire therapeutic undertaking, based as it is on the promise of 'absolute honesty,' becomes a 'lost labour if a single concession is made to secrecy.' For secrecy provides the self with, in Freud's appropriately religious image, a 'right of sanctuary' for disreputable citizens of the mental underworld. There are to be no refugees from honesty in Freud's program.[102]

The role of self-analysis and the rejection of sham and deception regarding one's motives are recognised to be of basic significance by the Buddha. Some very useful material on this question has been systematised by Rerukane Chandavimala Thero in a recent book in Sinhalese.[103] The first part is called 'Defilers of the Mind' and the second 'Desires in Disguise'. The latter part is of great significance and accordingly will be referred to below.

These broad similarities between the two systems of psychology should provide a background for comparing the structure of motivational theory in Buddhism and Freud.

III

THE UNCONSCIOUS

The concept of unconscious motivation is the focus around which the Freudian concept of mind has been constructed. The Freudian concept of unconscious motivation will be taken up first followed by the Buddhist theory of unconscious motivation. This is necessary, because before the role of unconscious motivation in Buddhism can be examined, the logic of its usage in the Freudian system has to be understood.

THE UNCONSCIOUS IN FREUD

There are six features of the Freudian unconscious which clearly define its place and function.[1]

1) 'The unconscious is formally distinguished from the conscious and the preconscious. The preconscious is what, not being in consciousness, can be brought to consciousness by ordinary introspective methods. The unconscious is the realm of that which cannot thus be brought into consciousness.'[2] This is the most important point about the unconscious and it clearly delimits its function. A preconscious idea or memory can become conscious without much difficulty. A little effort may be necessary to recall something that is in one's memory, but no special technique is necessary to unravel it. But an unconscious idea or memory is hard to recall, because the resistance is great. Though there can be varying degrees of unconsciousness, a special technique is necessary to uncover the deeper levels of the unconscious processes. Freud first used the technique of hypnotism and then free association to unravel the unconscious. The psychic experiences, which cannot be brought to the surface due to some kind of resistance, belong to the unconscious, or can be described as 'unconscious.' A passage from the works of Freud will better illustrate this point:

> It is by no means impossible for the product of unconscious activity to pierce into consciousness, but a certain amount of exertion is needed for this task. When we try to do it in ourselves, we become aware of a distinct feeling of repulsion which must be overcome, and when we produce it in a patient we get the most unquestionable signs of what we call resistance to it. So we learn that the unconscious idea is excluded from consciousness by living forces which oppose themselves to its reception, while they do not object to other ideas, the preconscious ones. Psychoanalysis leaves no room for doubt that the repulsion from unconscious ideas is only provoked by the tendencies embodied in their contents.[3]

This explains why the unconscious can be considered as that which cannot be brought into consciousness.

2) The unconscious can also be considered the area of the primary processes. This is a very important aspect of the unconscious, and some psychologists like Jones and R.S. Peters consider this Freud's greatest discovery. Peters says:

> I have argued in my monograph (1958) adopting Ernest Jones' interpretation that Freud's great discovery was not of the unconscious, but of the fact that what he calls the primary processes of thought, in terms of which the unconscious works, are of a quite different type from those of thinking proper.[4]

Freud says there are two fundamentally different kinds of mental processes: the primary and secondary. The primary processes are governed by reason and follow the pattern of logical thinking and recognition of temporal and spatial relationships. The secondary processes represent the functionings of ego. Laws of logic do not hold for primary processes. As was mentioned in our analysis of the id, contradictory impulses, negation and opposition exist in the id, but there are really no negatives. The infantile mind, the primitive mind, and the existence of dreams are all aspects of primary processes. These are also referred to as autistic emphasising the omnipotence of the wish element, which is not modified by rational or realistic processes.

3) The unconscious is also considered as that which is 'repressed,' by Freud. Though Freud later admitted that the repressed and the unconscious do not coincide, he accepted the repressed as a very significant aspect of the unconscious. In fact, his initial concept of the unconscious as the area of the repressed was never totally abandoned, only modified. Repressed wishes take a significant place in Freud's psychology.

4) Freud also considers the unconscious as the 'background link between infancy and adult life.' Due to the failure to cure mental disorders by purely physical methods, Freud's psychology took a very significant turn. He came across many mental disorders for which there was no corresponding physiological cause and then he discovered that hysterical paralysis is rooted in purely psychological factors. He also emphasised the significance of the early life of the patient, especially in infancy. Freud unravelled the fact that many personality disorders could be traced to traumatic experiences buried in the past. So he held that childhood wishes persist and influence adult behaviour.

5) The unconscious is an omnipresent background to conscious and overt mental life and to behaviour. It exerts a continual causal influence upon conscious thought and behaviour.

6) The unconscious is a 'place' or 'realm'. This concept of the unconscious as an entity raises the question of whether Freud was merely using spatial imagery or was claiming anything more than that.

Having outlined the basic features of the unconscious, let us briefly touch upon the type of material that he brought to bear on this concept, mostly drawn from the clinical study of case histories. There are a number of directions from which he arrived at the concept of the unconscious: the failure to cure mental disorders by the physical methods of neurosurgery, self-analysis, work on dreams, the psychopathology of everyday life, study of myths, anthropology, art, etcetera. On the one hand, the unconscious is analysed in terms of the neurotic, yet on the other, is a very interesting analysis in terms of the normal personality.

THE ABNORMAL AND THE UNCONSCIOUS

Long before the advent of psychoanalysis, experiments in post-hypnotic suggestion demonstrated the operation of the unconscious. A post-hypnotic experience is a laboratory production and an artificial fact. But if we adopt the theory of hysterical phenomena that was first put forward by Pierre Janet and elaborated by Breuer and Freud, the psychological character of post-hypnotic suggestion is even more distinctly seen. The mind of the hysterical patient is full of active yet unconscious ideas; all his symptoms proceed from such ideas. It is in fact the most striking character of the hysterical mind that it is ruled by these unconscious ideas. If the hysterical woman vomits, she may do so because of the idea of being pregnant. She has no knowledge of this idea, although it is easily detected in her mind and made conscious to her by the technical procedure of psychoanalysis. If she is executing the jerks and movements constituting her fit, she does not consciously represent to herself the intended actions. Nevertheless, she is acting her part in the dramatic reproduction of some incident in her life, the memory of which is unconsciously active during the attack.

The preponderance of active unconscious ideas is revealed by analysis as the essential fact in all other forms of neurosis. Furthermore, an analysis of neurotic phenomena shows that a latent or unconscious idea is not necessarily a weak one. There are some latent ideas that do not penetrate into consciousness, however strong they become. The term 'unconscious' is properly reserved for these, while the term 'preconscious' is used to describe the latent ideas that are accessible to consciousness under ordinary conditions. The term 'unconscious 'designates not only latent ideas in general, but especially ideas that are kept apart from consciousness, in spite of their intensity and activity.

Freud discovered this fact by the methods of hypnosis and free association. In obsessive neurosis, the patient's mind is occupied with thoughts that do not really interest him, he feels impulses that seem alien to him, and he is impelled to perform certain actions that not only afford him no pleasure, but which he is powerless to resist. What he does commit are certain very harmless trivial acts, repetitions and ceremonial elaborations of everyday performances, like going to bed, washing, dressing, etcetera. The patient is, of course, aware of his condition, but the meaning of the symptom is unknown to him. Analysis invariably shows these symptoms are derived from unconscious mental processes which can however under various favourable conditions become conscious.

Freud says the fact that it is possible to find meaning in neurotic symptoms by means of analytic interpretation is irrefutable proof of the existence of the unconscious. The unconscious process contains the meaning of neurotic symptoms. Breuer's discovery still remains the foundation of psychoanalytical therapy, viz. that symptoms vanish when their unconscious antecedents have been made conscious.

THE NORMAL AND THE UNCONSCIOUS

If someone should maintain these are conclusions drawn chiefly from the study of pathological conditions, it could be said that Freud supplemented them by a study of the everyday life of the normal man. Certain difficulties of function of frequent occurrence among healthy people, slips of speech, errors in memory, false actions, etcetera, were shown to depend on the action of strong unconscious ideas in the same way as neurotic symptoms. This work is significant, as the supposedly impossible gap between the normal and the abnormal person was shown to be false. As Maclntyre says:

> Freud's is not an explanation simply of the abnormal and the exceptional but also of the normal. The scope in principle of Freudian explanation is all human behaviour; had it been less than this Freud would have been unable to draw the famous comparison between the effect of his own work and that of Copernicus. It is not surprising therefore, that happenings as normal as dreams, slips of the tongue and jokes should receive attention along with melancholia, obsessive habits, and excessive anxiety.[5]

In the case of forgetting, for example, the motive is an unwillingness to recall something which may evoke painful memories. The same conflict governs the phenomenon of erroneous actions. Motor expressions serve as the expression of numerous unconscious or restrained feelings. For the most part they symbolically represent wishes and fantasies. Most of these faults in speech, memory and action are the expression of repressed emotions in the psychic life. Even in healthy persons, egotistic, jealous and hostile feelings and impulses, burdened by the pressure of moral education, often utilise the path of faulty action to express themselves in some way. A thought does not seek expression in its complete form, but in a parasitic form, as a disturbance and modification of another thought. That is how the unconscious and the repressed seek a relationship with the conscious: unwelcome, repressed psychic material which, though pushed away from consciousness, is nevertheless not robbed of all capacity to express itself.

There is one more mental product to be met in normal persons that yet presents a striking analogy to the wildest production of insanity, namely dreams. A dream is itself a neurotic symptom, but which possesses for us the advantage of occurring in all healthy people. A dream is the life of the mind during sleep. Dreams are the reaction of the mind to stimuli acting upon it during sleep. Dreams in general appear confused, unintelligible and often senseless, and their contents may contradict all that we know of reality. Freud, on the other hand, insisted that they have a very significant meaning and made an attempt to understand them. He maintained that we can interpret dreams if we assume that what we recollect as a dream after we have awakened is not the true dream-process, but only a facade behind which the true dream-process lies concealed. Here we make a distinction between manifest dream material and latent dream thoughts. The process which produces the former out of the latter is the dream work. The study of dream work affords us a very good example of the way in which unconscious materials from the id force themselves upon the ego, become preconscious, and owing to the efforts of the ego undergo the modification we call distortion.

The formation of dreams can be provoked in different ways. On the one hand, an instinctual impulse which is as a rule suppressed (an unconscious wish) finds enough strength during sleep to make an impression upon the ego. On the other hand, a desire left over from waking life, a preconscious train of thought with all the conflicting impulses belonging to it, obtains reinforcement during sleep from an unconscious element. The unconscious id plays a dominant role in the formation of dreams. Memory is far more comprehensive in dreams than in waking life. Dreams make unlimited use of linguistic symbols. Memory very often reproduces impressions from the dreamer's early childhood in dreams. Beyond this, dreams bring into light material which could not originate either from the dreamer's adult life or from his forgotten childhood. Freud considers this aspect of dreams has to be understood in terms of the child's 'archaic heritage'. This reference to the archaic heritage brings us to a rather complex question that has to be analysed separately.[6]

THE UNCONSCIOUS AND THE ID

Now let us briefly sum up the relationship between the unconscious and the id. Though Freud presented a very systematic and comprehensive picture of the unconscious in his essay *The Unconscious*,[7] he modified his position in the *Ego and the Id*[8] and this is of very great significance for a comparative study of Buddhism and Freud.

Freud's conception of the unconscious up to 1915 was basically 'rooted in pathology, with an emphasis on repression'.[9] Thus it was restricted to repressed impulses. With the publication of the *Ego and the Id*, 'Freud took account of the total personality, of normal as well as pathological functioning, and the repressed is explicitly described as only part of the id. The primary system is no longer only the repressed but includes normal impulses as well. It contains the passions.'[10]

The conception of the id was more productive and comprehensive than the concept of the unconscious as the repressed. When a patient exhibits signs of resistance, generally he is aware of his repugnance. But it appeared to Freud that sometimes he is quite unaware of it. Thus there must be some kind of unconscious resistance and this unconscious resistance comes from the ego. The unavoidable conclusion that follows is that the ego is not limited to what the subject consciously calls his 'self', but is continued below the threshold of consciousness; part of the ego is conscious, part of it is unconscious. And the latter part is not merely preconscious; it is unconscious in the fullest sense, since much work is needed to make it conscious.[11] This recognition of the 'greater depth of the ego' is a significant point in the development of Freudian psychology and one which is interesting in the light of Buddhist psychology. Early Buddhism upholds the operation of ego drives at subliminal and unconscious levels.

THE SUBCONSCIOUS AND THE UNCONSCIOUS

Often the words 'unconscious,' 'subconscious' and 'subliminal conscious' are used indiscriminately to describe one and the same phenomenon.

This type of loose usage is often found in popular expositions of psychology. *The Dictionary of Psychological and Psychoanalytical Terms* states that in 'popular psychoanalysis, the unconscious and subconscious are thoroughly confused'.[12] In his analysis of the *bhavaṅga* theory, Sarachchandra seems to use both 'unconscious' and 'subconscious' to describe the concept of *bhavaṅga* without implying any shift of meaning. This is a significant point, because the logical status of the concept of *bhavaṅga* is partly determined by the usage of words like 'unconscious' and 'subconscious,' especially when they are used to translate certain Pāli terms in Buddhist works.

Under the entry 'subconscious,' the *Dictionary* cites the following definitions: 1) not clearly conscious, but capable of being made so, 2) the preconscious of psychoanalysis, 3) subliminal, and 4) pertaining to what is on the margin of attention.[13] The psychoanalytic meaning of preconscious has already been discussed. The term 'subliminal' is not very much used by psychologists now. Historically F.W.H. Myers is associated with the conception of the subliminal. The psychologist's concept of the subconscious (whether we call it what is dimly conscious or at the margin of attention) is historically associated with the work of psychologists like Janet, Prince and Sidis. There have been various attempts to analyse the different shades of meaning of the word 'subconscious' as used by psychologists. Six definitions are given below from a symposium on subconscious phenomena:[14]

1) That portion of our field of consciousness which at any given moment is outside the focus of our attention; a region, therefore, of diminished attention. It can refer to the fringe of consciousness. The prefix sub- denotes 'diminished' or 'partial'.

2) In abnormal psychology, 'subconscious ideas are dissociated or ideas that are split-off from the main personal consciousness—from the focus of attention, if that term is preferred—in such way that the subject is entirely unaware of them, though they are not inert but active.' This split-off or secondary consciousness can under exceptional circumstances be the dominant consciousness.

3) Subconscious states may become personified and are then spoken of as the 'subconscious self,' 'subliminal self,' 'secondary self,' 'hidden self,' etcetera. What is of interest in these definitions is first of all the idea of marginal or partial awareness and then a dissociated state tending

toward a personified self.

4) Dissociated states which are 'active' and those which are 'inactive'. The inactive refers to the forgotten and may be recalled as memories.

5) This is the theory of 'subliminal consciousness' held by Myers. 'The subconscious ideas, instead of being mental states dissociated from the main personality, now become the main reservoir of consciousness and the personal consciousness becomes a subordinate stream flowing out of this great storage basis of subliminal ideas as they are called.' As Northbridge points out, there are two distinct aspects to this concept of the subliminal self, and Myers himself did not make this clear: 'It consists of those mental elements that are too weak to attract our attention. It refers to the intuitions of a "profound faculty," which are submerged by the constitution of man's personality.'

6) Lastly there is the hypothesis of the physiological psychologist that the subconscious refers to neural processes unaccompanied by any mental processes.

These shifts of meaning in the word as used by psychologists (not laymen) show how inadequate the concept was in classifying certain types of psychological phenomena. The shift went from preconscious phenomena (in the Freudian sense) such as those that lie at the margin of consciousness, to dissociated states and forgotten and inactive memories. It is because of this that Freud suggested his own terminology instead of the term 'subconscious'. Though he used this term in his *Studies on Hysteria,* [15] he rejects it later. In the *Introductory Lectures* he says:

> I should also like to hear you admit that our designations unconscious, preconscious and conscious, are less prejudicial and more easily defensible than some others which have been suggested or have come into use, e.g. subconscious, inter-conscious, co-conscious, etcetera.[16]

To facilitate the analysis of the concepts subconscious, subliminal and unconscious sixteen different shades of meaning of the word 'unconscious' are given below based on the treatment by J.G. Miller:[17]

1 *Inanimate:* this refers to what does not discriminate or behave.

2 *Absent-minded:* day-dreaming or anaesthetised.

3 *Not-mental:* a concept rejected by Freud as a popular but a wrong

view. Mind and consciousness cannot be equated. The mental or the psychical is a wider realm than the conscious.

4 *Undiscriminating:* though in the case of the inanimate, discrimination between stimuli is not logically possible, here it is possible but there is a lack of it. E.G. Boring, who has made a clear statement on this position says, 'Discrimination is the psychical function of the organism. It is the criterion of mind, of consciousness, of knowing. Animals, children and irresponsible adults are recognised as conscious only as and in as far as they discriminate, that is to say as they react differentially to a differentiated situation'.[18] This is essentially a behavioural criterion of consciousness and does not depend on any 'private awareness'.

5 *Conditioned:* this refers to those who act on the basis of conditioning or conditioned response.

6 *Unsensed:* under this heading are various aspects of unsensing, such as stimuli not reaching the organism, inadequate stimuli affecting the organism, subliminal stimuli affecting the organism.

7 *Unnoticed or unattended*: when unconscious is used in the sense of unattended, one's actions, ideas, emotions, needs and drives are unconscious merely because he is thinking of something else.

8 *Insightless*: Miller says that this is essentially a 'gestalt concept' and refers to doing a task without awareness of what is being learned or intent to learn it.

9 *Unremembered:* Miller cites seven types of forgetting which can be brought under this heading: extinction, simple forgetting, incorrect remembering, new material preventing the reproduction of older memories, dissociation, suppression and repression. This is a very important sense of the word unconscious connected with the psychoanalytic usage.

10 *Instinctive or inherited*: Miller says that this instinctive aspect is the most important characteristic of the unconscious in psychoanalytic theory. L.E. Emerson stated this well when he said that to a great extent the unconscious refers to cravings, instincts, impulses and reflexes or psychochemical reactions.

11 *Unrecognised*: Sometimes this implies that the existence of the process is not known and at other times that the existence is recognised, but the character of the process is not understood.

12 *Involuntary*: According to A. A. Brill, Freud believed that what is unconscious cannot be voluntarily recalled. Academic psychologists have never been certain what 'voluntary' means and have come to neglect studying the will almost entirely. The value of this strand of meaning in the word 'unconscious' depends on unravelling a lot of ambiguity in the use of the word voluntary.

13 *Incommunicable*: Miller says that this does not refer to what is not verbalised, but rather to what is incapable of verbalisation or of communication of any sort.

14 *Ignoring*: Describing the usage of this word, Broad says, 'A method which we very commonly use is to put a ring-fence around a certain region, to label it as dangerous, and to avert our attention from the whole of it.'[19]

15 *Psychoanalytic meaning*: Miller mentions three elements that he considers to be the meaning of unconscious in its psychoanalytic use: 1) they are dynamically repressed away from consciousness; the organs of perception, 2) they can be made available to consciousness only by special techniques such as hypnosis and psycho-analysis, and 3) they are not under voluntary control. Freud used a special abbreviation Ucs, to emphasise and mark the special way in which he used the word.

16 *Unavailable to awareness*: definition number four refers to the basic sense of the unconscious for those who accept only behavioural evidence, but this meaning is accepted by those who admit the validity of introspective testimony.

THE LOGIC OF UNCONSCIOUS MOTIVES

There appears to be some kind of contradiction in juxtaposing the words 'motive' and 'unconscious' and thus speaking of 'unconscious motives.' If motives are reasons for actions, 'unconscious motives' seems like an unhappy hybrid. It is necessary therefore, to explain the significance of this concept as a working hypothesis for understanding human behaviour. The preceding examination of the meanings of the word 'unconscious' should facilitate the attempt made here to explain the 'unconscious' in terms of dispositions. Both Else Frenkel-Brunswik and Arthur Pap refer to the possibility of explaining the unconscious in terms of dispositions:[20]

> From the standpoint of the logic of science, unconscious tendencies are a special case of latent or dispositional characteristics. They are comparable to such physical characteristics as magnetism – provided that we do not insist on assigning them to the mind in a metaphysical sense. Such composite terms as 'unconscious hostility' or 'dependency' describe a disposition to display aggression or dependency under specified conditions, for example, in therapy.[21]

Regarding the meaning of the word 'unconscious,' Pap says that though it has several meanings:

> Its characteristic psychoanalytic meaning however, seems to be dispositional, or more accurately, the meaning that remains after it is divested of misleading metaphorical connotations.[22]

Even MacIntyre, in his analysis of the concept of the unconscious, makes a good attempt to absorb the concept of disposition to his interpretation of unconscious motivation.[23] The best way to make a philosophical analysis of the concept of unconscious motivation is to make our way through some of these studies, especially MacIntyre's monograph on the unconscious, because these illuminating insights will help to clarify a concept that claims to grasp the dark and inner depths of human motivation. Freud himself accepts the fact that the poet, the novelist and the philosopher had before him discovered the unconscious, but that he discovered the scientific methods which give it objectivity and the stamp of a scientific hypothesis. As MacIntyre says:

> One of the central features of the novel is the depicting of how much of human action and passion is not the fruit of conscious intention. This uncovering of our own ignorance of ourselves Freud did not fail to see that he shared with the imaginative writer.[24]

Thus must be emphasised the fact that Freud was not a mere theoretician, but rather dealt with grim human realities.

PRE-FREUDIAN AND FREUDIAN SENSES OF UNCONSCIOUS MOTIVATION

Maclntyre says that to claim Freud's theory of unconscious mental activity is at fault, because wishes, motives, fears and the like must be conscious, is not a correct claim. The terms 'wish' and 'fears' do not in ordinary usage describe and refer only to private moments of consciousness, but are in part descriptive of patterns of behaviour which are publicly observable. These patterns go unrecognised and they may be denominated 'unconscious'.

Freud shows that some types of neurotic behaviour are the result of unconscious motivation. The neurotic has purposes and intentions of which he is unaware. Since he is unaware of them, he cannot avow them. By 'intention' here Freud means apparently a pattern of behaviour. A neurotic patient's intention or purpose is betrayed in his behaviour, and if he were not prevented by his disorder, he would avow it. Thus, the meaning of 'intention' is elucidated by a categorical reference to behaviour supplemented by a hypothetical reference to avowals. Maclntyre says that this is how the concept of intention and kindred concepts should be understood in the pre-Freudian sense.[25]

If we follow this line of thought, to ascribe a motive to someone is not merely to say he has a tendency to behave in a particular way, or to say there is a pattern in his actions. To find what else there is in intention, we must distinguish between causal properties in things and the disposition of human beings. The evidence that proves the solubility of salt in water is simply that it dissolves. But if you want to prove that Smith is ambitious, more evidence is needed than his behaving in a certain fashion.

The difference between things and people is that people can talk about their behaviour. It makes sense to say that Smith seems to be ambitious because he behaves in certain ways, but the fact is he may not be ambitious. If I tell Smith that he is ambitious and illustrate my point in various ways, it is possible that Smith will ultimately accept the fact of his being ambitious. If so, we should have a case of 'unconscious,' in the ordinary pre-Freudian sense. But if, on pointing out in suitable ways to Smith that he is ambitious, we discovered an inability in Smith to recognise his own ambition, we should have a case of unconscious ambition in the Freudian sense.

THE IGNORED AND THE INACCESSIBLE

It is possible that there are certain intermediary stages between the two senses of 'unconscious' discussed above, certain gradations that fall between the two usages. Maclntyre does not discuss this problem in detail, but it is important. The value of Maclntyre's analysis certainly lies in working out the connecting links between the pre-Freudian use of 'unconscious' and the Freudian use of the word. While he does a good job in dispelling the atmosphere of mystery that surrounds it, he ought to have discussed the problem of gradations and degrees of unconsciousness. In the case of Smith's inability to recognise his ambition, it is possible he is dimly aware of it, but does not really grasp its nature. In our daily activities, our actions often do not proceed from deliberate thought and reflection. We make decisions and pursue goals without being clear about the reasons for our actions. We sometimes decide on the spur of the moment and have only a vague awareness of the motives that enter into our decisions.

Freud emphasises the fact that many people have an aversion to honestly recognising their own attitude, especially if there is something uncomplimentary involved. When this tendency to ignore certain aspects of one's personality is repeated, it may be said that he systematically biases his opinion about himself. The question arises whether this systematic bias can be analysed by the person himself simply by trying to examine himself honestly, or whether one of the Freudian techniques like free association is necessary. According to Broad this aspect of unconscious motivation can be described as 'ignored, misdescribed or dislocated desires and emotions'. He adds:

> Desires and emotions are the experiences *par excellence* about which we pass judgments of praise or blame on ourselves and others. If we find that we have certain desires and emotions we are obliged to think badly of ourselves; and if we confess such desires and emotions to others, they will think badly of us. We thus have a strong tendency not to discriminate these desires and emotions; or if we discriminate them to ourselves, or if we discriminate and describe them rightly to ourselves, to acknowledge them to others.[26]

Now in what sense are these desires and emotions to be described as 'unconscious'? Regarding these desires and emotions, Broad says these states are quite literally conscious. They are really ordinary desires and emotions about whose existence, nature and objects, we need make no mistake if we introspect honestly and carefully enough. But, of course, we do not do this. He adds:

> If there be anything literally unconscious in the whole business, it is not the desire or emotion itself, but the process of ignoring, dislocating or misdescribing it.[27]

This aversion to introspective attention, which begins by being deliberate, quickly becomes habitual. What is interesting in this analysis is that there can be gradations of personalities, in some of whom the ignored and the misdescribed become one with the 'inaccessible' in the Freudian sense, and in some of whom the process has just begun and not taken root in the personality. With the latter group, an ordinary effort to look at themselves honestly should help them get at the self-knowledge required to transform their personalities. Though there is a close connection between ignored and inaccessible experiences, many experiences which have become inaccessible were not ignored when they happened, and some which were ignored have not become inaccessible.

Broad thinks there is a close connection between the 'ignored' and the 'inaccessible.' But the accessible and the inaccessible are two limits within which gradations of awareness, discrimination, sophistication and insight are possible. The distinction between the 'accessible' and the 'ignored' has been treated at length because of its great significance for an analysis of the Buddhist concept of the unconscious.

SELF-KNOWLEDGE AND SELF-CONTROL

Summing up the analysis of the concept of unconscious motivation, it could be said that there are two ways of mastering the unconscious. They are the twin methods of self-knowledge and self-control; two methods that really supplement each other. Though morbid self-analysis that paralyses action has to be condemned, rational behaviour is made possible by enlarging the area of self-control and self-knowledge. L.W. Beck makes a useful examination of this problem:

> As the agent comes to see his unconscious desires and wishes, he is not just learning a fact about his past; he is experiencing an enlargement of his sense of self through taking something into his personal makeup whose existence he did not know or whose existence he regarded as something alien and external to himself.'[28]

It is only when the unconscious intentions become as well known as consciousness that the agent can overcome his self-alienation. With the help of the psychoanalyst, the agent can come to see himself as others see him. In this way, the analyst takes the first step in encouraging the patient to go smoothly on the road to discovering his real nature. In fact, insight and wisdom regarding oneself makes excessive self-control superfluous. This emphasis on self-knowledge and the enlargement of one's personal horizon is a common ideal for Freud and the Buddha. Thus our interest in the nature of unconscious motivation is not merely theoretical. It is related to the therapeutic basis of Freudian and Buddhist psychology.

THE UNCONSCIOUS IN EARLY BUDDHISM

Now we come to our basic thesis that there is a concept of the unconscious in early Buddhism. This notion seems hardly to have engaged the attention of scholars. Sarachchandra's exposition of the *bhavaṅga* theory is the closest thing to any systematic examination of the unconscious in Buddhist thought. However, our study of this problem differs from his views in a number of ways:

> The *bhavaṅga* theory is not a central doctrine of the *Nikāyas*. This idea was not thought by the Buddha at all. It is hardly even mentioned until the *Milinda Pañha* and was developed by later expositors of the Abhidhamma, like Anuruddha and Buddhaghosa. There is a single occurrence of the word in the *Aṅguttara Nikāya* which Sarachchandra himself says 'is evidently a wrong reading for the commentary reads and

explains it as bhavagga'.[29]

His main concern is with the psychology of perception, whereas we are concerned with the psychology of motivation. A concept of the unconscious cannot be understood purely by discussing its function within the realm of theories of perception. A concept of the unconscious is basically related to motivation. Strictly speaking however, Sarachchandra was limiting himself to perception, his major theme having been the Buddhist psychology of perception.

He uses the terms 'unconscious' and 'subconscious' somewhat indiscriminately. Obviously this can be misleading, and a little care ought to have been observed regarding the usage of these words. Thus, in introducing the *bhavaṅga* theory he says, 'In the course of our description of the Abhidhamma philosophy of mind we found the occurrence of a new term, *bhavaṅga* which we have translated as the unconscious.[30] But later he says, 'The series of mental states from subconsciousness to active cognition would be, in order, *bhavaṅgaviññāṇa, mano, indriyaviññāṇa* and *manoviññāṇa*.'[31] Similarly, in commenting on the *yogācāra* theory, he says, 'From the subconscious *ālaya* there evolved the object-discriminating mind, and from the mind the five kinds of sense-perception.'[32] It is difficult to discover any reason for these shifts from one term to the other.

One of his basic contentions is that *viññāna* is considered a sort of anoetic sentience in the earlier texts, which he thinks is a view consistent with the usage of the word in later Abhidhamma theory. Opposing this view, Jayatilleke has shown that *viññāna* in the context of the process of perception is a general term for cognitive consciousness. Further, Sarachchandra states that the belief in *viññāna* as a transmigrating factor appears to be a later view.[33] That this thesis cannot be accepted has been made clear in chapter two.

In fairness to Sarachchandra, however, it must be said that the *bhavaṅga* concept is certainly of importance in Buddhist psychology, though the Buddha himself apparently did not mention it. It is used by many expositors and teachers of the Abhidhamma in Ceylon today and this makes it all the more important to learn to what extent it is found in the early stages in the development of Buddhism. But Sarachchandra errs in considering *viññāna* in the sense of 'a survival factor' to be a later intrusion into Buddhist thought. It is on this assumption that he employs the *bhavaṅga* theory to solve so many problematical issues. The *bhavaṅga* concept may be used to explain certain points in the Abhidhamma, but it should be applied with full awareness of its nature and limits.

Apart from the concept of *bhavaṅga* there are a number of interesting concepts in early Buddhism, like *anusaya, āsava, saṅkhāra, saṃvatta nika viññāna, bhavasota* and even *viññānasota* which make a close study of the Nikāyas of early Buddhism rewarding.

THE PROBLEM OF UNCONSCIOUS MOTIVATION

There are various guidelines to follow in working out the concepts of mind, matter or causation in early Buddhism. The discourses of the Buddha shed a great deal of light on such matters, as has been shown in chapter two, where a critical analysis of the *nāma-rūpa* concept was given. Details are often problematic, but anyone who wants to work out the concept of mind or matter in Buddhism can find his way about. The issue of the unconscious presents a more difficult problem. Before a clear picture can be gained, a large amount of critical study of many different texts must be undertaken and many little facts pieced together from here and there and interpreted.

THE BHAVAṄGA THEORY

Sarachchandra says that certain problems were raised regarding the metaphysics of the mind by later Buddhist thinkers for which the early Buddhism of the Nikāyas does not provide an answer, and in this way the *bhavaṅga* theory was introduced. These are some of the questions that were grappled with by the later Buddhist thinkers: 1) what is the relationship between the higher consciousness *(jhāna)* and the ordinary empirical consciousness? 2) what is the source of the intuition faculty? 3) does it lie hidden within the individual in a potential and non-manifest condition? 4) what is the difference between a trance state, deep sleep and dream consciousness? 5) can we account for the concept of human survival after death without introducing a notion of the soul? These were the questions that needed an answer. Sarachchandra sums up the position thus:

> How could states like deep sleep, trance and dream be explained without the assumption of a permanent, residing consciousness within the human body, manifesting itself at one time in mental activity, and lying potential and dormant at another? To say that there was nothing else besides empirical consciousness would be to expose Buddhism to the charge of materialism.[34]

Thus Sarachchandra's basic contention is that the concept of *bhavaṅga* was used later to explain the states of deep sleep, dream and trance and give a satisfactory theory of survival. According to Sarachchandra, *bhavaṅga* originally meant a link in the causal chain. The twelve factors beginning with *avidyā, saṃskāra* and *vijñāna* were called the 'factors of becoming' *(bhavaṅgāni)*. After some time *bhavaṅga* in the sense of 'factor of becoming' came to be used in the sense of 'cause of existence'. Thus there came into being a tradition which explained *bhavaṅga* as the cause of the individual in various existences.

When *bhavaṅga* is applied to the process of thought, it refers to the fact that at the end of every thought process the mind changes into its original state. When the mind is entirely vacant, as in dreamless sleep, it is *vīthimutta* (thought-free). It is often described as a state below the threshold of consciousness. S.Z. Aung says it corresponds to Myers' 'subliminal consciousness'.[35]

Aung compares the term *bhavaṅga-sota* or the 'stream of existence' to the current of a river when it flows calmly on unhindered by any obstacle. When the current is opposed by an obstacle of thought from the world within, then thoughts arise. 'But it must not be supposed that the stream of being is a sub-plane from which thoughts arise to the surface,'[36] he says, adding that there is only a juxtaposition of momentary states of consciousness, subliminal and supraliminal throughout a lifetime, from one existence to another. But there is no superimposition of such states. Now this process can be described by the term subconscious or subliminal. By that we mean that which is outside the threshold of awareness or below the threshold of normal sensory excitation.

On the other hand, if we use the term 'unconscious,' it can be confusing. For instance, in the Freudian use of the dynamic unconscious, there are definitely unconscious processes that attempt to emerge to the surface through various circuitous and devious ways. That connotation is rejected by Aung, when he says it cannot be regarded as a sub-plane from which thoughts arise to the surface. This shows that it is not wise to use terms like unconscious and subconscious indiscriminately to translate the word *bhavaṅga.* There are works on Buddhism where the *bhavaṅga* concept has been likened to a kind of dynamic unconscious in the Freudian sense. Nyanatiloka Thera says:

> Herein, since time immemorial, all impressions and experiences are, as it were, stored up, or better said, functioning but concealed as such to full consciousness from where however they occasionally emerge as subconscious phenomena and approach the threshold of full consciousness...'[37]

Nyanatiloka concludes:

> This so-called 'subconscious life stream' or undercurrent of life is that by which might be explained the faculty of memory, paranormal psychic phenomena, mental and physical growth, Karma and rebirth, etcetera.[38]

It is interesting to compare this statement with that of Aung mentioned above. Aung says that the *bhavaṅga-sota* is not a sub-plane from which thoughts rise to the surface; according to Nyanatiloka stored up impressions concealed to the consciousness emerge as subconscious phenomena and approach consciousness.

Thus, in spite of Sarachchandra's claim that the *bhavaṅga* theory is a useful concept to deal with certain problems unanswered by early Buddhism, the concept of *bhavaṅga* involves a great element of interpretation and sometimes contradictory interpretations. This danger has been perhaps averted by Nyanamoli Thera in his translation of *bhavaṅga* in *Visuddhimagga* by 'life continuum,' whereas Sarachchandra has 'unconscious continuum.'[39] In fact throughout his translation Nyanamoli uses this phrase consistently.

VIÑÑĀNA-SOTA AND THE UNCONSCIOUS

According to Sarachchandra the term *viññāna-sota* found in the *Dīgha Nikāya* is a later interpolation:

> One isolated expression *viññāna-sota* appears in the Nikāyas, used evidently in connection with continuance of the individual in a series of births. Since this conception of mind is alien to the ideology of early Buddhism, we might well surmise that as a later interpolation.'[40]

It has already been noted that in certain contexts *viññāna* is used in the sense of the 'factor of survival' and that Sarachchandra is wrong in considering this alien to the Buddhist concept of mind. On the other hand, this passage which he regards as a later interpolation is very significant and contains notions that are found elsewhere in the Nikāyas. It reads as follows, '*purisassa ca viññāna-sotaṃ pajānāti ubhayato abbocchinnaṃ idha-loke patitthitañ ca para-loke patitthitañ ca.*' Rhys Davids translates this passage thus:

> He goes on after that to discuss the 'unbroken flux of human consciousness established both in this world and in another world.'[41]

The context refers to certain degrees of discernment (*dassana-samāpatti)* attained by the recluse who practises meditation. First he meditates introspectively on the bodily organism 'from the sole of the feet to the crown of the head'. In this way he discerns the nature of the body. In the second stage he discerns the nature of the human skeleton. In the third degree of discernment, with which the passage quoted is concerned, the recluse discerns the consciousness of the living person *(purisassa)* as related both to this world and to the world beyond. The fourth state refers to the absence of such a consciousness in the *arahat* who will not be born again. Jayatilleke renders this passage somewhat differently from Rhys Davids.[42]

He thinks that the 'stream of consciousness' (i.e. the 'flux of human consciousness' in Rhys David's translation) is not 'unbroken' but actually 'divided into two parts'. This interpretation requires the Pāli word *'abbocchinnaṃ'* to be read as *'abbhocchinnaṃ'*. According to the *Critical Pāli Dictionary* (presumably following the view given in the *Pāli Text Society's Pāli-English Dictionary) abbocchinnaṃ* is a wrong spelling for *'abbhocchinnaṃ.'* This form without the -h- would have to correspond to Sanskrit *avyavachinna* which has a negative meaning, i.e. 'not divided' and this is the version adopted by Rhys Davids, as we have seen. But it is difficult to see why *abbhocchinnaṃ* must be regarded as a misspelling, though admittedly the traditional interpretation culminating in Rhys David's translation supports the negative view. The context, however, seems more naturally to favour the original reading with -h-. For if the reading *'abbhocchinnaṃ'* be kept, the sense of the passage, consonant with Jayatilleke's translation, would be:

> He discerns the stream of consciousness of the living persons as (being) divided into two (parts), viz. as established in this world and established in the world beyond.'

Now this passage would seem to suggest a twofold nature of the 'stream of consciousness' in the individual or living person, the one part of which he is not ordinarily aware. To attain an awareness of it requires passing into the third stage of meditation which the passage refers to. This part of the stream of consciousness of which the individual is not aware may well be the dynamic unconscious comprised of the dispositions *(saṅkhāra)* that determine the particular character of the next birth.

This interpretation can be strengthened by citing another significant passage (D. III, 104). In fact this passage precedes the one quoted above (D.III, 105) and is also found in the *Aṅguttara Nikāya* (I, 171). It refers to four methods of revealing the mind of another person. Firstly, a person can, by means of a sign *(nimitta),* infer the thought of another person, however much that person may deny it. Secondly, he can infer the thought of another by means of a sound made by a human or a non-human being. Thirdly, the thought of another can be known 'through hearing a rational sound made intelligently and deliberately'. Lastly, it is said that when the person attains a state of concentration which is void of conception and discursive thinking *(avitakka avicāra),* then he is able to discern the thought of another. This also gives him an insight into the mental dispositions of the other person. According to the mental dispositions of the other person he is able to predict that he will at a later time think 'such and such a thought'.

Since the person is not conscious of the mental dispositions *(mano-saṅkhāra)* which subsequently influence his process of thought, they are perhaps not present in his consciousness when they are discerned by the other with telepathic powers. Jayatilleke commenting on this passage says that this is perhaps the earliest historical mention of unconscious mental processes.[43]

ASAMPAJĀNA MANO-SAṄKHĀRA

In chapter two, a detailed analysis of *saṅkhāra* was made and in this chapter the dynamic of *saṅkhāras,* which persist in the unconscious and influence the subsequent behaviour of an individual have been discussed. In addition to these dynamic *saṅkhāras,* there are two subdivisions called *sampajāna mano-saṅkhāras* and *asampajāna mano-saṅkhāra.*

In the passages where they are mentioned, it is said that there are *mano-saṅkhāras* (mental dispositions or trains of thought), which are self-instigated or instigated by others, while we are aware of them (*sampajāno)* or while we are unaware of them (*asampajāna*).[44] The same analysis is made of *vacī-saṅkhāra* (verbal dispositions) and *kāya-saṅkhāra* (bodily dispositions). But the analysis of *mano-saṅkhāra* is more interesting to our theme as it implies the presence of unconscious motives.

The concept of *asampajāna mano-saṅkhāra* clearly implies the existence of unconscious tendencies. It does not imply the existence of a substrate called the 'unconscious,' but rather the presence of certain dispositions which can be described by the adjective unconscious. The Buddha rejected substance theories of mind and body whether they have reference to one's conscious experience or unconscious propensities. That is why we wish to understand the nature of unconscious motivation in terms of dispositions rather than substrates.

ANUSAYA

The term *anusaya* has been variously translated by Pāli scholars as 'proclivity, underlying tendency, inherent tendency, lurking tendency, inclination.' It must be made clear however, that the *anusayas* are distinct from the *saṅkhāras;* the latter function both at conscious and unconscious levels, whereas the former lie dormant at the unconscious level. What is the meta-psychological status of this concept? Using Freudian terminology, are we to say that the *anusaya* functions at a preconscious level or at the unconscious level? The *Pāli Text Society's Pāli-English Dictionary* defines *anusaya* as 'bent, bias, proclivity, the persistence of a dormant or latent disposition, predisposition, tendency.'[45] The characterisation of the *anusayas* as 'dormant' is psychologically interesting. The term 'dormant' as in ordinary language gives a good idea of the nature of the *anusayas,* as they are persistent, latent dispositions. They have been aptly described as 'lurking tendencies.' As a consequence of their pertinacity they tend to provide the foundation for sensuous greed, anger and pride, etcetera.

Their pertinacity is well illustrated in a passage from the *Saṃyutta Nikāyas.* 'Suppose, friends, there is a dirty soiled cloth, and the owners give it to a washer man, and he rubs it smooth with salt earth, or lye or cow-dung, and rinses it in pure clean water. Now though that cloth be clean, utterly cleansed, yet there hangs about it, still unremoved, the smell of the salt earth.'[46] This is especially true of the bias of conceit (*mānanusaya),* which will not be removed till one attains arahatship. This continuous upsurge of such proclivities is made possible by their very nature. Thus, the *anusayas* differ from passing mental states. They have eaten into one's nature and settled there and found a habitat there. The most striking fact regarding the *anusayas* is their irrational and impulsive character. The majority of people are not aware of the strength of these biases, though subject to them.

The *Yāmaka* (Book of Pairs) has a comprehensive breakdown of the *anusayas.*[47] It mentions seven *anusayas,* and this is also referred to in the *Dīgha Nikāya.*[48] They are:

1 The *anusaya* of sensuous craving (*kāmarāga*).
2 The *anusaya* of anger *(patigha*).
3 The *anusaya* of conceit *(māna*).
4 The *anusaya* of erroneous opinion *(diṭṭhi*).
5 The *anusaya* of scepticism *(vicikiccha*).
6 The *anusaya* of craving for existence *(bhavarāga*).
7 The *anusaya* of ignorance *(avijjā*).

The question is raised as to where the *anusaya* originate, and the following answers are given:

1. Where does the *anusaya* of sensuous craving adhere? It adheres to the two feelings (pleasant and indifferent) of the sensuous sphere.
2. Where anger? It adheres to painful (bodily or mental) feeling.
3. Where conceit? It adheres to the two feelings of the sensuous sphere (see one) and the fine material and immaterial sphere.
4. Where erroneous opinion? It adheres to all phenomena included in the existence group *(sakkāya).*
5. Where scepticism? The same as answer four.
6. Where craving for existence? It adheres to the fine material and immaterial sphere.
7. Where ignorance? The same as answer four.

The strength and the power of different *anusayas* are known, some are eliminated at an early state of development, while others remain until the attainment of the holy state (*arahat*). The 'stream winner' (*sotāpanna)* and the 'once-returner' (*sakadā gāmi)* have five *anusayas,* viz. numbers. 1, 2, 3, 6 and 7. The 'never-returner' (*anāgāmi)* is subject to three *anusayas,* viz. 3, 6 and 7. This shows that numbers 3, 6 and 7 are more powerful and persist until the attainment of holiness.

Conceit and the craving for existence, then, are more difficult to eradicate than the drive for sensual pleasures, a significant point that should be kept in mind with reference to the psychology of Freud. Though Freud later emphasised the power of the ego instinct and the destructive urge as different from the sexual drives, some people have been influenced by the libido theory to such an extent that they feel the spell of sensuous desires can never be mastered.

There are one or two other points that are worthy of note here. It is said that everyone to whom the *anusaya* of *rāga* (sensuous greed) adheres so does the *anusaya* of *patigha* (anger) and vice versa. These two always go together. Pleasant feelings induce an attachment (*upādāna)* to pleasant objects and there is potency in pleasant feelings to arouse latent sensuous greed (*rāgānusaya).* Painful feelings, on the other hand, arouse latent anger and hatred (*patighānusaya).* It is said that 'a tendency to attachment lies in pleasant feeling, a tendency to repugnance lies latent in painful feeling, and a tendency to ignorance lies latent in neutral feeling.'[49]

Clinging (*upādāna)* emerges always with craving as a condition. Craving is like aspiring to an object that one has not reached, like a thief stretching out his hand in the dark; clinging is grasping of an object that one has reached, like the thief grasping his object. But clinging is very deeply rooted and once a person clings to pleasure-giving objects, some latent tendencies or *anusayas* are excited and stimulated. Fixation on pleasure-giving objects is always fed by the undercurrent of the *anusayas.*

An interesting passage in the *Majjhima Nikāya* says of a baby boy that 'a leaning to attachment to sense-pleasures (*kāmarāgānusaya)* indeed lies latent in him.'[50] Four other *anusayas* latent in the 'innocent baby lying on his back' are referenced here, viz. *byāpādānusaya* (a leaning to malevolence), *silabbata-parāmāsānusaya* (a leaning to cling to rites and customs), *vicikicchānusaya* (a leaning to perplexity) and *sakkāyadiṭṭānusaya* (a leaning to the 'view of own body').

The Freudians are at a loss to explain the origin of these traits and sometimes they resort to biology and physiology. There are others like Otto Rank, who have introduced the hypothesis of the birth trauma. Early Buddhist psychology, however, considers these tendencies or traits to be the heritage of innumerable previous lives.

We have already seen how the polarity of attachment to pleasure and repugnance to pain dominate the mind. Now let us consider the *anusaya* of conceit (*mānānusaya).* This *anusaya* together with *bhavarāga* and *diṭṭhi* function within a common framework, since they are all directly or indirectly connected to the ego-concept. But while the *diṭṭhānusaya* is eliminated by the 'non-returner' (*anāgāmi),* the other two exist till the attainment of the holy state of arahat. Conceit (*māna)* has to be differentiated from ego-belief (*sakkāyadiṭṭhi)* which is connected with the *diṭṭhānusaya* and implies a definite view regarding the assumption of an ego. *Māna* can vary from a crude feeling of pride to a subtle feeling of one's distinctiveness which prevails till the attainment of arahantship.

Conceit is such a deeply ingrained trait of man that it remains dormant till one becomes an arahat. It is said that to realize arahantship, a monk has to give up six things: pride (*māna),* self-debasement (*omāna)* vain-glory (*atimāna),* excessive self-esteem (*adhimāna),* stupefaction (*thamba)* and excessive self-debasement (*atinipāta).* All these facets of egoism emphasise the fact that the ideal monk should not harbour any sort of pride. Conceit is manifested in three ways: first, the superiority feeling (*seyya-māna*); second, a feeling of equality with another (*sadisa-māna*); third, the inferiority feeling (*hīna-māna*). These three manifestations of *māna* can arise in connection with wealth, learning, personal charm and beauty, social standing, physical vigour, etcetera.

This concept of *māna* offers an interesting analogy to the Freudian concept of 'narcissism' and the Adlerian inferiority complex. *Māna* can be rendered as 'pride' but it really implies the illusion or conceit connected with pride. So long as the lurking tendency to conceit (*mānānusaya*) prevails, man is the slave of an arbitrary valuation of his own making. The *diṭṭhānusaya* is essentially connected with twenty types of personality beliefs and is eliminated at an early stage, i.e. by the *sotāpanna*.

When there is merely a complex consisting of body, feeling, perception, dispositions and consciousness, the individual being subject to the ego illusions assumes the existence of an ego. The twenty types of personality beliefs can be summed up thus:

1-5: Ego as identical with corporeality, feeling, perception, dispositions and consciousness
6-10: Ego as contained in them
11-15: Ego as independent of them
16-20: Ego as the owner of them.

The *anusaya* concept is helpful in explaining certain patterns of personality. The *kāmarāga anusaya* can be related to the libido theory, the *patigha anusaya* with the death instinct and *māna, diṭṭha and bhavarāga anusaya* with the ego instincts of Freud.

Having described the nature of the *anusayas*, we shall now try to determine their meta-psychological status. In the *Visuddhimagga* it is stated that the defilements (*kilesas*) pass through three periods or stages, the first of which is that of the *anusayas*.[51] A detailed analysis of this has been made by Ledi Sayadaw.[52] It runs as follows:

1) *Anusaya-bhūmi* or the period of latency. Sayadaw says this is the period during which the defilements lie latent around the life continuum.

2) *Pariyuṭṭhāna-bhūmi* or the period when defilements become manifest as thought processes. When these thought processes take place at the mind-door, any stimuli outside can arouse them.

3) *Vītikkamma-bhūmi* or the period when the defilements become so fierce and ungovernable that they produce sinful actions in word and

deed. Transgression by word and deed can be abandoned by substituting its opposites, which are the virtues (*sīla*).

> Evil thought processes have to be suppressed by concentration (*samādhi*). This kind of suppression called *Vikkhambana* can put the defilements into the background. *Jhāna* can dispose of the defilements for a considerable time so that they do not arise soon again, for meditation is more powerful in combating the defilements than morality.[53]

But yet, since they have not been completely rooted out, *paññā* (understanding) is needed to eliminate them. Thus the *Visuddhimagga* says:

> The abandoning of defilements by substitution of opposites is shown by virtue; that by suppression is shown by concentration; and that by cutting off is shown by understanding.'[54]

At the first level we deal with transgressions, at the second with obsessions and at the third with inherent tendencies *(anusayas).* In determining the meta-psychological status of the *anusayas,* we are confronted by a problem of terminology. They are often called 'subconscious,' 'subliminal' and 'unconscious'; the term 'latent' can be used in a neutral way.

Jayasuriya refers to the *anusaya* stage as a hidden or a potential state and concludes that this latent level of activity 'may be regarded as the level of the unconscious mind of the psychologists.'[55] 'Unconscious' is probably a better term to describe the *anusayas* than 'subconscious,' whereas *bhavaṅga* can be better termed 'subconscious' in the sense of a state of semi-awareness or the lowest degree of consciousness.

For as Conze says regarding *bhavaṅga,* 'It is, however, never completely "unconscious" but always accompanied by some degree of awareness.'[56] Another very significant aspect of the *anusayas* is that they have to be penetrated by a special kind of knowledge and can be rooted out completely only by the development of higher spiritual powers. The *anusayas* lie latent in the deeper levels of our personality and continue to influence our behaviour without our knowledge and thus they constitute an aspect of unconscious motivation.

ĀSAVA

The *āsava* concept closely resembles that of the id in Freud. The *Dīgha Nikāya* mentions four *āsavas:* sensuality, lust for life, speculation and ignorance. It has been translated by a number of words like canker, influx, intoxicant, bias, taint, etcetera. It is derived from a root corresponding to the Sanskrit 'flow' combined with the adverbial prefix a- which, with verbs of motion, suggests movement 'toward'.

Literally, then, *āsava* seems to mean 'flowing toward'. Horner suggests 'influx'. 'Canker'[57] implies that which frets, corrodes, corrupts or consumes slowly and secretly. Horner also says that if the prefix a- be taken in the sense of 'around' or 'from all sides', the translation 'canker' is quite apt. *Āsavas* is often rendered by 'intoxicant', a usage that has an important implication. As Mrs. Rhys Davids says, 'The *āsavas,* moreover, are like liquors *(āsava),* such as spirits, etcetera, in the sense of that which may be kept for a long time. For, in the world, spirits, etcetera, which have been laid down for a long period are called *āsavas.*[58] This point is taken up in the *Atthasālinī* where we read:

> As the juices of the madira fruits become intoxicants by fermentation for a long length of time, so certain states which are like these intoxicants are termed *asavas.*'[59]

All these facets of the concept of *āsava* bring us closer to the archaic bases of man symbolised by the Freudian concept of the id.

DESIRES IN DISGUISE (VAÑCHAKA DHAMMA)

Now we come to a very interesting phenomenon that definitely illustrates how some of the theories of Freud can be used beneficially to get an honest picture of oneself through introspection. We may translate the Pāli term for this phenomenon by 'desires in disguise'. It is used by Chandavimala Thera, who has made a systematic study of them in a Sinhalese work entitled *Vañchaka Dhamma Prakāsaya.*[60]

Those 'desires in disguise' generally refer to certain aspects of self-deception and can be better termed 'dislocated' or 'misdescribed desires,' to borrow from the terminology of Broad. We 'dislocate' them when we ascribe to them a different object from that which they have and we 'mis-describe' them by putting them into a certain class of mental attitudes when we ought to put them into a certain other class.

This phenomenon by which a person can succumb to lustful thought under the guise of compassion or where *kilesas* (defilements) can creep in under cover of *kusala dhamma* is of great significance. It has been clearly described in the *Atthasālinī,* where it is treated with reference to the four sublime states, viz. loving-kindness *(mettā),* compassion *(karuṇā),* altruistic joy *(muditā)* and equanimity *(upekkhā).*[61]

Loving-kindness and vengeful conduct cannot coexist by nature. But where love and its object are, they can be threatened by lust, for like love, lust is a positive attitude toward an object. Hence, lust is referred to as the 'near enemy' of love, since it lurks close to love. But ill-will is considered as a 'distant enemy'. Regarding compassion it is said that the distant enemy is cruelty, but it has a more insidious near enemy; this near enemy is a kind of self-pity filled with worldly sorrow. Sympathy and equanimity are also analysed in a similar manner in the *Atthasālinī.* The near enemy of sympathy is joy regarding worldly and material prosperity. Indifference is referred to as the near enemy of equanimity.

In chapter two, the statement 'secrecy is the category of moral illness for it provides a resting place for false motives' was referred to. Freud claimed that sham and deception have to be rejected to obtain mental health. The *vañchaka dhammas* form an interesting parallel to this view. Chandavimala Thera speaks of two groups of *vañchaka dhammas.*[62] One group is mostly applicable to monks and yogins and to a small extent also to ordinary people. The other group contains twelve types of *vañchaka dhammas* based on the discussions found in the Abhidhamma. This group is applicable to ordinary people and throws a good deal of light on the nature of unconscious processes. All these *vañchaka dhammas* are described within a certain framework, as is true of most ethico-psychological inquiries in Buddhist works.

There is a tension between *kusala* and *akusala* or wholesome and unwholesome states. Since we are dealing with the person who is actively and sincerely practising the Dhamma or with the monk and the yogin, the defilements and passions take an outward appearance of wholesome states. As people do illegal things under cover of legality so immoral dispositions under cover of moral dispositions take shelter in the abode of a person's mind. That is why these are called 'desires in disguise'. They are in the final analysis a subtle form of self-deception.

It is not necessary to review in detail all these desires in disguise. A few may be selected for the purpose of illustration. Let us take greed *(lobha)* first. Giving to others what belongs to you is a fine manifestation of self-sacrifice and consideration for others. This can take the form of giving wealth, goods, food or even your time for the sake of others. Now a person who practises this after a while may feel that, if he helps a person, he gets something in return or that he can give little to a person and expect something more in return. When this aim becomes dominant, his mind is defiled and he becomes dishonest. Of course, it is often very subtle and the person concerned may not be aware of the change in his aim.

The subtle working of passion *(rāga)* is especially interesting in the light of a comparison with Freud. A hypothetical illustration will serve to explain it. A married man of deeply religious nature, devoted to the Dhamma, is attracted by a woman who is beautiful, but stricken with dire poverty. He has compassion for the poverty-stricken woman, but in reality, though he is unaware of it, his compassion is due more to his love for her than to her poverty-stricken state. It is possible for passion to take an acceptable form by the outward appearance of compassion. This is a very subtle mechanism and a great deal of honest introspection and self-criticism is necessary to safeguard one from it.[63]

Hatred and anger *(dosa)* also take certain subtle disguised and counterfeit forms. Chandavimala Thera says anger can take four forms: that of ferocity, fear, disgust and sorrow. Even these forms can manifest through various disguised and counterfeit desires. Hatred can manifest as patience. Thus, if a child is punished by his parents, the child may say, 'I don't mind what my parents do to me. I will bear it all patiently.' Though he calls it 'patience', within him there is a great amount of unrevealed anger and hatred, albeit in another form. Certain demonstrations of nonviolence to show one's disapproval of an employer may also be born out of great anger and hatred. Chandavimala Thera works out in detail twelve types of desires in disguise: greed, hatred, jealousy, stinginess, pride, sloth and torpor, remorse, shamelessness, non-dread of evil, wrong view, delusion and doubt. All these unwholesome states can emerge through the guise of wholesome states.

ĀLAYAVIJÑĀNA (STORE-CONSCIOUSNESS)

This concept is sometimes compared to the 'collective unconsciousness' of Jung. Ninian Smart says 'the store-consciousness, which underlies the individual and is not part of what constitutes the individual, cannot be considered as the name for an entity peculiar to any individual. Thus it corresponds (very roughly) more to Jung's collective unconscious than to Freud's concept.'[64] Jung's attempt to develop the notion of the collective unconscious against the background of eastern religions is interesting.

He especially says that karma is essential to the understanding of the nature of an archetype.[65] In a sense the theory of karma and the law of dependent origination provide us with such general patterns in human behaviour. But there are an element of obscurity and a speculative vein in his writings that often make it difficult to understand what he is attempting to say. Thus, Jung's development of the Freudian notion of the archaic heritage is somewhat mystifying and a clear analysis of the psychological implications involved in the concept of the archaic heritage might prove very rewarding.[66]

The clinical implications in the light of the early Buddhist hypothesis of rebirth ought also to be studied. Jung, however, reached out into so many fields (anthropology, sociology, archaeology and art) that his results are obscure and complex, and, on the whole, do not answer the Freudian query about the archaic heritage. Though Jung's ideas are by no means crystal clear it would seem that his notion of the 'collective unconscious', shrouded as it is in speculative theories, bears some kinship to the *ālayavijñāna* concept of later Buddhism, whereas the Freudian unconscious, rooted in a scientific and empirical framework, resembles the concept of the unconscious in early Buddhism.

ĀLAYAVIJÑĀNA AND EARLY BUDDHIST PSYCHOLOGY

Is the concept *of ālayavijñāna* a natural and logical development of the *viññāna* of early Buddhism, or is it something diametrically opposed to it? Conze feels that it is opposed to the spirit of early Buddhism. He says:

> All these theoretical constructions are attempts to combine the doctrine of 'not-self' with the almost instinctive belief in

> a 'self', empirical or true. This climax of this combination of the uncombinable is reached in such conceptual monstrosities as the 'store conscious' of Asanga...[67]

The *ālayavijñāna* concept performs all the functions of a 'self' in a theory which almost vociferously proclaims the non-existence of such a 'self.' While Conze considers the *ālayavijñāna* as an unhappy hybrid of two philosophical positions diametrically opposed to each other (viz. the self and the non-self), others, like the Venerable Walpola Rahula, think otherwise. Venerable Rahula says:

> One may see that, although not developed as in the Mahayana, the original idea of *ālayavijñāna* was already there in the Pāli canon of the Theravada.[68]

His contention is based on a reference to passages in the Nikāyas where words like *ālaya* and *bīja* (seed) have been used and these occurrences suffice to convince him that the elements that make the concept of *ālayavijñāna* are found in the Pāli canon. He analyses the three layers of the mind (*citta, manas* and *vijñāna)* as presented by *Asanga* which he says are synonymous in the Pāli canon, in the *Lankavatara-sutra* and Asanga. Asanga also considers them as different aspects of the aggregates of consciousness. 'Thus we can see that *vijñāna* represents the simple reaction or response of the sense organs when they come in contact with the external objects.

This is the uppermost or superficial aspect or layer of the *vijñānaskanda. Mānas* represents the aspect of its mental functioning, thinking, reasoning, conceiving ideas, etcetera. *Citta* which is here called *ālayavijñāna,* represents the deepest, finest and subtlest aspect or layer of the aggregate of consciousness. It contains all the traces or impressions of the past actions and all good and bad future potentialities.'[69]

The Venerable Rahula also points to certain significant phrases in the Theravada texts, like *ālayasamugghāta* ('uprooting of *alaya')* used as a synonym for *nibbāna,* and *anālaya* also a synonym for *nibbāna*. In *ālayarāma, ālayabhirata* the word *ālaya* is explained in the Pāli commentaries as 'attachment to five sense-pleasures.'[70] Thus, *ālaya* and *vijñāna* being used in various passages in the Nikāyas, the concept of *ālayavijñāna* is not a creation of the Mahayana. But the fact that *ālaya and vijñāna* do occur separately in early Buddhist texts does not imply that the later compound *ālayavijñāna* is actually a development of any notion in that early tradition.

Further, if we follow the logic of the history of ideas that underlie the emergence of the Yogacara School, we can discern certain trends of thought that made possible the postulation of concepts like that of *ālayavijñāna*. The central criticism of the *ālayavijñāna* by the Theravadin is that this theory has been responsible for the infiltration of substance theories into Mahayana. In any case, whether or not the seeds of the *ālayavijñāna* concept existed in early Buddhism, no evidence is needed from this quarter to prove that there was a concept of unconscious motivation in early Buddhism.

It was pointed out in chapter two, that the word *viññāna* has four strands of meaning. It is reasonable to suppose that these same strands of meaning are found also in the compound *ālayavijñāna*.

1) A basic use of *viññāna* is in the sense of cognition. The five forms of sense-consciousness mentioned in the *Lankavatara Sutra*, i.e. visual, auditory, olfactory, gustatory and tactile, appear to be the only parallel to the cognitive import of *viññāna* found in the Theravada. But in the case of *ālayavijñāna* it does not have any intellectual function. 'It simply accumulates all the impressions, all the memory seeds *(bīja)* that are produced and left behind by the activities of the *vijñānas*.'[71]

2) *Viññāna* in the sense of anoetic sentience. This, as we have seen, is not a central usage of early Buddhism. But it is one of the strands of meaning found in the *ālayavijñāna* concept. As Sarachchandra notes, the idealist regards the functioning consciousness as a manifestation of the *ālaya*. '*Ālaya* seems to remain as a sub-plane all the while, even during the activity of its manifestations. This is the implication of the simile of the sea and the waves on it.'[72]

3) *Viññāna* as the medium in which progress in meditation takes place. This sense is of help in understanding the *yogācāra* preoccupation with the concept of consciousness. While the Madhyamaka School for instance laid emphasis on the dialectic of reason, the Yogacara School emphasised the contemplative process. That perhaps explains why the *yogācārins* conceived the absolute in terms of consciousness. In early Buddhism the stages of spiritual development are considered as the foot-

holds of *viññāna*. However, *viññāna* ceases to manifest itself in the final state of the cessation of all conceptual and empirical experience. Thus, in the final stage of spiritual development early Buddhism goes beyond the Yogacara School.

4) *Viññāna* as the factor of survival. Obviously this has a parallel in the concept of *ālaya* as the 'depository of karma seeds, good as well as bad.'[73] Though there is a parallelism to the *alaya*, the *yogācārin* metaphysics seems to consider the *ālaya* as some kind of substrate, thus perhaps inviting the comment that it is a 'soul in disguise'. In spite of Suzuki's attempt to dispel this criticism, he admits: 'There is no doubt that this idea of *ālayavijñāna* caused confusion in the minds of some Mahayana Buddhists who have been brought up in the teaching of *anātman* (non-ego).'[74] What the critics of Suzuki, like Conze, say is not that there is a fully-fledged substance theory of soul in the *yogācāra* system, but rather that it is an 'unhappy hybrid' of the soul and the non-soul theories.

NORMAL CONSCIOUSNESS AND SPIRITUAL AWAKENING

Fromm says when we speak of consciousness and unconsciousness in psychoanalytic contexts, there is the implication that consciousness is of a higher value than unconsciousness, but 'yet it is quite obvious that consciousness as such has no particular value; in fact, most of what people have in their conscious minds is fiction and delusion…'[75] If we accept the fact that most of our consciousness is delusion, to achieve something valuable the hidden unconscious must be revealed. Thus we arrive at a new concept of conscious-unconscious according to which the average person, though he thinks he is awake, is actually half asleep. Fromm says:

> By 'half asleep' I mean that his contact with reality is a very partial one; most of what he believes to be reality (outside or inside of himself) is a set of fictions which his mind constructs.[76]

Fromm's underlying idea is the fictional and unreal character of our normal consciousness. And he compares this with the awakening or enlightenment advocated by Zen Buddhism. 'To enlarge consciousness means to wake up, to lift a veil, to leave the cave, to bring light into the darkness.[77] This brings us to the concept of awareness in early Buddhism. With regard to the Buddha's message we can speak of those who are conscious of it and follow a method of self-discipline; of others who know of the Buddha's message but fail to manifest it in their behaviour; of others who are completely uninformed and insensitive to it, and so on.

In this connection are we going to say, as Fromm does, that what most people have in their conscious minds is fiction and delusion? If we compare those who are perfect and have attained the holy state *(arahat)* with the 'stream-winner' *(sotāpanna),* the 'once-returner' *(sakadāgāmi),* the 'never-returner' *(anāgāmi),* those who are ardently following the path of the Buddha but have not attained any such stage, those who call themselves the followers of the Buddha, either as monks or laymen, but fail to carry this out, then we should discover various stages of imperfection. In the context of the norms of Buddhism the arahat can be regarded as the awakened one who is fully aware and mindful to the utmost.

If so, there is a wide gap between the arahat and the *puthajjanā* (the worldling) who is still possessed of all the ten fetters binding him to the round of rebirths. If we proceed in this way, we come to that profound axiom *Sabbe puthajjanā unmattakā* (all worldlings are deranged). This parallels Freud's assertion of the world as a patient and civilisation as essentially pathological. In the context of Buddhism the normal personality can be defined to the degree to which one is not dominated by craving and the delusion of self-hood.

The levels of spiritual development referred to above are important because they bear upon the Buddhist concept of the 'conscious' and 'unconscious'. Let us examine some of the key words for awareness, like *sati* and *sampajāna.* The Buddhist therapeutic system has four significant elements of which *sati* (mindfulness) is one. They are faith *(saddhā),* mindfulness *(sati),* concentration *(samādhi)* and wisdom *(paññā).* In varying contexts *sati* has been translated by 'memory, recognition, wakefulness of mind, mindfulness, alertness, lucidity of mind, self-possession', etcetera. The word *sampajāna* is often used similarly to mean 'thoughtful, aware and attentive'.

There are other phrases with a similar meaning, like *yoniso manasikāra* (wise attention) or *paccavakkhati* (to reflect or look at oneself). Of course, mindfulness in Buddhism refers to concentration and wisdom to which it provides a footing. All these together imply a very high state of 'wakefulness' according to which ordinary consciousness seems fictional and confused. Against this background a number of polarities can be projected that illuminate the concept of consciousness in Buddhism:

1 Calm and quiet as contrasted to turmoil and agitation
2 Clarity and lucidity as contrasted to confusion and obscurity
3 Mastery and control of desires as contrasted to domination by involuntary impulses
4 Insight and knowledge as contrasted to delusion and ignorance.

Some of these are paralleled in the Freudian system but there is no mystical and spiritual development in Freud.

THE NATURE OF DREAMS

There is no systematic theory of dreams in the early Buddhist scriptures. However, the problem of the moral responsibility of the dreamer is discussed in the *Vinaya* where the question of whether a person who sins in his dreams is to be condemned, is taken up.[78] From this can be inferred an attitude to dreams. There is some interesting material in the *Milinda Pañha* as well as in some works on the Abhidhamma.

This material has been examined by Sarachchandra and Aung.[79] Since our aim is to describe the nature of unconscious processes according to the early Buddhism of the Nikāyas, only a limited reference to the Abhidhamma will be made. A brief reference to the *Milinda Pañha* is made only so far as it is relevant. In the latter work the question is raised whether a man dreams when he sleeps or when he is awake.[80] The answer given is that dreams do not belong to sleep or to waking experience, but to an intermediate stage comparable to a monkey's sleep. Dreams do not occur in deep sleep, for the mind has to be active in some way for the occurrence of dreams. How does the mind become active during sleep, and what are the causes of dreams? Dreams are classified thus:

1 Dreams due to organic and muscular disturbances
2 Dreams due to the impact of previous experience
3 Dreams due to the influence of supernatural agencies
4 Prophetic dreams.

Regarding the problem of mental responsibility the reference to previous experiences is significant. It is natural for a mind that is preoccupied with evil thoughts to extend this disposition to dreaming. Freud says that dreaming is a way of satisfying unfulfilled wishes. It is stated in the *Vinaya* that a monk who commits an offence in a dream is not morally responsible for his acts.[81]

This suggests that there is no volitional control over dream thoughts. According to another view, dream thoughts are not ethically neutral, but from the point of ecclesiastical offences they are of a negligible nature. If we accept this view that there is an element of volition, though negligible, it suggests a certain similarity with the Freudian hypothesis that dreams are wish fulfilments.

The fact that the arahat does not dream also shows that dreams are the product of imperfection. Freud, of course, believed that dreams gave an insight to the real nature of a person and this thesis is not inconsistent with early Buddhism, though the discussion in the *vinaya* does not shed much light on this point.

THE EARLY BUDDHIST UNCONSCIOUS IN LIGHT OF THE FREUDIAN THEORY OF THE UNCONSCIOUS

THE META-PSYCHOLOGICAL STATUS OF THE UNCONSCIOUS

We have already referred to the statement of Pap that the characteristically psychoanalytic meaning of the word unconscious is dispositional, and that is the meaning that remains after it is divested of metaphors and analogies that are misleading. Though Freud has used a number of spatial images to describe the unconscious, to Freud unconscious tendencies are a special case of latent tendencies and dispositions. If we accept this view maintained by people like Pap and Brunswik, we can see some very interesting points of contact between Freud and Buddhism.

In our analysis of the early Buddhist unconscious we have referred to the *anusayas* (latent tendencies) and *asampajāna mano saṅkhāras* (dispositions of the mind or trains of thought of which we are not aware). It was noted that a person who has telepathic powers can discern the mental *saṅkhāras* of another and predict what he will think at a later time. In the passage containing *viññāna-sota* was pointed out that a part of the stream of consciousness consisted of certain *saṅkhāras* which persisted in a state of flux in the unconscious influencing his later behaviour. Now most of these references indicate that the early Buddhist concept of the unconscious can be explained as a disposition concept similar to Freud's. One significant difference is that the *saṅkhāras* have a wider dimension extending from innumerable births. The hypothesis of rebirth is certainly something that the clinical psychologist and psychiatrist should seriously examine.

METHOD OF UNRAVELLING THE UNCONSCIOUS

According to Freud, an important difference between the preconscious and the unconscious is that the unconscious is not accessible to ordinary introspection like the preconscious. A special technique like the hypnotic method or that of free association is necessary to get at unconscious processes. A little effort may be necessary to recall a preconscious memory, but no special technique is necessary to unravel it.

According to early Buddhism too, whether it be one's own or another's recognition of unconscious processes, a special kind of cognition like telepathic power or extrasensory cognition is necessary to unravel the unconscious. Both systems, then, require a special procedure to unravel the unconscious. However, Freud would not claim any powers of extrasensory cognition but would merely say that it is a development of the usual powers of reason and sensory experience at a mature level that helps us to unravel the unconscious.

MEANING OF UNCONSCIOUS MOTIVES

A number of meanings of 'unconscious' were outlined with the help of the list suggested by Miller. Most of these can be brought under two heads: 1) motives that go unrecognised, the nature of which is not correctly understood by the person, 2) those which lack any 'control' by the agent and often appear almost compulsive. Beck's analysis of unconscious motives recognises these two aspects of unconscious motives.[82] Both are certainly found in Freud as well as in early Buddhism. Lack of insight into one's motives was well illustrated by the 'desires in disguise'.

Insight, whether it is transcendental or well developed introspection of the ordinary level can illuminate the sources of one's deeds, speech and thought according to the Buddha. Lack of control is equally discussed in the Buddhist texts. There is an emphasis on the unguarded and uncontrolled senses for when there is no control over them, evil states flow in. When the senses are unguarded, delightful and pleasant stimuli or disagreeable and painful stimuli can excite certain dormant traits. The person who is undergoing training is expected to analyse his own mental states carefully, for if one dwells with the organ of sight uncontrolled, evil states will creep in, or if he is obsessed with thoughts about sense-pleasure (*kāmavitakka)* evil tendencies emerge.[83]

CONTENTS OF UNCONSCIOUS MOTIVES

It is on this point that popular opinion rejects any comparison of Buddhist and Freudian psychology. It is true that Freud somewhat over-emphasised the role of sexuality. But one who follows the development of Freudian thought will notice that later Freud admitted the existence of both ego instincts and aggression. The points of similarity between the threefold desires of early Buddhism (*kāma, bhava* and *vibhava-taṇhā)* and the libido, ego and the death instinct are very significant. Thus there are also similarities regarding the content of the unconscious in the two systems, especially the role of sensuality, self-love and aggression.[84]

There is also the problem of whether the unconscious consists of only the evil aspect of man. On this, Jung has criticised Freud, saying that there is a profound and good aspect to man's personality buried in his unconscious. Buddhism certainly admits that man has dispositions which are both good and bad. Often it is possible that certain wholesome dispositions in some men can recede into the background and the evil traits dominate due to a bad environment, frustrations, upbringing, etcetera. The dynamic *saṅkhāras* that determine the nature of one's next life consist of both good and bad dispositions.

The defilers (*kilesas*), the cankers (*āsavas*), the latent tendencies (*anusayas*), the hindrances (*nīvaranas*) and allied concepts are aspects of personality that darken the mind. The moral aspect is rather defined in terms of powers (*bala)* like confidence, mindfulness, concentration, effort and wisdom. It is difficult to describe these as 'unconscious' because as the individual gets trained in morality, concentration and wisdom, the wholesome aspects of personality emerge with mindfulness. Hence, when the Buddhist focuses his attention on the unconscious, he is interested in the latent traits that distort and darken one's consciousness without his awareness. However, in a man's life through successive births the wholesome aspect can recede to the background and remain mute and find expression in the most unexpected circumstances. The classic case of the spiritual transformation of the criminal Aṅgulimāla may be a case in point.

MASTERY OF THE UNCONSCIOUS

This is certainly the point at which the early Buddhist system of therapy is superior to that advocated by Freud. Rieff concludes his classic work on Freud with the sentence:

> Aware at last that he is chronically ill, psychological man may nevertheless end the ancient quest of his predecessors for a healing doctrine. His experience with the latest one, Freud's, may finally teach him that every cure must expose him to new illness.[85]

This is the Freudian dilemma: the sense of despair of man who sought a cure for the ills of man. Freudian therapy is essentially a process of bringing into consciousness that which has been unconscious. But the mere unravelling of the unconscious sources of a personality disorder does not completely eliminate the re-emergence of similar or substitute formations. Though Freud preferred the method of obtaining insight into oneself to the technique of releasing one's pent-up emotions (catharsis) he could not find a radical solution such as advocated by the Buddha.

There are two significant aspects to the mastery of the unconscious advocated in Buddhism in keeping with two basic senses of the term unconscious motive already referred to: 1) the cognitive level at which insight and awakening break through the unconscious, 2) a conative level at which man achieves perfect self-control over his unruly desires and also stabilises the growth of wholesome tendencies within himself. In a very general way it can be said that the disciplines of *sīla* (morality) and *samādhi* (concentration and tranquillity) function at the conative level and *paññā* (wisdom) at the cognitive level.

Freud himself shifted from a position which emphasised emotional relief and tranquillity in catharsis to a system that emphasised insight and understanding of the sources of mental sickness. In spite of this similarity, the Buddhist therapy is more radical than the Freudian since the Freudian goal was limited to an attainable ideal of happiness and the translation of hysterical misery into everyday unhappiness.[86] Others say that his goals were far-reaching, that he aimed at ideal psychic normality, but that his techniques were not far-reaching.[87] Freud himself admitted that 'there is a bit of unconquerable nature in each of us.'[88]

IV

THE THEORY OF MOTIVATION

MOTIVATION IN FREUD AND BUDDHISM

The study of motivation deals with the diverse factors which 'incite and direct an individual's actions'.[1] Freud was basically interested in the unconscious determinants of human behaviour and this, according to him, was the most important aspect of motivation. A recent analysis of the complexities of the word 'motivation' sums up the situation thus:

> The term has no fixed technical meaning in contemporary psychology. It is often used in reference to the conscious feeling of desire and the whole complex of ideas and feelings which together seem to constitute the conscious antecedents of behaviour according to traditional wisdom. Just as often, 'motivation' is used to refer to the unconscious determinants of behaviour which Freud emphasized, to the purposive character of overt behaviour which Tolman identified as an empirical problem in its own right, to a coherent theoretical account of the contemporaneous determinants of action like the Lewinian scheme or Hull's principle of performance, or to some particular variable in a particular theoretical conception of the contemporaneous determinants of the impulse to action—for example, as a synonym for drive in S-R behaviour theory.[2]

John Atkinson who makes the above statement offers a key to accommodate these theories by saying that there are 'different languages' of motivation or 'several levels of discourse': 1) the experiential language, which refers to the conscious experience of desire, emotion, feelings of determination, and the inclination to act; 2) the neurophysiological language, which describes motivation in the technical language of the neural and organic processes; 3) the behavioural language which considers motivation in terms of the direction, vigour, and persistence of observable behaviour in relation to observable environmental conditions; and 4) the mathematical language, which describes motivation in terms of abstract mathematical concepts.

This is a useful way of looking at the problem. But the question really crops up when one of these languages, for example, the neurophysiological, is used to explain all motivational phenomena. Peters describes the situation well when he says that some misguided attempts have been made by psychologists to present 'over-all theories of human behaviour'.[3] 'There are many different sorts of questions which can be asked about human behaviour and the differences, as I shall hope to show, are such that an all-embracing theory is inappropriate. These different sorts of questions are especially confused in theories of motivation.'[4] In this context, Peters pays a compliment to Freud by saying that he was perhaps a great exception in this respect. 'For he was genuinely puzzled about concrete phenomena and developed some very fertile assumptions to explain them.'[5]

The basic structure of Freudian motivation is essentially based on his theory of instincts which is worked out clearly in his paper 'The Instincts and their Vicissitudes'.[6]

THEORY OF INSTINCTS

At a very early stage, Freud discovered that the symptoms of certain neurotic patients disappeared through the process of abreaction, when painful ideas are brought to the awareness of the patient. It was also assumed that there were memories of some traumatic experiences buried in the past. Then Freud discerned these ideas, which were usually fantasies, were rooted in wishes. His discovery that wishes underlie the apparently meaningless content of one's dreams had very significant consequences for the theoretical development of psychoanalysis. In the words of David Rapaport, 'It was to explain the origin of these fantasies and dream wishes that Freud introduced the concept of instinctual drives.'[7] He adds that:

> This step was the beginning of the end of that phase of

> Freud's theory-making in which he considered the crucial factors determining behaviour as predominantly environmental. It ushered in a new phase in which intra-psychic determiners—of the type I am defining as motivations—became the crucial causes of behaviour postulated by the theory.'[8]

In his *Three Essays on the Theory of Sexuality*,[9] Freud introduced his concept of instinct. But since the concept of the libido was given great importance in this book the problems of the nature of instinct receded into the background. It was in his I*nstincts and Their Vicissitudes*,[10] that Freud finally gave a systematic presentation of instinct. This theory took complete form in his papers entitled 'Repression' and 'The Unconscious'.[11] In a further enlargement on the theory, he emphasised the significance of ego instincts (as contrasted with sex instincts) in a paper called 'On Narcissism'.[12] Finally he emphasised the significance of aggression in *Beyond the Pleasure Principle*,[13] where he postulated the death instinct as one of the dominating instincts. Thus, in his final conception of the theory of instincts, he upheld the existence of three basic instincts: 1) the libido or instinctual desire for sense-gratification, 2) the ego instinct and its allied manifestations (self-preservation, self-love, self-assertion, self-continuity, etcetera) and 3) the death instinct and the roots of aggression.

The term *trieb* is translated as 'instinct' by Strachey, as 'desire' by some other scholars, and as 'instinctual drive' by Rapaport. Freud himself describes the concept of an instinct as something that falls between the frontiers of the mental and the physical. Whether we call the term *trieb* an instinct or an instinctual desire, we cannot lose sight of the psychological nature of the concept. As Rapaport says:

> Hunger, thirst or other metabolic needs are poor paradigms for instinctual drives; they are usually treated as somatic conditions rather than as mental representations of somatic conditions, and partly because they cannot be delayed for any significant length of time nor are they flexible in their object choice and consummatory pattern.[14]

No insight into the dynamic psychology of Freud is possible without an understanding of the vicissitudes of instincts, their conflict and their fusion. Freud has a clear insight into the ambivalent structure of instincts that continually prepare the ground for further conflicts, a remarkable echo of the early Buddhist psychology of craving (*taṇhā*). But what gives depth to the Freudian theory of instincts is the notion of unconscious motivation, the analysis of which is our primary concern.

THE CONCEPT OF MOTIVATION IN BUDDHISM

In early Buddhist psychology, the springs of human action are traced to six roots, which fall into two classes: the immoral and moral. The immoral roots are 1) greed (lobha), 2) hatred (dosa), and 3) delusion (moha). The moral roots are 1) liberality or charity (*alobha* or *cāga*), 2) kindness or goodwill (*adosa* or *mettā*), and 3) knowledge (*amoha* or *paññā*).

Greed (*lobha*) has two manifestations, viz. in the form of *kāma-taṇhā* (craving for sensuous gratification) and *bhava-taṇhā* (craving for self-preservation). Hatred (*dosa*) manifests itself in varied types of aggressions and ultimately issues forth as *vibhava-taṇhā* (desire for annihilation). Delusion (*moha*) is the primary root of evil that prevents man from seeing the true nature of things. As a result of this root, he does not grasp the three signs, viz. *anicca* (impermanence and transience), *dukkha* (suffering) and *anattā* (non-self or insubstantiality).

As mentioned in chapter two, there are two patterns of causal analysis in the Buddhist texts according to which motivational phenomena are treated: 1) the law of dependent origination (*paṭicca-samuppāda*) and 2) the method given in the manual called *Paṭṭhāna*, which contains an analysis of twenty-four relations (*paccaya*). Now, according to the law of dependent origination, feeling is conditioned by contact (*phassa-paccaya vedanā*) and craving is conditioned by feeling (*vedanā-paccaya taṇhā*) and so on, everything being dependent on something else for its particular state. Thus, due to the stimulation of the five sense organs and the mind organ there result six kinds of feelings based on eye-impressions, ear-impressions, nose-impressions, tongue-impressions, body-impressions and mind-impressions. These feelings have a certain hedonic tone according to which they are pleasant (*sukha*), painful (*dukkha*) and indifferent (*adukkha, asukha*). Pleasant feelings can induce a desire for pleasure giving objects and then the craving for sensuous enjoyment emerges. If pleasant feelings also cause a yearning for prolonged existence and for continuity, then there arises the desire for self-preservation. Painful feelings, on the other hand, can arouse our hatred and aggressive nature and finally issue forth as the craving for annihilation. There is potency in pleasant feelings to arouse latent sensuous greed (*rāgānusaya*) and for painful feelings to arouse latent anger and hatred (*patighānusaya*). Pleasant feelings can induce an attachment or clinging (*upādāna*) to objects through the emergence of craving. Thus, the next sequence in the law of dependent origination is: attachment is conditioned by craving. There are four kinds of attachment:

1 Attachment to sensuous pleasures (*kāmūpādāna*);
2 Attachment to erroneous opinions (*diṭṭhūpādāna*);
3 Attachment to mere rule and ritual (*silabhatūpādāna*);
4 Attachment to the ego-belief (*attavādūpādāna*).

The concept of *ūpādāna* is a very interesting psychological phenomenon. Jayatilleke has suggested translating it as 'entanglement' rather than 'clinging,' which is the translation commonly given. He says:

> *Upādāna* literally means 'grasping' or 'clinging' ...but since these words express a pro-attitude in that we grasp what we like or desire but not what we hate or are averse to it would be better to translate the word as 'entanglement' or act of 'involvement'. For it is obviously intended to include the object that we like as well as dislike.[15]

This is a very illuminating insight into the psychology of the word *upādāna* and helps us understand concepts like the Oedipus-complex where we discover the subtly ambivalent display of love and hate together.

Having illustrated how the theory of dependent origination helps to understand motivational phenomena, let us tabulate all the links in it in order to make the picture complete, since this will prove helpful in understanding the twenty-four relations in the *Paṭṭhāna*.

1 *Avijjā-paccayā saṅkhāra*: by ignorance karma formations (dispositions or rebirth-producing volitions) are conditioned.
2 *Saṅkhāra-paccayā viññāṇam*: by the karma formations or dispositions

(in past life) consciousness (in present life) is conditioned.

3 *Viññāna-paccayā nāma-rūpam*: by consciousness the psycho physical complex (*nāma-rūpa*) is conditioned.

4 *Nāma-rūpa paccayā salayatanam*: by the psychophysical complex the six bases (viz. the five sense organs and the mind) are conditioned.

5 *Salayatana-paccayā phasso:* by the six bases contact is conditioned.

6 *Phassa-paccayā vedanā*: by contact feeling is conditioned.

7 *Vedanā-paccayā taṇhā*: by feeling craving is conditioned.

8 *Taṇhā-paccayā upādānam*: by craving attachment is conditioned.

9 *Upādāna-paccayā bhavo*: by attachment the process of becoming is conditioned.

10 *Bhava-paccayā jāti*: by the process of becoming rebirth is conditioned.

11 *Jāti-paccayā jarāmaraṇaṃ*: by birth (as well as rebirth) old age and death (sorrow, lamentation, pain, grief and despair) are conditioned.

THE METHOD OF PAṬṬHĀNA

The *Paṭṭhāna* generally concentrates on the plurality of causes rather than a single cause that brings about an effect. For instance, take the case of a seed growing into a plant. The seed must be good, it must be planted well; there must be earth and water or the plant will not grow. Now these conditions can have different relations to the effect and the *Paṭṭhāna* works out twenty-four such relations as follows.

1 Root condition (*hetu-paccayā*)
2 Object condition (*ārammaṇa-paccayā*)
3 Predominance condition (*adhipati-paccayā*)
4 Proximity (*anantara-paccayā*)
5 Contiguity condition (*samanantara-paccayā*)
6 Co-nascence condition (*sahajāta-paccayā*)
7 Mutuality condition (*aññamañña-paccayā*)
8 Support (*nissaya-paccayā*)
9 Decisive-support condition (*upanissaya-paccayā*)
10 Pre-nascence condition (*purejāta-paccayā*)
11 Post-nascence condition (*pacchajata-paccayā*)
12 Frequency condition (*āsevana-paccayā*)
13 Karma condition (*kamma-paccayā*)
14 Karma-result condition (*vipāka-paccayā*)

15 Nutriment condition (*āhāra-paccayā*)
16 Faculty condition (*indriya-paccayā*)
17 *Jhāna* condition (*jhāna-paccayā*)
18 Path condition (*magga-paccayā*)
19 Association condition (*sampayutta-paccayā*)
20 Dissociation condition (*vippayutta-paccayā*)
21 Presence condition (*atthi-paccayā*)
22 Absence condition (*natthi-paccayā*)
23 Disappearance condition (*vigata-paccayā*)
24 Non-disappearance (*avigata-paccayā*)[16]

As it is not possible to examine all the relations mentioned in the *Paṭṭhāna*, a brief analysis of *hetu-paccaya* should suffice to illustrate the method of the *Paṭṭhāna*. The term *hetu*, though often used to mean 'cause' means in this case 'root' (*mūla*).[17] Just as a tree rests on its roots and cannot exist without them so also is the existence of all wholesome and unwholesome phenomena entirely dependent on the simultaneity and presence of their respective roots, and cannot exist in their absence. The metaphor of the 'root' is very suggestive, pointing out as it does the fact that our action and thought-processes have a certain stability as they emerge on certain foundations. It is stated in the Nikāyas that if a tree is cut down and the tree-stump left firm on its roots it can sprout again, but if the tree is completely rooted out it cannot grow again.

Greed, hatred and delusion should thus be considered as basic motives of unwholesome motivation. All other unwholesome states, like jealousy, pride and envy, can be understood in relation to *lobha*, *dosa* and *moha* (greed, hatred and delusion). As was stated in chapter two, in addition to the dependent origination doctrine and these twenty-four relations, there is another analysis in the Abhidhamma based on the eighty-nine forms of thought and fifty-two mental factors. Since a good discussion of this is found in the *Abhidhammattha-Saṅgaha*, there is no need to repeat it here. Some aspects of motivation, however, can be understood on the basis of this scheme.

THE LIBIDO

Freud's concept of sexuality is a subject that should be approached with a great deal of caution. Often, controversy regarding the meaning of the word 'sexuality', has been caused by an inability on the part of critics to understand the way in which Freud used the technical term 'libido'. Ernest Jones says:

> By 'sexual' Freud meant sexual in the ordinary sense, but he widened the popular conception of what things are sexual. The psychoanalytic study of early childhood and adult perversions compelled him to recognise that sexuality has many manifestations besides the simple genital union of coitus.[18]

Freud extended the use of the term sexuality in two directions—on the one hand, Freud extended its usage to cover all bodily pleasure; on the other hand, he extended its psychological dimensions to cover feelings like affection and tenderness.

The word 'libido' comes from the Latin word for lust. Just as the word hunger is used in ordinary language to represent the aims of self-preservation, so the word libido is used to indicate the presence of sexual longing in man.

> The popular view distinguishes between hunger and love, seeing them as representatives of instincts that aim at self-preservation and reproduction of the species respectively. In associating ourselves with this very evident distinction, we postulate in psychoanalysis a similar one between the self-preservative or ego instincts on the one hand, and sexual instincts on the other; that force by which the sexual instinct is represented in the mind we call 'libido'—sexual longing—and regard it as analogous to the force of hunger, or the will to power, and other such trends among the ego-tendencies.[19]

Thus if Freud had used the term 'love' or a phrase like 'desire for union' instead of the word sexuality, he could have avoided misunderstanding on the part of his critics. Freud's chief aim was to separate sexuality from its narrow connection with the genitals. He regarded sexuality as a more comprehensive bodily function, having pleasure as its goal and only in a subsidiary form serving the ends of reproduction. With the gradual development of the libido theory, the term sexuality became synonymous with the word love. Freud says that the nucleus of what we mean by love consists in sexual love with sexual union as its aim. But we cannot separate this from certain affectionate and friendly impulses, which are referred to by the word love. The love for parents and children, friendship, love for humanity and even the devotion to abstract ideals are the expression of the same instinctual root.[20]

During a later stage in the development of Freud's theory, he introduced the notion of two basic instincts, eros and destructive instinct. This was offered as an alternative to the three-fold scheme of the libido – ego instinct and the death instinct. He says:

> After long hesitancies and vacillations we have decided to assume the existence of only two basic instincts, eros and the destructive instinct. (The contrast between the instincts of self-preservation and the preservation of the species, as well as the contrast between ego-love and object-love, fall within eros).[21]

According to the new theory, both sexuality and the ego instinct fall within the eros. But Freud also gave a more general (almost a metaphysical) picture of the universe when he said that the aim of eros is to unify and that of the destructive instinct to separate. However, the concept of the libido (as different from the eros) can be broadly described as a 'pleasure-striving force'. Hence we should first examine the Freudian concept of the pleasure principle.

THE PLEASURE PRINCIPLE AND THE REALITY PRINCIPLE

Freud's psychology can be discussed under two broad principles of mental functioning: the pleasure principle and the reality principle. The entire psychical activity is bent upon 'procuring pleasure and avoiding pain'; it is automatically regulated by the pleasure principle.[22] Freud considers this as a fundamental purpose apparent in the working of the human mind.

Pleasure is connected with lessening or extinguishing the amount of stimulation present in the mental apparatus and pain involves a heightening and increasing the amount of stimuli. The mental apparatus serves the purpose of mastering the masses of supervening stimuli, and discharging the quantities of energy. Since pleasurable excitation is bound up with the distribution of quantities of energy, this consideration is referred to as economic. The sovereign tendency obeyed by these processes is called the 'pleasure-pain principle'.

The task of avoiding pain is equally as important as that of obtaining pleasure. The ego learns that it must inevitably go without immediate satisfaction, postpone gratification, learn to endure pain and renounce certain sources of pleasure. Thus, a new principle of mental functioning is introduced; conceived of as no longer that which is pleasant, but that which is real, even if unpleasant. The ego becomes reasonable and follows the reality principle. Freud says that this 'reality principle' also at bottom seeks pleasure, although it is a form of delayed pleasure.

In the final analysis, the reality principle is also based on the pleasure principle. Actually, the substitution of the reality principle for the pleasure principle does not imply a dethronement of the pleasure principle, but only a safeguarding of it. A momentary pleasure, uncertain in its results, is given up, but only in order to gain an assured pleasure later.

Then Freud links up the pleasure principle with religion and says that even religion postpones pleasure to the next life. Religions have been able to preach absolute renunciation of pleasure in this life by means of the promise of compensation in a future life; they have not, however, achieved a conquest of the pleasure principle in this way.

LOVE AND HATE

The pleasure-pain antithesis is bound up with the antithesis between love and hate. When the stage of auto-erotic activity changes into the object-stage, pleasure and pain denote the relations of the ego to the object. When the object becomes a source of pleasurable feelings, a motor tendency is set up which strives to bring the object near to and incorporate it into the ego. We then speak of the 'attraction' exercised by the pleasure-giving object and of loving that object. When the object is the source of painful feelings, there is a tendency which endeavours to increase the distance between object and ego. We feel a 'repulsion' for the object and hate it. This hate can be intensified to the point of an aggressive tendency towards the object, with the intention of destroying it.

The ego hates, abhors and destroys all objects which are for it a source of painful feeling. The source of pain is not essentially the frustration of sexual satisfaction but the frustration of the needs of self-preservation. Love and hate did not originate in a cleavage of any common primeval element but sprang from different sources.

Love originates in the capacity of the ego to satisfy some of its instincts auto-erotically through the obtaining of 'organ-pleasure.' Though love is primarily narcissistic, it is transferred to those objects which have been incorporated in the ego. It is intimately connected with the activity of the later sexual instincts and when these have been completely synthesised, it coincides with the sexual trends as a whole.

THE NORMAL AND THE ABNORMAL

It must be emphasised that Freud's theory of motivation was based on clinical data derived from the study of abnormal people. But he ultimately declared that there is no rigid gap between abnormal and normal sexuality. First, we will deal with adult perversions and then with infantile sexuality.

Sexual perversions can be grouped into two classes, according to the object or aim of sexuality. The sexual object is the person toward whom sexual attraction proceeds, while the act towards which the instinct tends is the sexual aim. The first group comprises changes in the sex, age or even species of the object. Under this head for instance he accepts the bisexual constitution of man and examined the problem of homosexuality.

Deviations about aim fall into two groups: anatomical transgressions and fixations on preliminary stages. Most of the deviations are found in a mild form in the normal man. They become pathological only when they become the object of 'fixation'.

These perversions are magnified and have their climax, for instance, in the neurosis of hysteria where symptoms are created in all systems of the body (circulatory, respiratory, etcetera). Impulses of a compulsive nature find substitutes for the genitals in the other parts of the body. It is precisely from the study of hysterical symptoms that Freud arrived at the concept of erotogenic significance.

Freud says that all this points to a very important factor and we are thus warned to loosen the bond between instinct and its objects.[23] Thus, the sexual instinct is in the first place independent of its objects.

> The most striking distinction between the erotic life of antiquity and our own no doubt lies in the fact that the ancients laid the stress upon the instinct itself, whereas we emphasize its object.[24]

Secondly, it is seen that even in the most normal sexual processes we may detect rudiments, which if they had developed would have led to deviations, described as perversions, e.g. certain intermediate relations to sexual activities which either (a) extend in an anatomical sense beyond the region of the body designed for sexual union, and (b) linger over the immediate relations to the sexual object, which should normally be traversed rapidly on the path towards the final sexual aim.

There are also other interesting elements of sexuality which are found in normal life. There is the infatuation or over-valuation of the object, where the subject becomes intellectually infatuated and his powers of judgment weakened. This over-valuation leads to a certain degree of 'fetishism', which is habitually found in normal sex-love. The contact between normality and perversion is very clearly seen in the two perversions that centre round looking and touching. There is the pleasure in looking, which as a perversion is called scopophilia (sexual gazing). 'Visual impressions remain the most frequent pathway along which libidinal excitation is aroused.'[25] This encourages the development of beauty in the sexual object.

Sometimes, instead of diverting the attention towards an extraneous object, there is the abandonment of the object and a turning of the scopophilic instinct towards a part of the subject's own person. Here there is a new aim: that 'of being looked at.' This is self-display, or as a perversion, becomes exhibitionism. Touch or tactile sensations is also a source of pleasure. Freud says that based on these pleasure-giving tactile sensations, there is a need in man to come into contact with the skin of another person. This is of course sometimes combined with sadism, to inflict pain, or to devour and destroy the object.

As regards sadism, the roots are easy to detect, for the normal sexuality of most human beings; it contains an element of aggression, a desire to subjugate, to overcome the resistance of the sexual object by a process other than wooing. Masochism comprises any passive attitude to sexual life, the extreme instance of which is the satisfaction which is conditioned upon suffering, physical or mental, at the hands of the sexual object.

The subject of sadism and masochism is significant for this comparative study, for it emphasises the aggressive factor in the libido. Various attempts have been made to understand the problem; it is said to be a relic of cannibalistic desire, an attempt at mastery, a product of repetition-compulsion, etcetera. What is certain is that towards the later stages, Freud came to posit a separate aggressive instinct.

This subject is also important in that it brings out a very important feature in the psychology of desire. Here we get the transformation of the content of an instinct into its opposite, the change of love into hate. Sometimes hate and love are simultaneously directed towards the same object and the phenomenon of their coexistence furnishes the most important example of ambivalent feeling.

Freud, in summing up the nature of perversions, makes a very significant observation. He says if such perversions admit of analysis, that is, if they can be taken to pieces, they must be of a composite nature. This gives us a hint that perhaps the sexual instinct itself may be no simple thing but put together from components which have come apart in the perversions. If this is so, the clinical examination of these abnormalities will have drawn our attention to amalgamations that have been lost to view in the uniform behaviour of normal people. Thus singular emotions of pride, jealousy, hatred, sorrow, pity, infatuation and excessive craving surge up in each abnormality as specific objectives are pursued with exclusivity.

INFANTILE SEXUALITY

Freud is aware of the revolutionary nature of his thesis and he raises the question, 'Is there an infantile sexuality?' 'Is childhood not rather that period of life which is distinguished by the lack of sexual impulse?'[26] Freud says that, on the contrary, the child has his sexual impulses and activities from the beginning, for he brings them with him into the world.

From those, the so-called 'normal sexuality' of adults emerges in a significant development through manifold stages.

The sexual impulse of the child manifests itself as a very complex one; it permits of an analysis into many components which spring from different sources. It is entirely disconnected from the function of reproduction which it is later to serve. It permits the child to gain different sorts of pleasure sensations which we include by the analogous connections which they show under the term sexual pleasures.

There are a large number of component instincts, arising from various regions of the body, which strive for satisfaction independent of one another. These component instincts find satisfaction in what may be called 'organ pleasure'. All of these pleasure seeking impulses are not incorporated in the final organisation of the sexual function.

In examining these component instincts, Freud made a detailed analysis of the levels of erotic development of the child. He says that the child moves through three phases: the oral, the anal and the phallic. In the satisfaction of the child's main needs like hunger, thirst and elimination, there is a kind of 'organ pleasure' that is stimulated. The parts of the body thus sensitised like the mouth, the anus and the genitals are referred to as 'erotogenic zones'. With the passing of time, activities like sucking and anal stimulation are performed because of the organ stimulation, rather than for any biological need of the body like hunger or thirst.

The first of the pregenital stages is called 'the oral phase.' The mother's breast is the original object of the infant's libidinal interest. The act of sucking gives him pleasure and this satisfaction is libidinal. Though this satisfaction is obtained by way of taking nourishment, the infant learns that sucking as such is pleasure giving. Then the child replaces the mother's breast by a part of his own body, like his thumb. The significance of thumb sucking lies in the child's ability to enjoy auto-erotic pleasures.[27]

According to Freud, sadistic and anal impulses come to the fore in the second phase, and thus it is described as 'the anal-sadistic stage.' Freud says that they emerge in connection with the cutting of the teeth, the strengthening of the musculature and the control of the sphincters. This stage can be subdivided into a preliminary one, where the destructive tendencies to annihilate and destroy things take an upper hand, and a later phase that is characterised by tendencies which are friendly to the object.

Finally, there is 'the phallic stage,' which is the climax of the development of childhood sexuality. The male genital organ is the centre of interest now. Freud says that regarding this stage, there is insufficient knowledge for the little girl and the phallic phase is merely presented as a male genital organ or a castrated condition. It is only the development of puberty when the polarity of sexuality coincides with male and female. Thus, the term 'genital phase' is used to distinguish it from the 'phallic stage' of the infant.

The sexual life of the child, rich but disassociated, in which each single impulse goes about the business of arousing pleasure independently of every other, is later correlated and organised. So by the close of puberty, the sexual character of the individual is practically determined.

The single impulses subordinate themselves to the over-lordships of the genital zone so that the whole sexual life is taken over into the service of procreation. On the other hand, object choice prevails over auto-eroticism so that now in the sexual life, all components of the sexual impulse are satisfied in the loved person.

But not all the original impulse-components are given a share in the final shaping of the sexual life. Even before the advent of puberty some undergo repression. Certain impulses might remain disconnected from the rule of the genital zone. Such disconnected impulses can bring about a perversion. Thus, some adult maladjustments have their beginning in the somatic and mental sexual life of the child.

The most revolutionary of all theories in connection with infant sexuality is the Oedipus-complex. The primitive object-choice of the child is derived from his need for help, and thus centres on the parents. Here again, anticipating objections, Freud says it may be objected that we never doubt the early awakening of affection but only that this awakening was of a sexual quality. Children between the ages of three and eight have certainly learnt to conceal this element but nevertheless, if we look attentively, we can collect enough evidence of the 'sensual' nature of this affection and whatever still escapes our notice will be amply and readily supplied by analytic observation.

The child takes both parents, although especially one, as an object of his erotic wishes. Usually, he follows the stimulus given by his parents, whose tenderness has very clearly the character of a sexual manifestation, though inhibited so far as its goal is concerned. One of the most important sources of the sense of guilt, which so often torments neurotic people, is to be found in the Oedipus-complex. *In Totem and Taboo*, Freud published a study of the earliest forms of religion and morality, where he expressed the idea:

> The sense of guilt of mankind as a whole, which is the ultimate source of religion and morality, was acquired in the beginnings of history through the Oedipus-complex.'[28]

One might object that the little boy's behaviour is due to egoistic motives and does not justify the concept of an erotic complex. This too is quite correct, 'but it is soon clear that in this, as in similar dependent situations, egoistic interests only provide the occasion on which the erotic impulses seize.'[29] Freud was interested in the behaviour of children for specific reasons. He was searching for the 'constitutional roots of the sexual instinct'. The postulated constitution containing the germs of all the perversions will only be demonstrable in children, even though it is with a modest degree of intensity that any of their instincts can emerge.

SEX AND LOVE

Freud is of the opinion that language has carried out an entirely justifiable piece of unification in creating the word love, with its numerous uses, and he says we cannot do better than take it as the basis of our scientific inquiry. The nucleus of what is meant by love naturally consists in 'sexual love with sexual union as its aim'. But we do not separate from this what in any case has a share in the name 'love'— on the one hand self-love and on the other hand love for parents and children, friendship and love for humanity in general, and also devotion to concrete objects and abstract ideas.

Freud says that all these tendencies are an expression of the same instinctual impulse. In relations between the sexes these impulses force their way towards sexual union. But in other circumstances they are diverted from their aim though always preserving enough of their original nature to keep their identity recognisable, as in longing for proximity and self-sacrifice. The depths, to which anyone is in love, as contrasted with his purely sensual desire, may be measured by the size of the share taken by the inhibited instincts of tenderness.

There is also the factor of the sexual over-estimation of the object. Due to this, the loved object enjoys a certain amount of freedom from criticism. If the sensual tendencies are somewhat more effectively repressed, the illusion is produced that the object has come to be sensually loved on account of its spiritual merits; on the contrary, those merits may really only have been lent to it by its sensual charm.

The tendency which falsifies judgment is idealisation. The object is treated in the same way as our own ego, so that when we are in love, a considerable amount of narcissistic libido overflows onto the object. It is obvious in many forms of love choice that the object serves as a substitute for some unattained ego ideal of our own. That is a roundabout way of satisfying our narcissism. In the over-estimation of the object, the tendencies towards sexual satisfaction may now be pushed back entirely, as happens in sentimental passion. The ego becomes increasingly modest and the object more and more sublime and precious, until at last it gains possession of the entire self-love of the ego.

It is now possible to define the distinction between identification and such extreme developments of being in love, which may be described as fascination or infatuation. In identification, the ego has enriched itself with the properties of the object. In the second case, it is impoverished; it has surrendered itself to the object.

Freud's conception of love has been subject to criticism. For instance, in Suttie's *Origins of Love and Hate*,[30] Freud's standpoint is vehemently criticised. Suttie says the neglect of the love element, as distinct from sex, has always appeared to be one of the blind spots of Freudian psychology.

There is an extremely interesting statement in the letters to Theodore Reik concerning Dostoevsky, which shows that the Freudian view of love is not one-sided:

> Consider his astonishing helplessness in face of the phenomena of love. All he really knew were crude, instinctual desire, masochistic submission, and loving out of pity.[31]

There is also a passage in *Group Psychology* where Freud says:

> In the development of mankind as a whole, just as in indi-

viduals, love alone acts as the civilising factor in the sense that it brings a change from egoism to altruism.[32]

EVALUATION

We have completed the exposition of Freud's theory of sexuality. However, we are more interested in the deeper insights he offered regarding the condition of man and his love-life. The Freud that came to grips with the tragic predicament of man in *Civilization and Its Discontents* did not just represent a minor episode in the life of a scholar who propounded a pan-sexual theory of man. If we glance at his essay entitled *Observations on Wild Psycho-analysis* we can almost see shades of Schopenhauer there. Freud says something in the nature of sexuality itself determines that there shall be ever a mental absence of satisfaction.[33] There is certainly something more than a purely frustration theory of sexuality.

Philip Rieff says that Freud's sensitivity to the transitoriness of sexual fulfilment deserves comparison with that of the novelists of romantic introspection—'the heart grows weary of all that it has and sighs for all that it has not'.[34] Freud saw the almost dialectical way in which the increase and decrease of pleasure is related to the presence of pain. 'Thus, contradicting hedonist theory, Freudian psychology reveals the ephemeral quality of pleasure as an end in itself.'[35]

We are not maintaining that this was Freud's most basic theme as such. But it would be seen that gradually, as Freud came to uncover the illusions of romantic love, he found a 'bit of unconquerable nature in each of us'. There is some kind of craving for sexual gratification that can never be satisfied, and thus renews and finds new and novel methods of satisfaction.

But Freud was so dominated by the theoretical construct of the Oedipus-complex, he could not find a radical answer to the dilemma outlined above. All he could do was to translate 'hysterical misery into common unhappiness,' and advocate that man achieve an attainable ideal of happiness. The Buddha, on the other hand, offers a more radical therapy to cure man's basic malady.

It seems, as Philip Rieff says, that to Freud an instinct is just the element that makes any response inadequate. The failure to respond can be traced not merely to societal rigidities, but further back to the ambivalent structure of instinct itself, which continually prepares the ground for conflicts.[36] If Freud maintained a thesis of the sort maintained by Philip Rieff, it brings us close to the Buddhist concept of *taṇhā*. If so, we can agree with Rieff and say that Freud's theory of instinct is the basis for Freud's great insight into the condition of man, '...the painful snare of contradiction in which nature and culture, individual and society, are forever fixed.'[37]

Apart from throwing light on the nature of instincts, Freud gave us a penetrating insight about the concept of self in relation to the problem of love. Though this is a concept that will be examined in detail under the concept of the ego, the concept of narcissism deserves our attention at the moment.

Freud made an analysis of two types of love called (1) narcissistic, and (2) anaclitic (leaning). In their choice of love objects, the narcissistic type selects a person who is like himself; the anaclitic type selects a person on whom the individual becomes dependent, essentially a mother substitute. Persons whose sexual development has suffered a setback in their choice of love objects, take as their model not the mother, but their own selves. They are seeking themselves as their love object.

The anaclitic type displays a marked sexual over-estimation, which is doubtless derived from the original narcissism of the child and then transferred to the sex object. 'That the self may chase love round an object back to itself again'[38] is a very brilliant insight of Freud, according to Philip Rieff.

Lastly, the fact that Freud did not present a purely pan-sexual theory can be seen by his recognition of the ego drive and aggression as a dominant source of behaviour. Though these aspects will be dealt with in the subsequent sections, it is relevant to mention some of the important facts at this stage. Anyone making a study of Freud's major works *Three Essays on Sexuality*, *Ego and the Id*, and *Beyond the Pleasure Principle* will find how he added new concepts as he came across new clinical data. The first concentrates on the sexual instinct, the second on the ego, the third makes an analysis of aggression and the destructive urge.

This shows that Freud was aware of the complex aspects of behaviour instead of offering a purely one-track theory of human motivation. In the works of Freud, we see a continuous struggle to grapple with the complex aspects of human personality.

KĀMA-TAṆHĀ: CRAVING FOR SENSE GRATIFICATION

THE PLEASURE PRINCIPLE

Kāma as 'sense desire' generally refers to the enjoyment of the five senses, but in a more specific and a more narrow sense *kāma* refers to sexual enjoyment as in the precept referring to evil conduct with regard to sexual behaviour (*kāmesu micchācāra*). In fact, the word 'methuna'[39] is used to refer to sexual enjoyment in a specific way; the words *methunasmin chanda* for instance refer to desires in sexual gratification. But the term *kāma* is used in a very broad manner and sexual pleasure may be one aspect of it.

Before we make a detailed analysis of the word *kāma*, let us review its position as a general pleasure principle. The Buddha considers the pleasure principle as one of the basic factors in human motivation. It is also the factor that reconciles man to suffering, tribulation and pain which overtake him in the search for pleasure. There is a passage in the *Samyutta Nikāya* that sums up the pleasure principle very clearly:

> ...if there were not this satisfaction that comes from the eye, beings would not lust after the eye. But in as much as there is satisfaction in the eye, therefore beings lust after it. If misery, brethren, pertained not to the eye, beings would not be repelled by the eye. But in as much as there is misery in the eye, beings are repelled by it.[40]

The same could be said of the other senses. Man is so constituted that he seeks what is pleasurable and avoids whatever is painful. The nature of pleasurable or painful feelings has been analysed in various ways. According to one classification, there are three types of feeling (*vedanā*): pleasant (*sukha*), painful (*dukkha*) and indifferent (*adukkhamasukha*).[41]

The term 'feeling' suggests a hedonic tone and is called pleasant if it is agreeable and painful if it is disagreeable. This could be further classified into bodily agreeable or disagreeable feeling or mentally agreeable or disagreeable feeling. Feeling is also classified as wholesome (*kusala*), unwholesome (*akusala*) and indeterminate (*avyakata*). What is of special significance in this analysis is the evaluation of feeling as *kusala* or *akusala*. This brings an ethical dimension into the analysis of pleasure in Buddhism that is not found in Freud.

Pleasant feelings induce an attachment (*upādāna*) to pleasant objects. There is potency in pleasant feelings to arouse latent sensuous greed (*rāgānusaya*). Painful feelings on the other hand arouse latent anger and hatred (*patighānusaya*). It is said that 'a tendency to attachment lies latent in pleasant feeling; a tendency to repugnance lies latent in painful feeling; a tendency to ignorance lies latent in a neutral feeling.'[42] Thus on the one hand, the craving for pleasure dominates human behaviour. On the other hand, there is a tremendous amount of suffering undergone in the pursuit of pleasures. It could be said that between pleasure and pain the worldling gets fatigued. This, in brief, is the dominance of the pleasure principle.

But there is a way out of this dominance of the pleasure principle. Though the Buddha agrees with Freud regarding this dominance, unlike Freud, the Buddha offers the religious ideal of the arahat; the arahat is free from the dominance of the pleasure principle. As he does not delight in sensual ease, the lurking tendency to sensual ease does not fasten on him. As he has no repugnance, the lurking tendency to repugnance fastens not on him. The question may be raised whether the arahat enjoys no bliss. Even if the arahat enjoys any bliss, the Buddhist scriptures say that it is a delight qualitatively different from human pleasures:

> ...there is this delight which, apart from pleasures of the senses, apart from unskilled states of mind, stands firm on reaching a deva-like happiness. Delighting in this delight, I do not envy what is low; I have no delight therein.[43]

Even if the states achieved by the recluse are described as 'pleasurable' states, they involve no attachment. Such a state has been described as 'rapturous and joyful', but no tendency to attachment lies latent there.[44] It is also said that there are pleasures of the householder and those of renunciation but the pleasures of renunciation are to be valued.[45] Having made an introductory exposition of the nature of the pleasure principle, let us examine the concept of *kāma* in more detail, especially the aspects that have a bearing on this study.

KĀMA AS OBJECT AND DESIRE (VATTHU-KĀMA AND KILESA-KĀMA)

The terms *vatthu* and *kilesa-kāma* are perhaps found for the first time in the *Mahā-Niddesa*.[46] But they are related to a distinction already made in the older suttas: *pañca kāmaguna* and *kāma-rāga*.[47] *Pañca kāmaguna* refers to the five types of pleasure objects obtained by the eye, ear, nose, tongue and body. *Kāma-raga* refers to the desires and passions of a sensual nature. Thus the term *pañcakāma gunika-rāga* refers to the fact that in beings there is a deep-seated proclivity for the enjoyment of the five senses.

The lure of these five types of sense-objects is often described in the discourses of the Buddha. There is a passage in the *Samyutta Nikāya* that sums up the position thus:

> There are objects, *puñña*, cognizable by the eye, objects desirable, pleasant, delightful and dear, passion-fraught, inciting to lust. If a brother be enamoured of such, if he welcome them, persist in clinging to them, so enamoured, so persisting in clinging to them, there comes a lure upon him.[48]

When beings cling to sensuous enjoyment they have a lure upon them; when there is a lure, there is infatuation; when there is infatuation there is bondage. Nyanatiloka Thera says that the term *kilesa-kāma* may be considered as subjective sensuality and the term *vatthu-kāma* as objective sensuality.[49]

According to the analysis in the *Niddesa Kāmasutta*, sense desire as object (*vatthu-kāma*) refers to pleasant forms, sounds, smells, tastes and touch. It could also refer to such objects as clothes, servants, goats, pigs, fields and land. When the concept is extended in that way, it would not be limited to sense gratification as such, but implies aspects of self-preservation, need for security, wealth, and so on. These may be considered the conditions necessary for sensuous gratification.

The term *kilesa-kāma* refers to factors like *kāma-chanda* (impulse), *kāma-rāga* (excitement), *kāma-sankappa* (thought), *kāma-nandi* (enjoyment), *kāma-sineha* (love), *kāma-parilāha* (consuming passion), *kāma-mucchā* (confused state of mind), etcetera. There are also more significant terms like *kāma-upādāna* (clinging), *kāma-taṇhā* (craving), *kāma-āsava* (canker of sensuality), all of which are covered by the term *kilesa-kāma*. The term *kilesa* gives an ethico-psychological basis to the analysis of sense desires in Buddhism that makes it somewhat different from the Freudian analysis. The word kilesas is generally translated as defilements. In the way that clear water can be made impure by the mixing of mud, lust can completely defile one's mind. Being derived from the word *kilissati*, it means stain, soil, impurity. In a moral sense, it means depravity or lust.

In the last analysis, it is not the existence of sense-organs or the impact of sense-impressions that is emphasised but the persistence of desire and lust. The eye is not the bond of object, nor are objects the bond of eye, but desire and lust that arise owing to these two. It is very significant that Freud makes a distinction between erotic instincts and objects, and considers the instincts as more important.[50]

According to the Buddha, unless there is the persistence of clinging (*upādāna*), excitation of the sense-organs is not sufficient to rouse the individual to activity. The pursuit of sense-pleasures, desire to possess, and tenacity in the presence of obstruction is present only when the individual clings to pleasures and pleasure-giving objects.

The *Mahā-nidāna Sutta* of the *Dīgha Nikāya* contains a good analysis of the emergence and persistence of sensuous craving.[51] Craving comes into being because of sensation; pursuit because of craving. Because of pursuit there is gain, and because of gain, decision regarding the desirability of the object; from decision emerges desire and passion, possession because of tenacity, avarice because of possession, watch and ward because of avarice, and many a bad and wicked state of things arise from keeping watch and ward over possessions. Clinging (*upādāna*) emerges always with craving (*taṇhā*) as a condition. But clinging (*upādāna*) as such works on a far deeper current and once a person clings to pleasure-giving objects, some latent tendencies (*anusayas*) have already been excited and stimulated. Fixation on pleasure-giving objects always feeds on the undercurrents of *anusayas*. These deeper instinctual forces are handed over through an innumerable number of lives.

ATTITUDE TO SENSUAL PLEASURE

On the one hand, pleasure is considered as a natural phenomenon and leaving the immaterial plane of existence (*arūpāvacara*), the world of earth is referred to as the sense-sphere (*kāmāvacara*).

There is a specific reference in the classification of the five destinies, where it is stated that the realm of human beings is abundantly pleasant when compared with the hell or the animal world.[52] In the hell (*niraya*), creatures experience feelings which are exclusively painful, sharp and severe. In the animal world there is experience of feelings which are painful. In the realm of the departed there are feelings which are abundantly painful. Among men there is experience of feelings abundantly pleasant and among gods exclusively pleasant. This is to emphasise the fact that in one sense there are more pleasures than pain in the world of men.

There is also the example of the homily to Sigāla laying down the fundamental virtues of a householder.[53] Here, enjoyment of desire is not condemned as such, what is condemned is desire that is vicious, excessive and illegitimate.

There is also an analysis of the types of people given to sensual pleasures, as paraphrased below.[54] A certain one, given to sensual pleasures, seeks wealth, unlawfully and by violence, so seeking wealth, he gets no ease, no pleasure for himself, shares it not with others, does no meritorious deeds. This is compared with the person who is given to sensual pleasures, seeks wealth by lawful means, without violence. So seeking it, he gets ease, gets pleasure for himself, shares it with others and does meritorious deeds. But he makes use of his wealth without greed and longing; he is guiltless of offence, he is heedful of danger and alive to his own salvation. Here instead of condemning the life of sensual pleasure, an effort is made to work out the difference between the life of pleasure lived on correct principles and the life of pleasure which is unlawful.

But on the other hand, in the majority of sermons given to the monks, sense-pleasures are referred to as sources of danger and as intrinsically incompatible with the life of renunciation. This is all the more emphasised in the attainment of higher states of mental development. The person seeking *jhānic* states (higher states of mental absorption or meditation) should seclude himself both from sense desire as defilement (*kilesa kāma*) and sense desire as object (*vatthu-kāma*). Sense desire as defilement refers to mental seclusion. Sense desire as object refers to bodily seclusion. Thus where in the ordinary layman, sense perception can be purely neutral in its ethical significance, it acquires a special bearing in the life of the monk, and more so in the seeker after *jhānic* states. In the acquirement of *jhānic* states even perception of diversity is given up.

Thus, in the life of the monk, it is clearly emphasised that lust is incompatible with concentration. And even the most trivial stimuli can excite lustful thoughts in a monk. Apart from the call to restraint and control of the sense-organs, the monks have been advised to judiciously avoid situations that can prompt unskilled activity. Thus detachment from sense-pleasure is the basis on which the monk has to work out his deliverance. This attitude to sensual pleasure is essentially a necessary prerequisite of the very nature of the therapy that the monk undertakes.

Basically the Buddhist attitude to sensual pleasures is rooted in a deeper awareness of the human tragedy. It is not possible to understand the Buddhist attitude to sensual pleasures without a reference to the doctrine of *dukkha* (anguish).

What sort of thing is the satisfaction in material shapes? It is like a girl in a noble's family who at the age of fifteen or sixteen is not too tall, not too short, not too thin, not too fat, not too dark, not too fair. She is at the height of her beauty and loveliness. And whatever pleasure and happiness arise because of beauty and loveliness, this is satisfaction in material shapes.[55]

What is the peril in material shapes? As to this, one might see the same lady after a time, at eighty or ninety or a hundred years old. Thus, that which was formerly beautiful and lovely has vanished, a peril has appeared. One might see that same lady, her body thrown aside in the cemetery, devoured by animals. Transience, change, decay and destruction are the nature of material shapes. Thus it is said, that birth is anguish, old age is anguish, disease is anguish and death is anguish. Grief, lamentation, suffering, tribulation and despair are anguish, and if one does not get what one wants that too is anguish; in short the five groups of grasping (corporeality, feeling, perception, disposition, consciousness) are anguish.

One who is under the spell of the craving for sense gratification (*kāma-taṇhā*) will ever be in a constant state of striving and wanting. In spite of incessant satisfaction, there will always be an inner restlessness. In fact, the word *taṇhā* connotes some kind of unquenchable thirst. The objects of satisfaction are themselves liable to change and decay. Even Freud says in his *Civilization and Its Discontents* that suffering comes from one's own body, which is destined to decay and dissolution.[56]

Even in the pursuit of sense-pleasures there are hardships and obstacles. In the *Majjhima Nikāya*, the suffering of a layman in the pursuit of the life of sense-pleasure is brought out in detail.[57]

Sensuous craving is thus to be given up because it is a source of ill. Sometimes they are described in the language of metaphor as a skeleton, a lump of meat, a dream, etcetera.[58] But apart from this figurative usage, it is quite clearly and emphatically stated that sense pleasures are a source of danger; empty, hollow and illusory, a stumbling-block to the attainment of salvation and neither worth rejoicing in nor worth approval.

In the final analysis, it could be said that this dual attitude to sense pleasures is partly due to the fact that the ideal of the monk commits him to a different way of life, once he accepts the way of renunciation. On the other hand, the layman accepts the life of pleasure as a part of his choice. This does not necessarily mean that the life of the monk and the life of the layman stand in an antithetical relation. But it is merely stated that the life of pleasure and the life of renunciation stand in contrast.

SEXUAL AND SENSUAL PLEASURE

There is a reference in the Suttas to the seven-fold associations with sexual feelings.[59] The seven-fold associations with sexual feelings (*methuna samyojana*) are given in their stages. Sensations of physical caresses, play and amusement with women, looking at and being enticed by feminine figures, being enticed by their voice, reminiscences and past associations with women, desire to see others enjoying the pleasures of sense—all these are considered as associations with sexual feelings, and lastly, even the living of a godly life in the hope of attaining a celestial abode. Any of these associations with sexual feelings are referred to as a breaking of the godly life, a tarnishing and blemish.

> (1) 'Consider, brahman, some recluse or godly man professing to live the godly life in full, who in sooth falls not so far as to couple with womenfolk, yet enjoys being rubbed, massaged, bathed, shampooed by a woman, relishes it, longs for it and is entranced thereby.' This is a tarnishing of the godly life.
>
> (2) ...jokes, jests and makes merry with them.

(3) ...eye on eye burns for them, stares after them.
(4) ...listens to them as they laugh, talk, sing or weep beyond the wall, beyond the fence.
(5) ...remembers the laughs, talks, jests he had with them of yore.
(6) ...watches some yeomen or yeoman's son, engrossed in, revelling in, the five pleasure-strands.
(7) ...lives the godly life in the hope of a deva-body.[60]

This context is significant because here sensuous excitement through eye, ear, body, etcetera are specifically referred to as associations with sex (*methuna*). There are other contexts where the power of women to enslave men is mentioned in general. A woman enslaves a man in eight ways: by appearance, by laughter, by speech, by song, tears, attire, garlands from the forest and touch.[61] Here it is not specifically mentioned that the bond is sexual. But a context like this is similar to the earlier one and is representative of both sexual and sensuous excitement.

It is difficult to differentiate sexual enjoyment from sensuous enjoyment. Even in the seven associations with sexual feeling they are mostly at the level of sensuous excitation through form, voice and touch. Apart from the usage of the word *methuna*, the term *kāma* is invariably used to connote sexual and sensuous enjoyment, which seem to shade off into one another.

Sexual conduct as such is a natural part of the layman's life though it is strictly prohibited for the monk. In the case of laymen there is even an attempt to distinguish legitimate sexual relations and illegitimate sexual relations.

A wrongdoer in regard to the pleasures of sex (*kāmesu micchācāri*) is referred to as one who has intercourse with girls protected by the mother, father, parents, a brother, a sister, or one who has a husband and whose use involves punishment, and even with those adorned with garlands of betrothal. The power of women to enthral is fully admitted in Buddhism:

> Monks, I know of no other single form by which a man's heart is enslaved as it is by that of a woman. Monks, a woman's form obsesses a man's heart.[62]

The Buddhist attitude to women is discernible from two standpoints; from the standpoint of the layman and then of the monk. For the monk, any kind of relation with women was considered as detrimental to a life of celibacy (*brahmacāriya*). That is why it is said that woman stains the higher life. Of course, on the other hand, a woman's life of celibacy can be stained by that of man.

But as the doctrine was mainly for monks, a woman's form almost symbolized the excitation of lustful thoughts and feelings. Woman's form, sound, taste, perfume and touch are referred to as the 'lust-linking strands'.

> Monks, take the case of a monk who lives dependent on a village or town... And there he sees a woman, with dress disordered, or not properly dressed, and at the sight passion overwhelms his mind...[63]

Thus the Buddha advises the monks to guard the doors of the sense organs.

LOVE AND AFFECTION

The English word 'love' is somewhat vague and has no specific connotation. Sometimes a distinction is made with the help of the Greek words: *eros* referring to the sensual aspects of love and *agape* to the spiritual aspects of love. However, we are forced to make finer distinctions as brotherly love, motherly love, sexual love, a love of God and so on.

Freud says that language is justified in using the same word to describe sexual love, self-love, love of parents, children, friendship, humanity and devotion to abstract ideas.[64] Though there may be a limited basis for bringing closer together self-love and sexual love, self-love and love of children, sexual love and friendship and so on to explain all forms of love by an overall reductive theory, does violence to the finer distinctions made by ordinary people even with this ambiguous word love. In the final analysis, Freud's theory seems most limited when we attempt to give an ethical basis to the emotion of compassion.

His critique of romantic love is certainly to be commended. His remarkable insight into the duality of love, between the sensual and the affectionate aspects, is of lasting significance. But his positive conception of love, spiritual or ethical, is very thin. Since Freud introduced the well-known Oedipus-complex[65] there has been much controversy regarding the emotions of love, affection and compassion. Suttie, for instance, says that Freud was blind to the tender emotion of selfless love that is found in a mother's love for the child. Suttie, in his *Origins of Love and Hate* refers to this as the 'taboo on tenderness'.[66] The Buddha considers the love of a mother for a child as the closest analogy to spiritual or universal love.

The Pāli word *mettā* has a specific meaning which helps us to distinguish between lustful love and compassion. Instead of considering *mettā* as even sublimated sexuality, Buddhism traces *mettā* to a different source altogether. All unskilful actions are traced to the morally unwholesome roots of *lobha* (attachment), *dosa* (ill-will) and *moha* (delusion). *Mettā*, on the other hand, emerges as a result of *alobha* (non-attachment), *adosa* (lack of ill-will), and *amoha* (non-delusion). *Mettā* (loving-kindness) is considered as one of the four divine states, others being *karunā* (compassion), *muditā* (altruistic joy) and *upekkha* (equanimity).

It is our chief aim in this section to work out a positive conception of loving-kindness (*mettā*) within the ethical dimension of Buddhism. It is all the more necessary as it is of contemporary significance. As Erich Fromm has indicated, it is the problem of love that should have an answer to the problems of human existence.[67] There have been many recent attempts to examine the basis of this most humane emotion of love. Erich Fromm's *Art of Loving*, Suttie's *Origins of Love and Hate*, and Theodore Reik's *Of Love and Lust*,[68] are some of the very recent attempts to deal with this fundamental conception of human love.

Fromm says that the experience of 'separateness' is the source of all anxiety.[69] He also says that the main condition for the achievement of love is the overcoming of one's narcissism.[70] In this sense the four sublime states of Buddhism (love, compassion, sympathetic joy and equanimity) could be of great therapeutic value in breaking through certain neurotic personality traits. The Buddha, however, is careful to note the distinction between *mettā* as loving-kindness and quasi-sexual affection (*pema*). *Mettā* is an extremely impersonal and detached emotion. *Pema* is an exclusive affection and does not radiate towards all beings. In fact, there are certain dangers to which persons practising *mettā* can succumb. For a beginner who wants to practise the contemplation of *mettā* it would be wise to avoid an antipathetic person, a very dearly loved one, a neutral person and a hostile person. These dangers are not limited to *mettā* but to other divine states as well.

Apart from the practice of the four divine states, the expression of love and devotion is given fitting expression in the *Sigālovāda Sutta.*[71] Here is mentioned the devotion of parents to children, that of the children to parents, learners to teachers, husband to wife, friend to friend, master to servant, layman to recluse.

The homily to Sigāla gives a charming code of domestic relations. As gods take compassion (*anukampati*) upon their devotees who pray for them with offerings, so in all six relations the seniors function as gods. The relationship between parents and children is significant as manifesting the tender emotion of love (*anukampati*). In five ways, parents minister to their child and show their love for him; they restrain him from vice, they exhort him to virtue, they train him to a profession, they contract a suitable marriage for him and in due time they hand over his inheritance.

All six relations cited earlier are based on healthy humane emotions and bring men together in mutual goodwill and contribute to the development of both domestic and social harmony. Motherly love is often taken as the very analogy of selfless devotion and sacrifice. Against the background of this homily, anything like the Freudian concept of Oedipus-complex stands rejected.

But Buddhism is a many-sided doctrine. Though in the *Sigālovāda Sutta* we get a fitting benediction to the domestic relations between parent and child, we get another attitude elsewhere. Of course, there is definitely no attempt in Buddhism to prove that parent-child relationships are of erotic origin. In fact any such phenomenon would be counter to the very grain of the *Sigālovāda Sutta*. However, there are a large number of contexts where, especially from the point of view of the monk, family relations are considered fetters; they are called *gihibandhana* (fetters of household life):

> Take the case, Dona, of a brāhman of similar birth and conduct...who weds in like manner... And when in wedlock he has begotten a child, the fondness for children obsesses him, and he settles on the family estate and does not go forth from the home to the homeless life.[72]

Even companionship (*samsagga*) is considered as chaining the heart of man. This is clearly brought out in the *Sutta-Nipāta* where the individual is asked to fare alone like a rhinoceros.

> Love cometh from companionship;
> In wake of love upsurges ill;
> Seeing the bane that comes of love,
> Fare lonely as rhinoceros.[73]
> In truth for all his bosom-friends,
> A man heart-chained, neglects the goal;
> Seeing this fear in fellowship,
> Fare lonely as rhinoceros.[74]

Both companionship (*samsagga*) and love (*pema*) for sons are referred to as ties of love (*piyavippayogam vijigucchamāno*). *Sineha* (fondness) and *pema* (affection) in this context are condemned not because they are erotic as such, but because of these ties the brāhman tends to neglect the goal. But expressions of human affection and fondness tend to be exclusive and possessive quite often, even if we would not call them erotic. They are also based on clinging (*upādāna*). This is clearly brought out in the *Saṃyutta Nikāya*.[75]

> 'Now, headman, what is the reason, what is the cause, why sorrow, suffering, woe, lamentation and despair would come upon you in respect of some, but not of others?'
> 'In the case of those, lord, owing to whose death or imprisonment, or loss or blame I should suffer such sorrow... it is because I have desire and longing for them... .'

Those for whom people have a special affection and love bring in turn sorrow and anxiety in the loss of the beloved. From affection (*pema*) springs grief, from affection springs fear. For him who is wholly free from affection there is neither grief nor fear.[76]

Most of these teachings of the canon are especially meant for the monk. But even for the householder, if his household ties are wrong, he will not get close to the goal. As for the monk, even worldly activity and delight in companionship is condemned.[77]

> 'When you are assembled and met together and live enjoying company, I think thus; surely those worthies cannot obtain at will and without trouble this happiness of renunciation... .'[78]

Delight in worldly activity, company, companionship, gossip, living a life of diffuseness lead to failure in a monk's training. *Raga, sineha, pema* and even *samsagga* (passion, fondness, affection and even companionship), are discouraged as not conducive to the life of renunciation.

THE LIBIDO AND THE CONCEPT OF KĀMA-TAṆHĀ

A basic point on which there is agreement between the psychology of early Buddhism and Freud is the dominating role of the pleasure principle. The Buddha has often declared that man is so constituted that he is attracted by what is pleasurable and is repelled by what is painful. Dr O. H. de A. Wijesekera, in an essay examining the concept of *dukkha*, says:

> ... critics of Buddhism may wonder whether it is justifiable to regard the whole psychology of the sentient being as being so strongly ruled by this principle of hankering for the pleasurable and shunning what is unpleasant. That a similar conclusion was arrived at by Freud, the founder of the modern School of Psychoanalysis, should cause such critics or sceptics to pause and reflect upon the scientific validity of such an observation.[79]

But there are two significant differences between Buddhism and Freud on this point. Firstly though the Buddha emphasised the dominance of the pleasure principle, he said that there is a way out of this dominance.[80] As mentioned earlier, the ideal Buddhist monk or arahat has renounced both attachment for pleasure and repulsion to pain. Freud, on the other hand, emphasised the repressed desires and restrictions imposed by culture and merely advocated the clearing away of social obstacles. He accepted the life of sense gratification and merely tried to reduce the neurotic ways of obtaining pleasure.

Yet Freud's attitude to sense-pleasures is not all that simple. As Philip Rieff has shown, at times Freud came very close to Schopenhauer when he said that an instinct is just that element which makes any response inadequate.[81] There seems to be a bit of unconquerable nature in each of us. But Freud unlike the Buddha had no radical therapy for human suffering and his *Civilization and Its Discontents* suggest that all this suffering has to be accepted with resignation.

Secondly, there is a difference of emphasis in the analysis of the concept of pleasure. Both psychologies use the concept of pleasure in a very broad sense to cover both sexual and sensual gratification, but there is a difference of emphasis. Buddhism traces all pleasures to the five senses, and there does not seem to be anything sexual in tasty food, the smell of scent or even a musical note. Buddhism certainly considers the desire for bodily pleasures and sexual satisfaction as a powerful factor in human motivation. Yet the concept of pleasure is much broader than the Freudian notion of pleasure.

Apart from these differences there are interesting similarities. The Buddhist scriptures always emphasise how people obtain sense gratification by way of the 'eye'. There is an interesting parallel in one of the perversions mentioned by Freud called 'scopophilia'. Here the eye is an erotogenic zone. The other perversion called exhibitionism or self-display is the inverse of this designed to attract the eye of the other person. Though these are perversions, they are not completely alien to the normal mind. In fact as Freud says the so-called normal often shades into the abnormal. Freud also says, 'Visual impressions remain the most frequent pathway along which libidinal excitation is aroused.'[82]

There is also the emphasis on tactile sensation in Freud. Freud refers to Moll's instinct of contractation—a need for contact with the other person's skin. This is given more general expression as the 'longing for proximity'.[83] The Buddhist scriptures give a very prominent place to tactile sensation. The body is the tactile organ.

There is also a noteworthy resemblance between Freud and Buddhism in emphasising the role of the 'instincts' more than that of the 'object'. In the last analysis what is emphasised in Buddhism is not the object or the sense organs, but the persistence of desire and lust. Freud says that the sexual instinct is in the first place independent of its object.

This brings us to the strength of instincts. The concepts of *kāma-rāga* (sensuous passion) and *kāma-upādāna* (sense clinging) and *kāma-āsava* (the canker of sensuous desire), refer to the persistence and upsurge of the craving for sense-gratification. Freud's analysis of instincts was influenced by a physiological orientation. The concept of *taṇhā* cannot be reduced to a somatic origin. Yet the Freudian concept of id seems to resemble the concept of *āsava*. Wishful impulses which have never got beyond the id, and even impressions which have been pushed down into the id by repression, are virtually immortal and are preserved for whole decades as though they had only recently occurred.[84] The fact that 'they are immortal' may be a close echo of *āsavas* (cankers) inherited through countless births. In commenting on this point, Freud says, 'This seems to offer an approach to the most profound discoveries. Nor unfortunately have I myself made any progress here.'[85]

Instead of getting involved in a rather vague notion of the 'collective unconscious,' if he had considered the hypothesis of rebirth as found in early Buddhism, he might have got at some worthwhile explanation. This is certainly significant in the light of Freud's observations on infantile sexuality. A passage in the *Majjhima Nikāya* maintains that there is a 'lurking tendency' for attachments to pleasure latent in a baby lying on his back.[86]

The Buddhist concept of *upādāna* (clinging) also should be of interest to the students of Freud. Since in recent years, scholars like Erich Fromm have shown that when the Freudian Oedipus-complex is rid of its sexual colouring, the lasting element is a father-centred or mother-centred symbiotic attachment. This, when combined with the notion of 'anaclitic object choice', seems to be an echo of the Buddhist notion of *upādāna* (clinging).

In spite of all these similarities there is one basic difference which must be mentioned now. There is a final evaluative element in the Buddhist analysis of pleasure into *kusala* (moral or wholesome) and *akusala* (immoral or unwholesome). Unwholesome pleasures are caused by passion, hatred and delusion, whereas the wholesome pleasures are caused by their opposites. It may be said at this point that even Freud advocates people to enjoy pleasures which are wholesome rather than neurotic. But there is an important difference as to what is meant by wholesome in the two systems. The Freudian concept of wholesome pleasures is derived from the Freudian concept of normal personality which is merely an 'average', the ability to adjust oneself to society. The Buddhist conception of what is wholesome is a 'norm' and thus has an ethical dimension.

It could be said of course that, as critics like Philip Rieff have maintained, the Freudian concept of the normal personality is not a statistical concept. But even so, according to the Buddha, mental illness is continual until the final stage of sainthood is attained. Thus it is a very high ideal, and gives us an absolute standard or norm to determine our own conception of the normal personality.

THE EGO

It must be emphasised that Freud did not present a complete finalised system of psychology at any time, but his thought grew over a long period of time. With the analysis of the concept of the ego, we come to another stage in the psychology of Freud. There are three significant areas in the Freudian analysis of the personality: id, ego, super-ego. The id is the source of instinctual drives of blind, undirected passion. The ego handles reality. In German the word for ego is *ich* which is the ordinary word for 'I'. The super-ego is a composite of commands, prohibitions and ideals that form the personality.

Here again as was the case with the analysis of sexuality, a number of linguistic questions arise. The word 'I' is such an elusive concept that it seems to almost defy analysis. Words like egoism, egotism, selfishness, self-regard and self-torture are the sorts of words that are often used vaguely and ambiguously. To add to this loose usage, there is another problem that comes up with Freud's analysis of the ego. Sometimes, the ego is referred to as the seat of order, harmony and balance; it represents sanity and reason. But at other times, the ego is referred to as a drive or an instinct. This aspect becomes very important as, while earlier Freud held that all the aspects of the ego coincided with the 'conscious', he later held that a part of the ego is 'unconscious'. The unconscious aspect has tremendous influence on the conscious. In *The Ego and the Id*, Freud says:

> A part of the ego, too—and Heaven knows how important a part—may be Ucs., (sic for unconscious), undoubtedly is, Ucs.[87]

Our main interest in this chapter will be in the second usage. The concept of narcissism is central to this comparative study and is an important point of contact between early Buddhism and Freud. Erich Fromm in a recent work says, 'one of the most fruitful and far-reaching of Freud's discoveries is his concept of narcissism.'[88] Fromm says that Freud himself considered it to be one of his most important findings, and employed it for the understanding of such distinct phenomena as psychosis, love, fear, jealousy, sadism, etcetera. Fromm goes on to say that it has not received enough attention at the hands of Adler and Jung or even Horner. Even in orthodox Freudian theory and therapy, attention has been focused only on the narcissism of the infant and the psychotic. This may be due to the fact that Freud tried to present his concept of narcissism within the framework of his libido theory. Let us make a detailed examination of the Freudian concept of the ego and then make an analysis of the concept of narcissism.

THE CONCEPT OF EGO

The ego is that part of the id which has been modified by the direct influence of the external world.[89] It serves the purpose of receiving stimuli and protecting the organism from them. This relation to the external world is decisive for the ego. The ego has taken over the task of representing the external world for the id and so of serving it; for the id blindly strives to gratify its instincts in complete disregard of the superior strength of outside forces. Thus the ego has the task of bringing the influence of the 'external world' to bear upon the id and its tendencies. The ego endeavours to substitute the reality principle for the pleasure principle, which reigns supreme in the id.

Thus the ego as an organisation of mental life, is derived from the primal structure of the id and modifies itself accordingly as limitations are imposed by the external world. Freud compares the relationship of the id and the ego to a man on horseback. The rider has to hold in check the strength of the horse, the only difference being that the rider seeks to do so with his own strength while the ego uses borrowed forces.[90]

Besides the impact of the external world, there is another factor that has been at work in bringing about the formation of the ego and its differentiation from the id. The body itself, and above all its surface, is a place from which both external and internal perceptions may spring. The ego is 'first and foremost a "body-ego".'[91] It is not merely a surface entity, but it is itself the projection of a surface. The ego is ultimately derived from bodily sensations and may be regarded as a mental projection of the surface of the body. This body-image is significant in the formation of the ego. In fact it lies at the root of the phenomena of narcissism, where one's own body is treated in the same way that a sexual object is treated.

PLEASURE EGO

Originally, at the very beginning of mental life, the ego's instincts are not directed towards the external world. The outside world at this time is generally not cathected with any interest and is indifferent for purposes of satisfaction. During this period, therefore, the ego-subject coincides with what is pleasurable and the external world with what is indifferent or even painful.

Insofar as the ego is auto-erotic, the ego has no need of the outside world, but in consequence of experience undergone by the self-preservative instinct, it acquires objects from that world, and in spite of everything it cannot avoid feeling internal instincts for a time as non-pleasurable. Under the dominance of the pleasure principle a further development now takes place in the ego. Insofar as the objects which are presented to it are sources of pleasure, it takes them into itself (introjection); on the other hand, the ego thrusts forth upon the external world whatever within itself gives rise to pain (projection).

Thus the original 'reality-ego', which distinguished internal and external by means of a sound objective criterion changes into a purified 'pleasure-ego,' which places the characteristic of pleasure above all others. This tendency to dissociate from the ego everything which can give rise to pain, to cast it out and create a pure pleasure-ego, determines the future development of the ego. Freud says, 'The limits of this primitive pleasure-ego cannot escape readjustment through experience.'[92]

REALITY OF THE EGO

> 'Normally there is nothing we are more certain of than the feeling of ourselves, our own ego. It seems to us an inde-

> pendent unitary thing, sharply outlined against everything else. That this is a deceptive appearance, and that on the contrary the ego extends inwards, without any sharp delimitation, into an unconscious mental entity which we call the Id and to which it forms a facade, was first discovered by psycho-analytic research... .'[93]

Thus instead of regarding the ego as a permanent and abiding entity, sharply delimited, Freud used the concept of ego as a hypothetical construct to explain the dynamic interaction of forces.

Though the ego makes an attempt to keep itself clearly and sharply outlined towards the external world at least, even this is not always preserved. In pathology there are instances where the boundary line between the ego and the outer world becomes uncertain, cases in which parts of a man's own body, even component parts of his own mind, perceptions, thoughts, feelings, appear to him alien and not belonging to himself. There are other cases in which a man ascribes to the external world things that clearly originate in him. So the ego's cognisance of itself is subject to disturbance, and the boundaries between it and the outer world are not very sharp. Freud also cites the case of a person being in love as a state which threatens to obliterate the distinction between the ego and the external world.

Further reflection shows that the adult's sense of his own ego cannot have been the same from the beginning. When the infant at the breast receives stimuli, he cannot as yet distinguish whether they come from his own ego or from the outer world. He learns it gradually.

It must make the strongest impression on him that many sources of excitation, which later on he will recognise as his bodily organs, can provide him at any time with sensations, whereas others become temporarily out of reach, e.g. the mother's breast. Thus he begins to consider the sources of pleasurable sensations in his body as his own. That is why Freud remarked in his *The Ego and Id,* that the 'ego is first and foremost a body-ego.' The ego is ultimately derived from bodily sensations, chiefly from those springing from the surface of the body.

Secondly, a further stimulus to the formation of the ego comes from the presence of frequent unpleasant sensations which it tries to abolish or avoid. The tendency arises to dissociate from the ego everything which can give rise to pain, to cast it out and create a pure pleasure-ego, in contrast to a threatening outside not-self.

Much that the individual wants to retain because it is pleasure-giving is nevertheless not part of the ego but of an object; and much that he wishes to reject because it torments him proves to be inseparable from the ego, arising from an inner source.

Freud attempts to make a distinction between the internal and the external, on what is part of the ego and what is part of the external world. Against certain painful excitations from within, the ego has only the same means of defence as that employed against pain coming from without. This fact is the starting point of important morbid disturbances. Thus in the case of the pathological the clear distinction between the ego and the external world gives way.

Instead of maintaining the existence of a unitary entity called the ego, Freud analysed the psychological origins of the ego-instincts. He saw quite clearly that at the beginning there is hardly any distinction between the ego and the id. The ego develops out of the id, and continues to merge into the id. Like the id, the ego is pleasure-loving, the difference being that the ego's striving for pleasure is savoured by a sense of reality. On the side of the ego the 'ego's own narcissism' must be reckoned with, in its dealings with the id.

EGO INSTINCTS AND THE CONCEPT OF NARCISSISM

Karl Abraham expressed the view (after a discussion with Freud) that the main characteristic of *dementia praecox* is that in this disease the investment of objects with libido is lacking. And then the question arose as to what happens to the libido of dementia patients when it is diverted from its objects. Abraham did not hesitate to answer that it is turned back upon the ego. Thus Freud came to interest himself in these phenomena where the libido abandons objects and sets the ego itself in their place. This problem is discussed at length in Freud's paper 'On Narcissism'.[94]

In certain cases, one observes that the ego takes itself as object and behaves as if it were in love with itself. Thus the term 'narcissism' which was taken from a Greek legend, was used to describe this phenomenon. The term 'narcissism' was used by Paul Nacke, and denotes the attitude of a person who treats his own body in the same way in which the body of a sexual object is ordinarily treated. Havelock Ellis had also used the term 'narcissus-like', to describe this parallel psychological attitude.

Though it was first discovered in people who suffered from disorders, Freud says that it seems probable 'that an allocation of the libido such as deserves to be described as narcissism might be present far more extensively, and that it might claim a place in the regular course of human sexual development.'[95] Narcissism in a sense is not a perversion, 'but the libidinal complement to the egoism of the instinct of self-preservation, a measure of which may justifiably be attributed to every living creature.'[96]

What happens to the libido in schizophrenia? The libido that has been withdrawn from the external world has been directed to the ego and thus gives rise to an attitude which may be called 'narcissism'. But the megalomania itself is no new creation. On the contrary it is a magnification and plainer manifestation of a condition which had already existed previously. This leads us to look upon narcissism which arises through the drawing in of object cathexes as a secondary one, superimposed upon a primary narcissism that is obscured by a number of different influences. Freud says that just as the transference neuroses enabled him to trace the libidinal instinctual impulses, so *dementia praecox* and paranoia will give an insight into the psychology of the ego.

The observation of the erotic life of human beings in general too has interesting data for understanding the nature of the ego. The first auto-erotic sexual satisfactions are experienced in connection with vital functions that serve the purpose of self-preservation. The sexual instincts are at the outset attached to the satisfaction of the ego-instincts; only later do they become independent of the ego instincts.

Even then, we have an indication of their original attachment. The persons who are concerned with the child's protection and care become the objects of attachment. This type of object choice may be called the attachment type, meaning 'leaning-type' (anaclitic). Psychoanalytic research has revealed a second type:

> We have discovered, especially clearly in people whose libidinal development has suffered some disturbance such as perverts and homosexuals, that in their later choice of love-objects they have taken as a model not their mother but their own selves.[97]

They are plainly seeking themselves as love-objects and exhibiting a type of choice that may be called 'narcissistic'. Freud says that in this observation he has the strongest reason which led him to adopt the hypothesis of narcissism.

The primary narcissism of children is less easy to grasp by observation than to confirm by inference. 'If we look at the attitude of affectionate parents towards their children, we have to recognise that it is a revival and reproduction of their own narcissism, which they have long since abandoned.'[98]

EGO IDEAL

Libidinal impulses are fated to undergo repression if they come into conflict with the subject's cultural and ethical ideas. From the point of view of the ego, the formation of an ideal is the condition for repression.

To this ideal ego is now directed the self-love which the real ego enjoyed in childhood. Thus the narcissism is now displaced onto this new ideal ego which, like the infantile ego, deems itself the possessor of all perfection. The child is reluctant to give up a once-pleasurable gratification, and he does not willingly give up his narcissistic perfection in childhood. As he develops he is disturbed by the admonitions of others and his own critical judgment is awakened. He seeks to recover the early perfection in the new form of the ego-ideal.

NARCISSISM AND EGOISM

For Freud, narcissism is the libidinal complement of egoism. One can be egoistic and yet maintain a strong interest in object-libido or can be egoistic and yet at the same time be preponderantly narcissistic. In the first instance his egoism will see to it that his desire towards the object involves no injury to his ego. The second alternative might either take the form of direct sexual satisfaction or the higher forms of love.

'In all these situations egoism is the self-evident, the constant element, and narcissism the variable one.'[99] But as psychological attitudes, 'egoism' and 'narcissism' go together. One of the essential characteristics of narcissism is the demand for ego-gratification through receiving the attention and consideration of others. In the Freudian sense, it is the 'need for receiving love'. In fact, there is an intimate connection between the instinct of self-regard and narcissistic libido. In paraphrenia, self-regard is exalted, in the transference it is debased, and where the erotic life is concerned, not being loved lowers self-regarding feelings while being loved raises them. To be loved is the aim and satisfaction in a narcissistic object-choice.

Further, it is easy to observe that libidinous object cathexis does not raise the self-regard. He who loves had so to speak forfeited a part of his narcissism, which can only be replaced by being loved. In all these the self-regarding feeling operates in a close relation to the narcissistic element in the erotic life.

The realisation of impotence, of one's own inability to love in consequence of mental or physical disorder, has an exceedingly lowering effect upon the self-regard. Here is the source of the feelings of inferiority of which patients suffering from the transference neuroses so readily complain to us.[100]

In the face of disappointment the innate sense of narcissism suffers set-backs. Thus with a sense of ego injury the pride of a person manifests in the form of secondary narcissism. Primary narcissism is the original libidinal ego-cathexis, part of which normally persists, while the rest is gradually transferred to objects. It was his study of the mental life of children and of primitive peoples that led Freud to this conception of a primary narcissistic stage. Freud defines secondary narcissism as that which arises when libidinal object cathexis is withdrawn. It results when renounced or lost objects are recreated within the individual and are loved as a part of himself, as secondary identification. If a person is rebuffed, his libido then returns to himself.

EGO AND ANXIETY

With the publication of *Inhibitions, Symptoms and Anxiety,*[101] we come across a very important change in his concept of anxiety. Freud's new theory of anxiety is that 'ego is the seat of anxiety,' and thus anxiety precedes repression. Repression does not lead to anxiety but anxiety leads to repression. The ego has the power of reproducing automatically a previously experienced fear. Thus anxiety is a signal given by the ego that there is a danger. The three main types of anxiety: objective anxiety, neurotic anxiety and moral anxiety can be related to the three directions in which the ego is dependent on the external world, on the id and the super-ego.

Freud made a detailed analysis of the danger that threatens the ego, and says that its essence lies in 'a separation anxiety.' The prototype of this is separation of the infant from the mother at birth. Though he agreed with Otto Rank that in every outbreak of anxiety there is reproduction of the original birth trauma, he discards Rank's exaggerated theory.

Freud accepts the importance of the association between fear reactions to the birth danger and later danger situations and fear reaction. But he says that it is not possible to assume that the foetus has any kind of knowledge that it is in danger of annihilation. Freud also rejects Rank's thesis that child phobias are based on birth impressions; for instance fear of small animals as they vanish into or emerge from holes. Rank is wrong in thinking that the infant has definite sense-impressions. This could not be anything more than a mere tangible or general sensibility.

This new theory made Freud emphasise the importance of the oral stage and the relationship between mother and child. This new theory of anxiety also made the mechanism of defence and its relation to the ego significant. The defence mechanisms were discussed in greater detail later by Freud's daughter Anna Freud.[102]

EVALUATION

As Erich Fromm pointed out, Freud's conception of narcissism is based on his theory of the sexual libido. Fromm thus makes an analysis of narcissism on a broader basis and shows how fanatical devotion to ideologies, personal vanities regarding one's honour, physical power, intelligence or pride in one's children are connected with his concept of narcissism. He also divides narcissism into two kinds: benign and malignant.

In the benign form a person may have a narcissistic pride in his work; his achievements are constantly balanced by his interest in his work. In the case of malignant narcissism, the object of narcissism is not anything the person does, but something the person has, like his looks or wealth. Fromm makes a very interesting analysis on these lines, and concludes by saying that the essential teachings of all the great religions could be summarised in one sentence: *It is the goal of man to overcome his narcissism.* Then he makes a very significant statement; 'perhaps this principle is nowhere expressed more radically than in Buddhism.'[103] Fromm says that according to the Buddha, to overcome suffering man should be rid of the illusions of narcissism, 'The "awakened" person of whom Buddhist teaching speaks is the person who has overcome his narcissism.'[104]

However, Fromm perhaps fails to see what is distinctive about the Buddhist analysis of the ego, which makes it so different from the Christian approach. While Christians uphold the existence of a permanent entity called the soul, the Buddha preached the *anattā* (non-self) doctrine. The *anattā* doctrine is the best remedy for an egoist, and the Buddha has made a detailed analysis of twenty kinds of wrong personality beliefs.[105] Fromm also seems to suggest that the omniscience and omnipotence of the God has a negative effect on man's narcissism. But, according to the Buddha, this kind of belief in an omnipotent God and absolute self-surrender can have the opposite effect of exciting one's inferiority feelings (*hinā mana*). Buddhism advocates man to develop self-confidence.

However, Fromm has struck the correct note in searching for a broader basis for the study of narcissism and also absorbing some of the insights of the Buddha to his own ways of thinking. Thus, we can say that the essay on narcissism will remain as the most significant point of contact between Freud and Buddhism.

BHAVA-TAṆHĀ: CRAVING FOR SELF-PRESERVATION

The ego instincts in Buddhism can be clearly described by an analysis of the concept of *bhava-taṇhā*, the thirst for selfish pursuits. *Bhava-taṇhā* arises with a false conception of personality, based on the dogma of personal immortality (*sassata-diṭṭhi*). This is the belief in an ego entity existing independently of those physical and mental processes that constitute life. And this entity is assumed to exist as a permanent, ever-existing thing, continuing after death. This wrong view or false opinion is referred to as *diṭṭhi*.

This ego-illusion is not merely an intellectual construction, but is fed by deeper affective processes like the desire for self-preservation, self-continuity (personal immortality), self-assertion (power), self-display, and self-respect. Some of these affective processes are manifest in ordinary behaviour. In the day to day existence of man, in his pursuit for pleasure and the problems of household life, by practical necessity he has to look after his self-interests. But the deeper undercurrents like the lurking tendency to cling to existence (*bhavarāga anusaya*) surge up only under special conditions, e.g. danger to life. The moment there is a danger to one's life, the craving for existence surges up and he seeks even violent means of self-defence.

When ambition dawns upon a man to achieve glory and fame, he goes all out to achieve his ambition and enhance his self-esteem. In the midst of success and flattery, he feels elated. In facing failure, he feels dejected and then the self-seeking instinct retreats and takes refuge in self-pity. In all these diverse manifestations of the ego-instincts, the root malady is that the individual clings to a false conception of his personality (*atta-vādupādāna*).

Buddhism also analyses the kind of illusion involved in self-humiliation, self-mortification and varying types of violence done to the self. These emerge from the ego-illusion connected with the annihilationist heresy (*uccheda-diṭṭhi*).

SOME ROOTS OF SASSATA-DIṬṬHI (THE DOGMA OF PERSONAL IMMORTALITY)

Nyanaponika Thera has made a very useful analysis of the roots of the dogma of personal immortality:[106]

> Thinking by way of such conceptual constructs as existence and non-existence has, however, a powerful hold on man, because that way of thinking is perpetually nourished by several strong roots deeply embedded in the human mind.[107]

Firstly, there is the practical and theoretical assumption of an ego or self. In the day to day existence of man, he takes for granted the existence of a separate entity that may be called the self.

Secondly, there is a linguistic root, because the nature of linguistic habits is such, that people tend to think there must be a thing if there is a word for it. Nyanaponika Thera says that the language of subject and predicate, noun and adjective, the tendency to simplify affirmative and negative propositions—all these used for the purpose of easy communication distort our views. This could be clarified by looking at these statements: 'I am five feet tall,' and 'My body is aching'. In the first instance, the self is identified with the body. In the second instance, the body is taken separately from the self, yet the self is considered the possessor of the body. Many such fine distinctions can be made as to how words like 'I', 'mine' and 'my' are used. The Buddha has analysed twenty such personality beliefs. The Buddha denies the concept of a soul in any form as an owner (*sāmi*), doer (*kāraka*), experiencer (*vedaka*) or an immortal resident in a body (*nivāsi*). It is said that the wise man, even though he uses language conforming to conventional usage, will be aware of its conventional nature and not fall into any pitfalls.

Thirdly, there can be emotional reasons expressing basic attitudes to life, like pessimism and optimism, hope and despair. If there is a wish to feel secure through metaphysical support this hope could lead us to the dogma of personal immortality. This aspect of personality belief is very vividly displayed in a work by Unamuno called *The Tragic Sense of Life*.[108] He suggests that the great proof for immortality is the desire for it. On the other hand, the desire to live freely in a materialistic world or a mood of despair and pessimism can lead to the annihilationist view. Thus a light-hearted pleasure-lover who wants to make the best of the present life, or one haunted by anxieties, guilt and fear of the next life could take to this fold. In fact the Freudian analysis of the God concept as issuing from a wish to have a magnified father-figure shows to a great extent how deep emotions can be disguised in the form of rationalisations.[109]

Lastly, there is an intellectual root. Here we come across the speculative and theorising preoccupation of certain minds, which is referred to in Buddhist works as *diṭṭhi-carita*. 'Conceptual opposites are played off against each other with an ingenuity that provides great satisfaction to those engaged in these thought constructions.'[110] Some of the metaphysical theories found in the history of philosophy like the Cartesian *cogito* display the preoccupation of the theorising type. Where Descartes says 'I think, therefore I am,' thus identifying the self with thinking, Unamuno says 'I feel, therefore I am,' thus identifying the self with feeling.

A word of warning is necessary regarding terminology before we conclude this analysis. Words like soul, self and ego are often used interchangeably. Whatever term is used by philosophers who introduced some of these fallacious theories, our term *sassata-diṭṭhi* refers to the belief in a permanent substance or entity, whether to a multitude of individual souls or selves, a monistic world-soul, or a deity of any description. The strength of these dogmas is seen in true form only against the background of the *anattā* doctrine, where the so-called 'self' is described as a continuous flux of material and mental processes arising from their appropriate conditions.

The Buddha says that people usually lean upon that duality—the dogma of personal immortality or the annihilationist view of the soul. Even the Buddhist ideal of nibbāna has been interpreted on the basis of this duality—existence or non-existence. Thus those who took the view of nibbāna as existence considered nibbāna as pure-being, pure-consciousness, pure-self, etcetera. Others gave it a purely negative and nihilistic interpretation. Even Freud, in his *Beyond the Pleasure Principle,* associates Buddhism with the negative approach and thus the identification of nibbāna and the death instinct. Thus the analysis of *bhava-taṇhā* in this chapter and of *vibhava-taṇhā* in the next chapter is of basic importance for this comparative study.

WRONG PERSONALITY BELIEF

Wrong personality-belief is the first of the ten fetters (*samyojana*). It is also one of the four clingings. There are twenty kinds of wrong personality belief.

People who are unskilled in the doctrine, either 1) regard body as the self (*attā*), 2) regard self as having body, 3) regard the body as being in the self, and 4) regard the self as being in the body. They say 'I am the body,' 'the body is mine' and are possessed by the idea.[111] They are enamoured by body and cling to it, and because of clinging, there comes a lure upon them. They pay full devotion to the body and its concerns. They are proud of the fact that the body is full of youth, vigour and beauty. Thus emerges the ego-illusion associated with their body. When it arises on *taṇhā* they think 'the body is mine;' when it arises on *māna*, they think 'I am this;' when it arises on theory (*diṭṭhi*) they think 'this is myself.' In the way that people misconstrue the nature of the body, so do they regard feeling, perception, dispositions and consciousness. Thus we get the twenty types of personality belief:

1-5: Ego as identical with corporeality, feeling, perception, dispositions and consciousness
6-10: Ego as contained in them
11-15: Ego as independent of them
16-20: Ego as the owner of them

Where there is merely a complex consisting of corporeality, feeling, perception, dispositions and consciousness, the individual subject to ego-illusions assumes the existence of an ego. Secondly, this complex called *nāma-rūpa* is subject to change and decay, but the individual considers it as permanent. Thirdly, this complex of *nāma-rūpa* is the source of ill, but the individual considers it as a source of pleasure. The individual subject to these ego-illusions will not be able to realise the three truths of *anattā*, *anicca* and *dukkha*.

ARCHAIC EGO FEELING

Thus, really there is no ego-entity, but only a psychophysical complex. The egoistic behaviour actually rests on a primitive and archaic ego illusion, which has been functioning through countless births. This archaic ego feeling lies dormant in the form of a sub-current. This aspect of personality is referred to in the Suttas as *bhava-rāga* and *bhava-āsava*.

The notion of *āsava* as describing certain powerful psychological traits, stretching back to countless births is one of those factors that make a revaluation of Freud in the light of Buddhist psychology useful. When we glance at one of Freud's last papers, 'Analysis Terminable and Interminable',[112] we find Freud raising some interesting questions. Is there a logical end to analysis? How is it that even after a successful analysis, patients fall into the same neurotic habits? Who is the fully recovered patient? What is normality?

Questions of this sort seem to suggest that at least some case histories were problematic in the light of one single birth. Freud seems to almost slip through this problem in his fascination for the repetition compulsion and his vague notion of the collective unconscious.[113]

At times, Freud considers both the ego and the libido as a kind of archaic inheritance, as some kind of 'abbreviated repetition' of the evolution undergone by the human race. There is a very significant passage in *Moses and Monotheism* where he says:

> In fact it seems to me convincing enough to allow me to venture further and assert that the archaic heritage of mankind includes not only dispositions but also ideational contents, memory traces of the experiences of former generations.[114]

However, in the last analysis, Freud's notion of collective unconscious is ill-defined and vague, while the Buddhist conception of dispositions which are 'samsaric' and which can be traced back to a number of previous births is something more clear and specific.

SELF-CONCEIT (MĀNA)

Another manifestation of the ego is very clearly noticeable in self-conceit (*māna*). Self-conceit of this nature has to be differentiated from ego-belief (*sakkāya-diṭṭhi*) which implies a definite view regarding the assumption of an ego. This is the first of the ten fetters and disappears when one becomes a 'stream winner' (*sotāpanna*). *Māna* is the eighth fetter and can vary from a crude feeling of pride to a subtle feeling of distinctiveness that prevails till the attainment of arahatship.

Self-conceit takes three forms: firstly, the form of a superiority feeling with the thought, 'I am superior to the other' (*seyya māna*); secondly, a feeling of equality with another, 'I am equal to the other' (*sadisa māna*); and thirdly, an inferiority feeling with the thought, 'I am inferior to the other' (*hinā-māna*).[115] The false feeling of superiority is based on ignorance. It is due to ignorance that one feels themselves a separate entity. One is subject to vain imaginings and subject to the latent conceit that 'I am the doer,' 'mine is the doer' (*ahankāramamamkāra mānānusaya*). This insidious tendency to vain conceits can emerge with reference to the body, feeling, perception, disposition or consciousness. Through the cause body, comes the conceit 'I am.' When one is proud of one's body, because it is vigorous and young or because of its personal charm, one associates oneself with the body and then emerge vanity and pride based on it.

Hinā-māna or 'inferiority feelings' are also a manifestation based on pride, but they are more subtle. It can be said for instance that superiority feelings emerge in kings and inferiority feelings in servants. Both are dependent on a measuring of oneself with others. But even a king can at one time feel superior in his relations with the people and inferior perhaps in his relations to the beloved.

In the same way that a beautiful woman can be intoxicated (*mada*) with the pride of her beauty, a very ugly woman can brood over her ugliness, compare her figure with those who are beautiful and always suffer from a sense of inferiority. The latter phenomenon has been analysed in detail by Adler in his well-known concept of the inferiority complex.[116]

People should neither be proud of their body and adorn and beautify it, nor should they loathe it, be ashamed of it and use methods of destroying and mortifying it. Body and mind have only a conditioned existence based on craving.

Thus pride and conceit emerges on the false valuation of oneself. Pride can issue due to gains, fame, flattery and happiness. A person who develops a sense of detachment through the practices of introspective self-analysis, could with equanimity face either victory or defeat. But so long as the lurking tendency to conceit (*mānānusaya*) prevails, man will be the slave of an arbitrary valuation of his own making.

SELF-SURRENDER AND THE DEPRIVED EGO

In the same way that the Buddha condemns arrogance and pride, he advocates due respect to others, to elders, teachers, parents and recluses. But any kind of self-surrender where the individual gives himself over to God, as in the Christian religion, is foreign to Buddhism. Buddhism advocates a person to develop self-confidence and a belief in each one to attain salvation. A person who lived an evil life will not be able to seek repentance, either by obsessive self-reproach or by passive submission and surrender to a higher authority. A person who lived an evil life should analyse his own impulses and understand why he succumbed to temptation. Then with confidence he should turn over a new leaf and lead a good life.

Excessive submission and self-surrender to a transcendent God has to be condemned as each one is his own master. Erich Fromm has made a very interesting analysis of this problem. By his distinction between the 'authoritarian' and the 'humanistic' personality he emphasises the importance of self-confidence and self-knowledge that should be developed by each person.[117] Freud makes some interesting observations as to how pathological manifestations of submission can crop up out of inferiority feelings, guilt and the need for punishment.

In the way that a person who is proud of his superior personal charm would indulge in self-display, a person with a deprived ego would sometimes advertise his melancholy. Both superiority and inferiority complexes seek self-advertisement. They are dual manifestations of the same root, an inflated sense of vanity (*māna-mada*).

Pride is one of the most dominant human impulses and remains dormant till the attainment of arahatship. In fact a recluse at each stage of perfection is subject to pride. He can be intoxicated by the very perfections in morality.

a) Because of honours, gains and fame he can be satisfied, and say 'I am famous,' but not the other recluse.
b) Because of success in moral habit he is satisfied and says 'I am good.'
c) Because of success in concentration he is satisfied and exalts himself, 'I am composed.'
d) Because of success in knowledge and vision, he says 'It is I who dwell knowing and seeing but these other monks dwell not knowing and seeing.'[118]

Thus, Venerable Sariputta says that in the attainment of the second *jhāna* he was not subject to any feeling of pride. 'The thought never came: "It is I who am attaining second *jhāna*" or "It is I who have emerged from second *jhāna*".'[119] Thus, for a long time, the leaning to I-making, to mine-making (*ahankāra-mamamkāra mānānusaya*) was rooted out from Sariputta.

SELF-REGARD

There is a very significant distinction between self-devoting motives and self-centred motives. Enlightened self-interest regarding one's own salvation (*sad-attha*) is approved.[120] It is said that we can love nothing as we love the inner self. This is the self-confidence and joy one gets from one's own spiritual and moral development and no narcissistic satisfaction.

It is also said that if one is overwhelmed by lust, he will not know his own profit or the profit of others. Thus the life of renunciation is the best expression of the other-regarding virtues. A person may express his altruistic nature by helping another by way of material benefits, such as giving food to a starving beggar. But the life of renunciation is the highest expression of the other-regarding instincts. The very nature of the good is such that no one can seek the salvation of others, without seeking his own. As it is said, 'He who of both is a physician, since himself he healeth and the other too.'[121] Again it is said:

> If a man discern his own good (*attha*) this is enough to call up earnestness; if he discovers another's good, this is enough to call up earnestness; if he discern both his own and another's good this is enough to call up earnestness.[122]

There is also a classification of beings into four groups where the nature of self-regarding virtues is clarified: he who is bent neither on his own profit nor on the profit of another; he who is bent on another's profit but not on his own; he who is bent on his own profit, not another's; and he who is bent on the profit both of himself and of another.

In the light of the self-regarding virtues which are self-devoting rather than self-centred, a person 'abandons evil, cultivates goodness, abandons things blameworthy, cultivates things blameless and keeps himself in perfect purity.' This is referred to as making the self predominant. 'This, monks, is called "dominance of the self".'[123]

THE EGO INSTINCTS AND BHAVA-TAṆHĀ

Narcissism as a term used by Nacke denotes the attitude of a person who treats his own body in the same way in which the body of a sexual object is ordinarily treated. Examining the connection between auto-eroticism and narcissism, Freud makes a very interesting comment that the ego is first and foremost a 'body-ego.' In stating that this 'body image' is significant for the formation of the ego, Freud comes very close to the analysis of ego impulses in the Buddhist scriptures.

This is similar to the operation of personality beliefs (*atta diṭṭhi*) regarding corporeality. Here one's own body is associated with one's ego. The majority who are unskilled in the doctrine regard body as the self. They are enamoured of their body and fond of their body. They adore it and beautify it. They are proud of their body and think that it belongs to them. Here one's own physical body becomes the object of one's attention and absorbs all interest. This primary sense in which egoism is associated with one's own body is a basic teaching of the Buddha.

Though we think that the ego is an independent and unitary entity sharply outlined against everything else, Freud says that this is a 'deceptive appearance.' Freud says that the ego is ultimately traced from bodily sensations. After the auto-erotic phase, the ego comes into contact with the external world. It associates itself with external perceptions insofar as they are pleasurable. The ego here is determined by the pleasure principle. This is similar to the operation of the *atta diṭṭhi* regarding perceptions and feeling. The ego is here considered as a pure pleasure ego.

Freud also says the ego as an organisation of mental life is derived from the primal structure of the id. This is somewhat like the relationship of the ego illusion to the *bhava-āsava*. *Atta diṭṭhi* is rooted in an archaic ego-feeling coming from previous births. This archaic feeling is essentially the emergence of the canker or bias for eternal existence (*bhava-āsava*).

These observations show some points of contact between Freud's analysis of the ego and the conception of the ego in the Buddhist scriptures. However, we do not get the distinction between the 'reality principle' and the 'pleasure principle' in the Freudian sense, in the Buddhist scriptures. The ego originates in the experiences of the perceptual system and it is designed to represent the external world instead of the world of wishes and whims. It represents sanity and sobriety in place of the wild, uncontrollable forces of the id. But Freud ends up by saying that at bottom the 'reality principle' also seeks pleasure, though delayed and diminished.

Hence in the final analysis this distinction into the reality and the pleasure principles is not very significant for the purpose of comparison with Buddhism. Freud, like the Buddhist scriptures, agrees that ultimately all activity is basically determined by the desire for pleasure. If we are to speak of a reality principle at all in the manner of a Buddhist, it is the realisation that all human pleasures are transitory and impermanent. The finest point of convergence between Buddhism and Freud is the concept of 'secondary narcissism'; this is what Theodore Reik renders as pride and is similar to the concept of *māna* in Buddhism. Hence, even at the risk of repeating what has been said on the subject of narcissism earlier, it is necessary to make a comprehensive comparison of the notions of 'secondary narcissism' and *māna*.

Freud's observation that self-love is the beginning of all love is an interesting one. When it flows out we call it 'object love', love for objects other than the self. But it can flow back again and once more be withdrawn into the ego. This is referred to as 'secondary narcissism,' superimposed upon a primary one 'a condition which had already existed previously.' This secondary narcissism with its withdrawal into self-preoccupation has its roots in the primary base of self-love.

Though this 'primary narcissism' is obscured by a number of different influences, it is the only key to the inroads that the later development of the ego makes. On these lines Freud sheds some profound insight in his *Mourning and Melancholia*. In melancholia we come across an extraordinary diminution in self-regard, an impoverishment of the ego on a grand scale. The self-reproaches and self-accusations against the loved object are shifted away from the loved object on to the 'patient's own ego'. Freud analysing the basis of the malady says, 'As Otto Rank has aptly remarked, this contradiction seems to imply that the object choice has been effected on a narcissistic basis, so that the object cathexis, when obstacles come in its way, can regress to narcissism.'[124] This represents 'a regression from one type of object-love to original narcissism.'

Freud continues his analysis by connecting this original self-love with sadism when hate comes into operation on the substitutive agent.

> If the love for the object—a love which cannot be given up though the object itself is given up—takes refuge in narcissistic identification, then the hate comes into operation on this substitutive object, abusing it, debasing it, making it suffer and deriving sadistic satisfaction from its suffering.[125]

And Freud says, 'It is this sadism alone that solves the riddle of the tendency to suicide, which makes melancholia so interesting... .'[126] Hence it seems that the paper on 'Mourning and Melancholia' provides a fine point of contact for Freud's theory of the ego instincts in his 'On Narcissism' and of the death instinct in his *Beyond the Pleasure Principle*.

If Freud had developed this hypothesis, it would have brought him still closer to the Buddhist theory of motivation. For self-assertion, self-display and self-respect on the one hand, and self-reproaches, self-vilification and self-destruction on the other, could have paradoxically been traced to a common source in self-love, primary narcissism. In fact, Freud almost slips through the idea when he says:

> So immense is the ego's self-love, which we have come to recognise as the primal state from which instinctual life proceeds and so vast is the amount of narcissistic libido which we see liberated in the fear that emerges as a threat to life, that we cannot conceive how the ego can consent to its own destruction.[127]

Theodore Reik has made some significant comments on this problem of masochism. He says that we should see the problem of masochism under a new aspect. It appears as nothing but a reaction to injured self-love, to a narcissistic offence. Reik refers to this secondary narcissism as pride, which in Buddhism would be rendered as *māna*. Pride originates as a reaction formation to an injury of the originally naive self-love of the ego, to a disturbance of narcissism.

> Narcissism is the original and natural love of the ego, pride the secondary ego amorousness, following as a substitute after this naive attitude has been disturbed.[128]

Though the problem of sadism and masochism is discussed in the chapter on the death instinct (where hatred and aggression play a significant role) the problem is discussed here to trace their relation to narcissism. Both gross egoism on the one hand and compulsive self-destruction on the other hand spring from a false valuation of personality.

Secondary narcissism or what Reik refers to as pride, has its equivalent in Buddhism. Pride is referred to as *māna* in the Buddhist scriptures. *Māna* is the measuring of oneself with another in point of beauty, wealth, class, etcetera and feeling that one is superior, inferior or equal to others.

If a person has attained fame and glory he could suffer from an inflated sense of vanity (*māna mada*). On the other hand, in the case of a person who is beset with constant disappointment and defeat, if his pride is disturbed, he will suffer from a deprived ego. All those situations of being slighted or disappointed excite inferiority feelings in people. This is referred to as *hinā māna* in Buddhism. This is the parallel impulse that is at the base of the patient who is suffering from melancholia.

Ego injury or ego elation exists according to Buddhism because there is a sub-conscious undercurrent which excites our 'ego-sense'. In the scriptures, this proclivity is called *ahankāra-mamankāra mānānusaya* (the leaning to 'I'-making or 'mine'-making). This 'I-conceit' is a central malady in the personality. Even when the five lower fetters have been put away the subtle remnant of the 'I-conceit' (*anusahagato*), the residual base of the ego persists.[129] In general, it could be said that Buddhism makes a clear distinction between *kāma-taṇhā* and *bhava-taṇhā,* i.e. the desire for sense gratification and the desire for self-preservation. This falls in line with the distinction in Freud between the sexual instincts and the ego instincts. Though Freud has been accused of pan-sexualism, his analysis of the ego instincts brings into focus another powerful source of human motivation. The desire for personal immortality, for personal glory and fame, the will to power, and subtle forms of self-love, self-importance and self-absorption are brought out through the aid of his case histories.

There was of course a significant problem that Freud confronted with the writing of the paper 'On Narcissism'. If the ego itself was libidinally invested, then it looked as if we should have to reckon its most prominent feature, the self-preservative instinct, as a narcissistic part of the sexual instinct. Ernest Jones, who raises the problem, says however, that the case is not so serious:

> To say there is reason to suppose that the ego is strongly invested with libido is clearly not the same thing as saying it is composed of nothing else.[130]

Jones says:

> ... the critics were quite wrong in asserting that Freud was aiming at a monistic libidinal conception of the mind. On

the contrary, he was obstinately dualistic as ever.[131]

In conclusion, it should be said that Freud's paper 'On Narcissism' is the most significant point of convergence between Buddhism and Freud. Thus, as an epilogue to this chapter, we reproduce the words of Ernest Jones on the subject of narcissism:

> The second phase in the development of Freud's ideas on instinct dates from 1914 when he published a disturbing essay 'On Narcissism' (I will explain in a moment why I use the word 'disturbing'). Self-love appears in its purest form in a sexual perversion Havelock Ellis was the first to describe by the name 'narcissistic', referring to the well-known myth of the Greek youth who fell in love with himself. But it is easy to detect numerous other manifestations of the same tendency elsewhere. They are to be found in the megalomania of insanity, in the attention the hypochondriac devotes to his body, in various observations easily made on children, on the aged, on patients desperately ill, and even in the phenomena of normal love. Common to all these fields is a remarkable reciprocity between the love of self and the love of others, between what analysts term narcissism and object libido respectively: when one increases the other diminishes, and vice versa. Freud supposed with good reason that the libido to begin with is all collected in the ego, that self-love is the beginning of all love. When it flows outwards we call it object-love, love for other objects than the self. That unfortunately it can flow back again, be once more withdrawn into the ego, is a familiar enough fact. In most marriages there are times later on when one partner reproaches the other that he (or she) does not love as much as formerly, that he (or she) has become 'selfish'. And as hinted above, there are many typical situations in life, such as in disease, after an accident, in old age and so on, when the tendency to this withdrawal into self-preoccupation and self-love is apt to become pronounced.[132]

THE DEATH INSTINCT AND BHAVA-TAṆHĀ

Professor Flugel points out that there is an element of paradox in the notion of a death instinct. He says that clinging to life seems to have a much more vivid instinctual quality than the decision to end it.[133] Freud himself is aware of the revolutionary nature of the concept:

> So immense is the ego's self-love, which we have come to recognize as the primal state from which instinctual life proceeds, and so vast is the amount of narcissistic libido which we see liberated in the fear that emerges as a threat to life, that we cannot conceive how the ego can consent to its own destruction.[134]

Freud had, by about 1915, formed the conclusion that hate, later to be called 'the aggressive instinct, 'was distinct and separate from the sexual instinct. This element of hate, which formed a part of the ego, stood in contrast to the libidinal instinct. However, Freud himself took time to introduce this concept of 'the death instinct' and it was finally worked out in his *Beyond the Pleasure Principle*, published in 1920. Here Freud examines the question as to whether man is always dominated by the pleasure principle, and introduces a rich variety of analytical experience which goes against the grain of the pleasure principle. And thus to account for such problematic clinical facts, he introduces the hypothesis of the death instinct. In fact, this hypothesis is introduced to explain a variety of factors. Flugel says that there are really six components of the death instinct.

1 The universal tendency of living organisms to suffer dissolution and die.
2 The tendency to achieve and maintain equilibrium in the inorganic as well as the organic world.
3 In the psychological and physiological aspects, the tendency to reduce or abolish tension. Pleasure accompanies reduction of tension caused by stimuli; lack of pleasure is associated with its increase.
4 Repetition, compulsion and restoration of earlier states.
5 Source of aggression, which aims at the annihilation of self and when redirected outwards, manifests itself as hostility to others.

6 Death instinct contrasted with the life instinct, or *thanatos* as opposed to *eros*, the former integrating and uniting organisms, the latter separating and disintegrating.

Let us have a glance at the variety of clinical data that Freud introduces in support of the hypothesis of a death instinct.[135]

BEYOND THE PLEASURE PRINCIPLE

Under the influence of the instinct of self-preservation, the pleasure principle is replaced by the reality principle. The reality principle does not give up the intention of ultimately attaining pleasure. Yet it enforces the postponement of satisfaction, abandonment of a number of possibilities of gaining satisfaction, and the temporary toleration of lack of pleasure as a step on the long, indirect road to pleasure. But this does not account for all painful experiences.

Another regular source of pain proceeds from the conflicts and dissociations in the psychic apparatus during the development of the ego towards a more highly coordinated organisation. Particular instincts or a portion of those prove irreconcilable and split off from the unity of the ego by a process of repression. For the time being, they are cut off from the possibility of gratification, and they often fight their way through circuitous routes. This success, which might have otherwise brought pleasure, is experienced by the ego as pain.

Then Freud came to be interested in deeper psychic processes. In the traumatic neuroses, the dreams have a very interesting peculiarity. These dreams continually take the patient back to the situation of his disaster from which he awakens in renewed terror. In their dreams, they tend to realise the traumatic situation. This made Freud come to a very important conclusion that there seemed to be a tendency to repeat earlier situations, even painful ones. This thesis was applied to the play of children. Freud cites the instance of a child at play. When the mother went away the child played a game of hiding a toy and finding it again, 'disappearance and return.'[136] It was connected with the child's remarkable cultural achievement, the forgoing of the satisfaction of an instinct. Thus, he could let his mother go away without making a fuss.

The departure of the mother cannot possibly have been pleasant for the child or merely a matter of indifference. How then does it accord with the pleasure principle that he repeats this painful experience as a game? By repeating the experience as a game in spite of its unpleasing nature, there is an attempt to obtain mastery of the situation.

Freud also suggests that the flinging away of the object so that it vanishes, might be the gratification of an impulse of revenge. It is known of other children also that they can give vent to similar hostile feelings by throwing objects instead of people.

This shows that even under the domination of the pleasure principle there are ways and means of making what is in itself disagreeable, the object of psychic preoccupation. Thus Freud came to emphasise the factor of automatic repetition and concluded that the tendency to repeat an earlier situation may be stronger than the pleasure principle.

Referring to psychoanalytical technique in general, he says that twenty-five years of intensive work has brought about a significant change in psychoanalysis. The patient is obliged to repeat as a current experience what is repressed, instead of as the physician would prefer to see him do, recollecting it as a fragment of the past. The repetition compulsion which psychoanalysis reveals in the transference phenomena with neurotics can also be observed in the life of normal persons.

THE REPETITION COMPULSION AND NORMAL PEOPLE

Here it gives the impression of a pursuing fate, a demonic trait in their destiny. Psychoanalysis has always taken the view that their fate is for the most part arranged by themselves, and determined by early infantile experiences. For instance we hear of lovers whose relationships with women, each and all, run through the same phases and end disastrously in the same way.

This 'perpetual recurrence of the same thing' causes us no astonishment when it relates to active behaviour on the part of the person concerned and when we can discern in him an essential character trait which always remains the same and which is compelled to find expression in a repetition of the same experience. We are much more impressed by the cases where the subject appears to have a passive experience over which he has no influence but in which he meets with repetition of the same fatality.

If we take into account observations such as those, based upon the life-histories of men and women, 'we shall find courage to assume that there really does exist in the mind a compulsion to repeat which overrides the pleasure principle.'[137]

INERTIA IN ORGANIC LIFE

The expression of the repetition compulsion shows in a high degree an instinctual character. Freud raises the question: how is the predicate of being 'instinctual' related to the compulsion to repeat? At this point perhaps we have come upon the track of a universal attribute of the instincts and perhaps of organic life in general—it seems that an instinct is a compulsion inherent in organic life to restore an earlier state of things which the living entity has been obliged to abandon under the pressure of external forces. It is the expression of the inertia that is inherent in organic life. This view of instincts strikes us as strange, because we have been used to see in them a factor impelling towards change and development, whereas now we are asked to recognise in them on the contrary an expression of the conservative nature of living things. This is compared with eros, the force which binds all things together.

AGGRESSION

Freud says, 'we started out from the great opposition between life and death instincts. Now object-love itself presents us with a second example of a similar polarity—that between love (or affection) and hate (or aggressiveness).'[138] How could these two polarities be related to each other? From the very first, it was recognised that there was a sadistic component in the sexual instinct.[139] It can make itself independent and in the form of a perversion dominate an individual's sexual activity. But how can the sadistic instinct, whose aim it is to injure the object, be derived from *eros* the preserver of life? In answer to this question Freud says:

> Is it not plausible to suppose that this sadism is in fact a death instinct which, under the influence of narcissistic libido, has been forced away from the ego and has consequently only emerged in relation to the object?[140]

Sadism is produced by combining some of the forces of the death instinct with the libido. This was for Freud an attempt at self-preservation. By eroticising the destructive forces, they become useful for life. Now, to make his concept of the death instinct consistent, he makes a modification of the theory. Earlier, he regarded masochism as sadism turned around upon the subject's own ego. But now he thinks rather that there is a primary masochism, a destructiveness directed against the self, and then secondarily turned against outer objects. Really, the aspect that has interested psychoanalysis most, is the relation of aggression to the death-instinct. Freud's final view was that aggression has its roots in the death-instinct. It is originally directed against the self as a death seeking urge and only secondarily deflected as a means of self-preservation against the outer world.

EVALUATION

Freud's work *Beyond the Pleasure Principle* has been one of the most controversial of his works. Ernest Jones says:

> It is, in many respects, a remarkable book. In dealing with such ultimate problems as the origin of life and the nature of death, Freud displayed a boldness of speculation which was unique in all his writings; nothing that he wrote elsewhere can be compared with it.[141]

The speculative nature of this work and the great amount of close thinking that has been compressed into one little book has made this certainly one of the most controversial books that Freud wrote. In fact, it seems that Freud has attempted to collect arguments for the existence of a death instinct from such diverse fields as physics, biology, physiology, chemistry, clinical psychology and even metaphysics. As mentioned earlier, Professor Flugel has discerned six components of the death instinct as discussed by Freud.

But, after some time, psychoanalysts have been able to concentrate on the more significant psychological aspects of it and today, analysts like Melanie Klein and Karl Meninger (who at least verbally supported the notion of a death instinct) use it in a clinical rather than in a biological manner. There have been attempts made, for instance, to compare the death instinct to the second law of thermodynamics, which leads to the conclusion that the universe is running down and will eventually be extinguished. However, we hope in this study to concentrate more on the clinical and psychological aspects of the so-called 'death instinct'. Professor Flugel says that as a scientific concept, the notion of a death instinct lacks precision, but that, if rid of its 'mystic implications,' it becomes very much like simple aggression.[142]

Of course, the genius of Freud lies in depicting the complicated and devious routes the instinct of aggression takes, for instance, the manner in which it can be turned against the self as well as the outer world. We should also give Freud the credit for having shown in a remarkable manner the intimate fusion of love and hate. Though superficially they look like opposites, excessive love and hatred seem to function in the same framework of human passions. All love-relations involve some degree of ambivalence; all love objects both satisfy and frustrate man. These are the psychological aspects of the death instinct analysis that are relevant for this comparative study and even come close to the analysis of hatred (*dosa*) and passion (*rāga*) in early Buddhism.

Having outlined the direction in which we should approach Freud's notion of the death instinct, let us look at the significant aspects of the death instinct from a purely psychological point of view. Though almost all psychologists would agree that aggression is a dominant source of motivation—as important as the libido or the ego instincts—we are in this chapter concerned with a special aspect of aggression; aggression turned against the self or what Flugel in following Rosenzwig calls, 'nemesism'. This can be compared with another attitude to the self that we have already discussed: narcissism or the process of love directed to the self.

Flugel cites an instance to show that nemesism is not merely found in extreme cases of suicidal behaviour but even in the behaviour of children to varying degrees:

> The other day I was watching a mother feed her little girl of two. The child resisted the soup that was being offered her in a spoon and endeavoured to push away the mother's

> hand with considerable show of force and displeasure. After a while, however, the mother still persisting, the child suddenly altered her behaviour, seized the spoon herself and, without changing in any other way the combative expression, pushed it into her own mouth with quite unnecessary violence and poured the contents down her throat.[143]

The problem arises as to whether what is displayed in this instance is aggression turned against the self. It seems merely that the child expressed her resistance to the parents in a certain way. A clear case of aggression turned against the self is really found where a person feels ashamed of himself and where this feeling of unworthiness leads to self-punishment. It also could emerge under conditions of extreme frustration. However, we could say that the child displayed a certain amount of aggression in this instance.

Much work has been done by psychoanalysts to understand the many facets of aggression—caricatured obedience, bringing humiliation to oneself, self-imposed handicaps, self-punishment and types of ascetic behaviour leading us ultimately to the final case of suicidal behaviour. The work done by analysts like Melanie Klein does show that children display a tremendous amount of aggression, much more than is commonly believed. Also many interesting studies have been made regarding the relation between aggression and the super-ego. Phenomena like guilt, punishment, anxiety, fear have been studied.

In conclusion, it could be said that no one will doubt the presence of a strong element of aggression in human behaviour. But the real problem is to explain the notion of a self-destructive urge in man. And those who sympathise with even a mild notion of the Freudian concept of the death instinct are more interested in it as a clinical concept than as a biological hypothesis.

The death instinct as such is not directly observable. Freud himself says that it manifests clinically only in the ways in which the destructive drive appears in the vicissitudes of sadism and masochism. It is hard to determine whether there is a biological basis for the death instinct.

Attempts have been made to find arguments from physics and biology. In physics an analogy has been drawn between the death instinct and the law of entropy, which leads to the conclusion that the universe is running down. Inquiries of this sort are highly speculative, and often not relevant to the Freudian concept of the death instinct. Thus analysts like Melanie Klein and Karl Meninger have concentrated on the psychological aspects of the death instinct.

VIBHAVA-TAṆHĀ: CRAVING FOR SELF-ANNIHILATION

In our analysis of the concept of *bhava-taṇhā,* we referred to the dogma of personal immortality (*sassata-diṭṭhi*) and annihilation view (*uccheda-diṭṭhi*) as two dogmas that have a powerful hold on man. As the Buddha very clearly said, 'men usually lean upon this duality;'[144] the belief in the existence or non-existence of an entity called the soul. The Buddha speaks of the duality (*dvayatā*) of existence (*atthitā*) and non-existence (*natthitā*). It is the aim of this section to examine the concept of *vibhava-taṇhā* in the light of this duality between existence and non-existence. In fact, a deeper understanding of the relationship between *bhava-taṇhā* and *vibhava-taṇhā* is necessary for us to clear the mystery that surrounds the word *vibhava-taṇhā.*

In general, *bhava-taṇhā* (the craving for personal immortality) implies a belief in the existence of a permanent entity, a persisting ego. *Vibhava-taṇhā* (the craving for self-annihilation) upholds the existence of an ego identical with the physical and mental processes that will be annihilated at death. But the word *vibhava* as used in the Buddhist works has two meanings: 1) power, wealth, prosperity,[145] and 2) non-existence, cessation of life and annihilation.[146] There seem to be two meanings of *vibhava-taṇhā* which may be connected with these two meanings of the word *vibhava.*

1 The love of the present life or craving for success in the present life based on the belief that there is no future state. The ego will be annihilated at death, so make the best of the present life.
2 The desire for self-annihilation accompanying the belief that there is a self-entity that is annihilated at death. This springs not from a desire for success in the present life, but from loathing and disgust of the body. This leads to suicide and self-inflicted tortures to do away with the body. While the earlier form of *vibhava-taṇhā* is connected with sensual craving (*kāma-rāga*) the latter emerges from the root hate (*dosa*).

Rhys Davids and Mrs. Rhys Davids seem to prefer the earlier meaning. Rhys Davids thus comments on the meaning of the word *vibhava*:

> This word usually means power, prosperity, success; the prefix 'vi' being used as an intransitive particle. In this particular connexion the traditional interpretation takes the prefix in a negative sense, and paraphrases the word by 'the absence of becoming (*bhava*).' This view is apparently supported by some *Nikāya* passages (S. III 57, It. No. 49) and by the *Dhammasaṅgani* 1314. It may be derived from them; and it is odd that the word should have been found nowhere else in that sense. It is quite possible that the original sense was the usual one.[147]

Mrs. Rhys Davids too, following the same line of thought, says:

> In the anthology called *Iti-Vuttaka*, a later very monastic work, the later meaning is clearly seen, and was enough to make Oldenberg hold that prosperity was incorrect. He did not allow for changing values in the pitakas, nor did he recognize that at first Buddhism was greater than a monk-gospel.[148]

Instead of getting involved in the controversy as to what is the early meaning of the word and what is the later meaning, let us determine whether these two meanings sound logically or psychologically possible according to the concept of craving in the psychology of Buddhism. Then we could also examine a few central passages in the discourses of the Buddha to see what sense we could make of the second meaning given to this word.

Logically both positions are possible. It is possible for a carefree pleasure-lover to be a materialist and only hope for success in this life. He will hold the position that death is the end of life. It is also possible for a man full of worry and anxieties to wish for the end of life even by committing suicide. The latter position is a more complex and interesting situation. Even Freud for instance says that so immense is the ego's self-love that we cannot conceive how the ego can consent to its own destruction. It took some time for him to accept that there is a basic aggressive aspect in the personality of man that makes the concept of a death wish meaningful.

Though early Buddhism does not depict the specific kind of death instinct upheld by Freud in all its details, Buddhism does trace the destructive urge to the root ill-will or hate (*dosa*). The destructive urge springs from the root hate. When this source is excited hatred and aggression surges its way continuously and finds temporary satisfaction. First one attempts to harm some thing or person 'external' to one's physical body and then if this is inhibited, self-inflicted torture or suicidal tendencies are possible. Painful sensations always excite dormant hatred (*paṭighānusaya*). In the way that the ignorant worldlings are attracted and infatuated by pleasant sense-impressions, when touched by painful feeling they seek violent methods of getting rid of pain; they become excited and come to bewilderment. There is a verse in the *Aṅguttara Nikāya* that summarises the aggressive behaviour of man:

> In wrath, the common folk kill self, by diverse forms distraught; by sword men kill the self; in madness poison take; and in some hollow of a mountain glen, they hide, and bind themselves with ropes and die.[149]

There is a crucial passage in the *Majjhima Nikāya* which we shall reproduce here along with the Pāli original, which gives a definite sense to the second meaning of *vibhava-taṇhā* as the craving for self-annihilation.

> *Ye kho te bhante samana brāhmanā sato sattasa ucchedaṃ vināsaṃ vibhavaṃ paññapenti, te sakkāyabhaya sakkāyaparijegucchā, sakkāyam ñeva anuparidhāvanti anuparivattanti.*[150]

Horner translates this passage thus:

> 'those worthy recluses and brahmanas
> who lay down the cutting off, the destruction,
> the disappearance of the essential being, these,
> afraid of their own body, loathing their own body,
> simply keep running and circling round their own body.'[151]

The three terms *uccheda, vināsa* and *vibhava* are used as synonyms here. The word *vibhava* is used here very clearly in the sense of destruction as in this context *vināsa* is used as a synonym. The sense of the word *vibhava* in this passage from the *Majjhima Nikāya* fits in well with two other passages: *Uddāna* 32, *Iti-vuttaka* 49. These passages will be referred to later in the course of our discussion.

This context also gives a fine insight into the nature of the vicious circle into which the individual falls. Though the individual attempts to get rid of the 'essential being' by destroying or cutting off, this paradoxically betrays a tremendous preoccupation with oneself. Theorising as to what will happen to the self in the future, and displaying a morbid preoccupation with one's body, or 'essential being,' displaying undue anxiety and fear regarding one's own body (*sakkāyabhaya*), loathing one's body (*sakkāyaparijegucchā*) one keeps running and circling around one's body. This is compared to a dog running and circling round a post to which it is tied. This kind of morbid preoccupation with one's body does not lead to insight as to its real nature.

This analysis can be applied meaningfully to a person who commits suicide or practises misguided methods of self-torture. Those who take to suicide as an escape from intolerable conflicts out of despair are subject to the annihilationist delusion. They too are subject to an ego-illusion. They have no insight into the nature of suffering. In the very intensity of their melancholy and sorrow, they fail to see that there is no sufferer but only suffering.

There is no shortcut; impatient and heightened forms of penances and self-torture will not take a person to nibbāna. In his very anxiety and impatience he is subject to craving, the craving for self-annihilation. People often confuse the desire for nibbāna and the craving for annihilation. It is very necessary to distinguish the concept of nibbāna from *vibhava-taṇhā*.

> In one who sees as it really is by perfect wisdom, the craving to become is left, he enjoys not in its slaying (*vibhava-taṇhā bhinandati*). But craving's utter ending, utter stopping is nibbāna.[152]

All violent and forced attempts to deal with states of pain and dejection lack insight and are subject to the delusion of the ego. It is in this light that the word *vibhava* could be analysed. The words *bhava-taṇhā* (*bhava* or 'becoming') and *vibhava-taṇhā* (*vibhava* translated in diverse ways, as non-becoming, de-becoming, ceasing to becoming, etcetera) are opposites only in a limited sense, for they are really like the two sides of the same coin. To use the words of the Buddha we could say, 'self-mirrored all these beings are'.

THE OPPOSITION BETWEEN BHAVA-TAṆHĀ AND VIBHAVA-TAṆHĀ

In what sense is the expression *bhava-taṇhā* the opposite of *vibhava-taṇhā*? They are opposites only in a limited sense as both work within the framework of human craving.

In a philosophical study of the nature of opposites by Roubiczek, a very illuminating point has been made that is quite relevant to this discussion.[153] If there is a book on the table, the book as a solid body is in opposition to the surrounding air, which has the qualities of a gas. But if we investigate a more comprehensive sphere, as for instance matter, the solid body and the air both appear as combinations of 'atoms or electrons;' within this greater context their opposite states exist at the same time and only form a contrast. 'Contradictory opposites become mere contrasts if we enlarge the sphere of consideration.'[154] 'Contrasts on the other hand become contradictory opposites when we restrict our attention.'[155] In the same manner *bhava-* and *vibhava-taṇhā* appear as opposites only in a very restricted context. But if we consider them against the larger background of the doctrine of dependent origination, they seem to be merely contrasting attitudes of a man bound to craving. If we compare them with the concept of nibbāna, we can see that the concept of nibbāna stands in opposition to both *bhava-taṇhā* and *vibhava-taṇhā*.

NIBBĀNA AND ANNIHILATION

The charge of being an annihilationist is brought against the Buddha and the Buddha duly answers it:

> There are some recluses and brahmāns who misrepresent me untruly, vainly, falsely, not in accordance with fact, say-

> ing: 'The recluse, Gotama is a nihilist (*venayika*), he lays down the cutting off, the destruction, the disappearance (*vibhava*) of the existing entity.' But as this monk is just what I am not... these worthy recluses and brahmāns misrepresent me untruly. Formerly I, monks, as well as now, lay down simply anguish and the stopping of anguish.[156]

Here the Buddha replies to the charge that he is an annihilationist. This charge is significant, for often people confuse the desire for nibbāna and *vibhava-taṇhā*. Even Freud, in his *Beyond the Pleasure Principle,* brings the Buddhist ideal of nibbāna to illustrate his conception of a 'death wish'. Buddha clearly states that what is aimed at is the stopping of anguish, and not the destruction of an entity. It is very well brought out with the help of an analogy:

> 'If a person were to gather or burn or do as he pleases with the grass, twigs, branches and foliage in this Jeta Grove, would it occur to you: The person is gathering us, he is burning us, he is doing as he pleases with us?'
> 'No Lord. What is the reason for this? It is that this, Lord, is not our self nor what belongs to self.'[157]

Thus there is no entity to be destroyed; it is at most a subjective illusion that has to be got rid of. If there is any annihilation it is the annihilation of *kilesa*. The Buddha says, in the sense that he advocates the annihilation of *kilesa*, 'I am also an annihilationist.'

Secondly nibbāna is not merely a negative concept; it is a positive ideal. Magandiya refers to Buddha as a destroyer of growth (*bhūnahu*).[158] What the Buddha taught was not destruction but the control of the sense organs and suppression of greed. Here nibbāna is compared to health and *dukkha* to the presence of a basic malady in beings. Thus the negativist interpretations of Buddhism have been rejected by the Buddha.

There are also contexts where feverish longing and desire for nibbāna as such is condemned. 'In beings subject to birth, the wish arises: Ah! If only we were not subject to birth, if only we could avoid being born!'[159] But nibbāna is not attained by mere wishing and longing. The path to salvation is a positive undertaking with a clear-cut therapy.

SUICIDE AND THE DESTRUCTIVE URGE

A man cannot by suicide escape the sufferings which are the result of his former deeds. But when a man is subject to the annihilationist delusion he sees the passing away of phenomena but he fails to see its origination and reappearance. He fails to see that according to the theory of dependent origination, things originate due to a condition. Hence the *kamma* of each individual cannot be offset by any violent means.

Even the saint who leads a religious life should not seek salvation by putting an end to his body. Even from religious motives suicide is not effective, as the Buddhist rejects the annihilationist heresy. A person who is under the spell of the destructive urge ('the thirst for non-existence') cannot attain nibbāna.

> He shakes not down the unripe fruit,
> but awaits the full time of its maturity.[160]

To illustrate this fact an apt analogy is given in the dialogues, where a woman ripped up her belly to find out whether her child was a boy or a girl:

> Moral and virtuous wanderers and Brahmins do not force maturity on that which is unripe; they, being wise, wait for that maturity. The virtuous have need of their life. In proportion to the length of time such men abide here is the abundant merit that they produce and accomplish for the welfare of the many...[162]

The Jains for instance believed that suicide by starvation and experiencing of physical torture will promote the purification from sin. 'Jains believed that vocal sins are destroyed through silence, mental sins through respiratory restraint, bodily sins through starvation and lust crushed through mortification.'[163]

Buddhism does not say that such methods of torturing and destroying the body could help a man to get rid of past *kamma*. The future has to be improved by earnest effort, patience and diligence. Buddhism teaches the non-substantiality of the ego, but that does not mean that people should go to the other extreme and fall into the snare of the annihilationist heresy. There is no substantial ego, but existence is the product of certain conditions.

BUDDHIST ATTITUDE TO THE PHYSICAL BODY

On the one hand, beautification and adornment of the body is condemned, but on the other hand, infliction of torture is unwise. The ability to live through any painful situation with detachment and equanimity is commended. There are cankers to be got rid of by endurance. Wisely reflective, a monk should bear cold, heat, hunger, thirst or any disagreeable and painful feeling.[164]

But under the spell of the annihilationist urge ordinary beings and recluses too, fail to develop insight into the nature of the body:

> And how, monks, do some go to excess (*atidhāvanti*)? On the other hand some are afflicted by becoming; humiliated thereby and loathing becoming they take pleasure in not-becoming (*vibhava*). They say, 'My good sir, inasmuch as when body breaks up after death, this self is annihilated, destroyed, it exists not after death'.[165]

These beings are afflicted by becoming, disappointed, disgusted, they loathe the body. They feel that they are humbled, humiliated and their sense of pride broken down. There are of course instances of people who commit suicide being overpowered by compulsive passions. Thus the thirst for destruction can stem from varying motives and can be prompted by different situations. But there is always at least an element of aggression. Freud has laid immense importance on the role of frustration, inferiority feeling, guilt, and anxiety, as sources of the death instinct. He made a very significant attempt to understand the strange indulgence in self-inflicted suffering called masochism.

In the light of the Buddhist conception of motivation the phenomenon of masochism is quite intelligible. Those who inflict severe torture on the body or aim at death through starvation make a fundamental confusion. They are subject to the annihilationist heresy in thinking that the 'body is the self'. Hence they indulge in morbid preoccupation with the body; feelings of inferiority (*hinā-māna*) fear and anxiety (*paritassa*) and compulsive passions (*rāga*) excite them, and they lose their sense of balance. The annihilationist solution is always referred to as an extreme, and those who take to it, even if they have religious motives go to excess (*atidhāvanti*). Thus those who are subject to the annihilationist theory are referred to as being obsessed by 'anxiety about something subjective that doesn't exist.' It occurs to him thus, 'I will surely be annihilated, I will surely be destroyed... .'[166]

There are however, certain instances where suicide was the occasion for the attainment of arahatship, though in other cases it may be premature, destructive or sinful. Sīha was distressed at not obtaining spiritual progress after seven years of endeavour. She queried the use of living and tried to die through hanging. As the rope was tied round her neck, she was turning her thought towards enlightenment. She attained arahatship and the rope loosened and fell. Sappadasa overpowered by passion and about to commit suicide realised enlightenment.[167]

The question as to whether an arahat should, because of pain, escape to nibbāna quickly by putting an end to the body has often been raised by critics. When he feels a physical pain, why does he not escape into final nibbāna by dying quietly? An arahat has no more likes or dislikes. The Buddhist attitude to the body is discussed in *Milinda Paṇha*.:

> The king raises the question thus, 'Is the body, Nagasena, dear to you recluses? If not, why do you look after it and cherish it so?' Then Nagasena replies thus, 'Has your majesty somewhere and some time been wounded by an arrow? In such a case is not the wound anointed with salve, smeared with oil and bandaged...? Is then this treatment a sign that the wound is dear to your majesty?' The king replies, 'No, it is not dear to me, but all this is done so that the flesh may grow again.' Nagasena replies, 'Just so, the body is not dear to the recluses; without being attached to the body, they take care of it for the purpose of making a holy life possible.' [168]

Thus in its attitude to the body, Buddhism adopts a middle path between extremes of sense-gratification, adornment and beautification of the body on the one side, and self-torture, mortification and severe asceticism on the other. Buddhism doesn't fall into either the heresy of eternalism or annihilationism.

THE DEATH INSTINCT AND VIBHAVA-TAṆHĀ

The concept of the death instinct contains within itself a number of components, and there is a very loose thread that puts them together. There is a certain amount of vagueness in this concept. Professor Flugel refers to Freud's work *Beyond the Pleasure Principle*, as a 'short but immensely pregnant work.'[169] There is undoubtedly a great amount of close thinking in this book that needs further analysis, for the purpose of comparison.

A comparison of these two concepts is very essential at least for one reason. Freud in his *Beyond the Pleasure Principle* calls the death instinct the 'nirvana principle,' and associates this with the teachings of the Buddha. However, nirvana is not annihilation. As discussed in the last section, Buddha made a specific attempt to reject the charge that he preached a doctrine of annihilationism. In fact, it is *vibhava-taṇhā* rather than the desire for nibbāna that can be compared with the death instinct.

Also it must be mentioned that the term *vibhava* has two meanings as discussed earlier.[170] In this comparison we are more interested in *vibhava* as 'annihilation' rather than as power or wealth.

In regarding hate as a distinct and separate instinctual root and emphasising the significance of the aggressive instinct, Freud brings his theory of motivation very close to Buddha's analysis of human nature. According to Freud, the role of frustration, inferiority feelings, guilt, revenge motives and suicide—all illustrate the play of the instinct of aggression.

Basically, Freud traces this to a preoccupation with painful feelings in contrast to pleasurable feelings. 'There are ways and means of making what is in itself disagreeable the object of psychic preoccupation.'[171] There is a tendency to gain mastery over pain. But very often it leads to anxiety and forms of self-inflicted torture. Buddhist scriptures mention the fact that ignorant worldlings when touched by painful feeling, 'weep, wail, cry, knock the breast and come to utter bewilderment.' Aggression also manifests itself in destroying the external objects if they are painful.

Thus both Freud and the Buddhist scriptures consider hate as a primal instinctual root. People are attracted by pleasure giving experiences, and repelled by painful experiences. These two factors offer a common basis for the purpose of comparison. Although the instinct of aggression was later to be interwoven with the biological principle of inertia and the tendency of living things to regress back to an inorganic state, Freud's primary insistence on hate as an instinctual root remains.

In Freud's essay *Instincts and Their Vicissitudes*, we can trace his attempt to find the springs of action in a basic antithesis of love and hate. This is the profound source from which emerged his concept of the death-instinct; love and hate reproduces the polarity of pleasure and pain. It is said in the Buddhist scriptures that greed arises through unwise reflection on attractive objects, and hate through unwise reflection on repulsive objects.

In comparison with Freud's death instinct which is later interwoven with biological concepts, the concept of *vibhava-taṇhā* remains basically psychological to the core. *Vibhava-taṇhā* springs from the root hate and surges its way continuously. It finds expression in all forms of aggression.

On the one hand, *vibhava-taṇhā* causes 'disgust, anxiety and fear regarding body'. On the other hand, it has a hold on the victim in the form of a repetition compulsion. The Brahmans who lay down the cutting off, the destruction of the essential being, 'loathing their body, simply keep running and circling their own body'.[172] All this is due to a false belief regarding the ego, the annihilationist heresy.

The annihilationist solution is always referred to as an extreme, and those who take to it even from religious motives go to excess (*atidhāvanti*). This may be compared with what Freud calls 'the need for punishment,' that was found among men of religion.

There is an important difference that emerges in our comparison. Freud finally regarded the death instinct as originally deflected against the self. He upheld that there was a fundamental death-seeking urge in man that was only tamed and made less vociferous by the eros. The Buddhist scriptures would consider the root of hate and aggression as basic, and suicide as merely a manifestation of aggression.

Repetition-compulsion is not a specific component merely of *vibhava-taṇhā*. It is basic both to *kāma* and *bhava-taṇhā*. In considering the death instinct as the nirvana principle, Freud did not classify this idea sufficiently. Undoubtedly Freud is supposed to have got the idea from the quietist teachings of Buddhism. If Freud associated the nirvana principle with the annihilation of instincts, then a parallel to his death instinct is found in *vibhava-taṇhā* and not in the Buddhist ideal of nibbāna.

Freud also considers the nirvana principle as a homoeostasis principle, maintaining that the ultimate idea is to maintain equilibrium. There he brings the death instinct and the pleasure principle together, maintaining that the ultimate ideal of life is rest. But nibbāna is a positive ideal of emancipation and does not fit in with a biological hypothesis of the order of the death instinct. Nibbāna is not an inorganic state of rest, or of pure quiescence. Nibbāna has been described in terms of perfect knowledge and perfect health. It is the culmination of one's spiritual growth, and not merely the annihilation of instincts.

As far as the mystery of *vibhava-taṇhā* is concerned, an analysis of the concept of craving makes it far more intelligible than the death instinct, which is a synthesis of diverse components. As shown in an earlier section, *bhava* and *vibhava-taṇhā* are not opposites in a real sense; they are rather like the two sides of the same coin. In the words of Nyanamoli Thera, 'Denial is as much an activity of craving as assertion is.'[173]

CONCLUSION

In evaluating the Freudian analysis of sexuality we mentioned some of the deeper insights of Freud into the condition of man and his love life. When Freud says that something in the nature of sexuality itself determines that there shall be ever an absence of mental satisfaction he seems to echo the thoughts of Schopenhauer. We have also commented on the significance of the Freudian concept of narcissism, and its remarkable similarity to the concept of pride (*māna*) in Buddhism. A critical analysis of the notion of the death instinct was made, where we pointed out that whatever be the status of this speculative concept, both Buddhism and Freud consider aggression as a dominant source of human motivation.

However, there are a number of limitations in the Freudian system which have emerged out of our study. Freud is often disappointing when we look for a positive conception of love and compassion. His conception of love is thin as it had no ethical determinants. We have commented on this in examining the Buddhist concept of compassionate love (*mettā*). Freud could not visualise the tender emotion of the love of a mother to a child without there being even a modicum of sensuality in it. We referred to this as the taboo on tenderness.

Freud's only ethical norm was that one must be rational. But he had no social philosophy that could give form and shape to this conception. If society is so constituted that men are subject to severe emotional disturbances, why not change society? Freud was in favour of revolutionary changes especially with regard to the sexual code. Reuben Fine commenting on this issue says that ultimately Freud would have recognised that it is impossible to change one aspect of society without touching upon the other aspects. Reuben Fine concludes:

> At the same time Freud became curiously hesitant. He began to consider other possibilities, that it is not society which is necessarily at fault, but the instinct itself.[174]

If we accept this interpretation of Fine, we have come to a point where the Buddha's radical therapy for the ills of man has meaning. Thus it seems that an answer to Freud's painstaking query in 'Analysis Terminable and Interminable'[175] as to whether there is a logical end to analysis is found in early Buddhism.

Apart from attempting an analysis of the methods of therapy in Buddhism and Freud, it is one of our aims in this chapter to reveal the strength of certain instinctual roots of human behaviour. Early Buddhism recognises the dominance of certain instinctual roots that can be traced to a number of past births. According to the Buddha, the three-fold desires (*kāma, bhava* and *vibhava*) continually seek and find temporary satisfaction (*tatratatrābhinandini*). But yet they cannot be satisfied and thus drive the individual to seek novel and variegated forms of satisfying these desires. That is why the Buddha advocated a radical therapy for rooting out these self-centred desires.

The real gulf that separates Freud from early Buddhism is the early Buddhist hypothesis of rebirth. While the Freudian analysis is limited to the childhood experiences of a single birth the Buddhist analysis is cast in a wider dimension. According to Buddhism, the psychological past of the individual can be traced back to innumerable numbers of past births.

Thus, it is a pity that Jung's development on the Freudian notion of the collective unconscious has been somewhat mystifying. A clear analysis of the psychological issues involved in what Freud called the 'archaic heritage' of man would have been more rewarding. Perhaps an attempt to work out the clinical implications of the early Buddhist concept of rebirth may prove to be a worthwhile venture.

V

THE THERAPEUTIC BASIS OF EARLY BUDDHIST PSYCHOLOGY

ROOTS OF MORALITY AND RELIGION

Early Buddhist psychology grew up within the dimensions of an ethico-psychological system. Its basic inspiration is religious. But if early Buddhism is termed 'religious,' some qualifications are needed. As we know, Buddhism does not uphold the belief in an all-powerful god or an unchanging soul. As a result, some consider early Buddhism rather as a system of practical psychology with a therapeutic basis. On the other hand, there is a very strong spiritual and mystical core in early Buddhism because of which we can say that it has an ethico-religious basis. Freud's criticism of current religions, that they display a non-psychological attitude, cannot be made against early Buddhism. The Buddha himself condemned current religions that perpetuated 'rite and ritual clinging'. This criticism is quite similar to the Freudian critique of religious fetishes. This is perhaps what made Rhys Davids remark:

> Compared with the ascetic excesses, as well with the imaginative and speculative obsessions of the age, the Buddhist standpoint was markedly hygienic.[1]

But in spite of its criticism of the religious practices of the age, Buddhism did uphold the reality of mystical and spiritual experience, and in this attitude it differs from Freud, although according to Fromm, the Freudian standpoint is not unsympathetic to a humanistic religion like Buddhism as compared to an authoritarian creed.[2]

Now it may be asked, 'What was Freud's specific aim in applying the findings of psychoanalysis to ethics and religion?' Flugel maintains that it was to reveal a certain clumsiness and crudity in the operation of man's powers of moral control. It was to show that conscience was a factor in the mind that was capable of doing harm as well as good.[3]

RITE AND RITUAL CLINGING (SĪLABBATUPĀDĀNA)

The Buddha's reference to some of the contemporaneous religious cults and rituals, echoes Freud's severe indictment of traditional morality in his *Future of an Illusion*. The Buddha came across a variety of religious cults that perpetuated misguided and pointless rituals. Buddha described their adherents as subject to 'rite and ritual clinging' (*sīlabbata-parāmāsa*). This is described as one of the four clingings (*upādānas*): 1) sense desire clinging, 2) false view clinging, 3) rites and ritual clinging and 4) self-doctrine clinging. Rite and ritual clinging was condemned by the Buddha on various grounds.

The term *parāmāsa* suggests that one clings to these rituals more with a feeling of compulsion than by a judicious understanding of their function, as it literally means 'being attached to or being under the influence of contagion, etcetera.' Thus, in the phrase *sīlabbata-parāmāsa,* it came to mean that one is excessively attached to the outer ceremonial aspect of morality or the contagion of mere rule and ritual.

It was earlier suggested that *upādāna* might be rendered by 'entanglement,' which unlike 'clinging,' suggests involvement in objects whether we like or dislike them. Some of the religious fetishes like hand-washing mentioned by Freud are primarily the expressions of such entanglements or obsessions. The Buddha exposed the vacuity of many superficial forms of self-purification practised in his time. There were those who used severe forms of penance to destroy sins, like fasting and starving.

The Buddha described this ideal of self-mortification as painful, unworthy and unprofitable. There were also other practices such as washing away impurity by bathing. The Buddha declared that no amount of washing can cleanse the hostile and guilty man. Some of the practices he condemned are enumerated in the following passage:

> Such ways as fastings, crouching on the ground, bathing at dawn, reciting of the Three, wearing rough hides and matted hair and filth, chantings and empty rites and penances, hypocrisy and cheating and the rod, washings, ablutions,

> rinsings of the mouth.[4]

Unless there is a basic transformation of character, a person who tries to purify himself by external ceremonies will miss the mark. As an unclean cloth when dyed will not be pure in colour, so is the man who tries to wash away the evil deed in the river.[5] The method of purification that the Buddha advocated is not external, but internal. It implies a basic transformation of character. The person who follows this method is said to have been washed with an 'inner washing.' The Buddha was of the opinion that ethical sacrifices were more worthy than physical sacrifices or rituals. The intense spiritual fire that burns within one puts to the shade even a thousand fires produced by burning wood.

> I lay no wood, brahmin, for fires on altars; only within burneth the fire I kindle. Ever my fire burns, ever tense and ardent, I, Arahant, work out the life that is holy.[6]

ASCETICISM AND SELF-MORTIFICATION

There was a group of religious teachers who believed that the mortification of the body would bring about the purification of the soul. This path of self-mortification was one of the methods tried by Gotama for eight long years and ultimately rejected. He rejected it when he discovered the true path of nibbāna. Actually the Buddha rejected two extremes: the way of self-mortification and addiction to sensual pleasures. His own way, the 'Noble Eightfold' path is referred to as the 'Middle Path' (*majjhimapatipadā*).

Thus the Buddhist attitude regarding anguish (*dukkha*) offers a striking contrast to the methods of self-mortification practised, for example, by the Jains. The deliberate attempt to live through painful experiences and the technique of purging and burning up the effects of karma is condemned by the Buddha. He declared that some of these methods were the manifestations of craving itself. For example, the immortality penance, self-tormenting exercises performed to attain immortality, were the product of the craving for self-preservation (*bhava-taṇhā*). Certain types of penance and self-torture excited latent hatred (*patigha anusaya*) and issued forth in the craving for annihilation (*vibhava-taṇhā*). The Buddha showed that there is no short-cut to end suffering; self-torture will not take a person to nibbāna. People often confuse the desire for nibbāna and the craving for self-annihilation. All violent attempts to deal with problems of suffering lack insight and are subject to the diffusion of the ego in a subtle form. The individual exhibits a tremendous preoccupation with the ego in spite of his attempt to 'destroy the essential being.' It is a vicious circle, and the Buddha analogically says it is like a dog running and circling round a post to which it is tied. Many forms of self-torture and suicide display this psychological pattern. A comparison of the concept of self-annihilation (*vibhava-taṇhā*) in early Buddhism with the death instinct in Freud is significant as Freud says that the super-ego is rooted in a tremendous amount of aggression.

The Jains believed that 'vocal sins are destroyed through silence, mental sins through respiratory restraint, bodily sins through starvation and lust crushed through mortification.'[7] The doctrine of the expiation and purge of former misdeeds upheld by the Jains is treated in the *Majjhima Nikāya*. The Buddha says that the Jains maintain the doctrine:

> Whatever this individual experiences, whether pleasant or painful or neither painful nor pleasant, all is due to what was previously done. Thus by burning up, by making an end of ancient deeds, by the non-doing of new deeds, there is no over-flowing into the future.[8]

This doctrine is definitely rejected by the Buddha. His own position is explained by an analogy. A man is pierced by an arrow smeared with poison. Then his friends procure a physician and surgeon. They cut open the wound, dress it with medicated powder and heal it. And when the skin is healed the patient is cured and his wellbeing restored. In the process of treatment, the painful feelings are incidental and have to be borne by the patient. In the same way, whatever bodily and mental hardships are incidental to the path of morality (*sīla*) and concentration (*samādhi*) have to be patiently borne by the monk. But the Buddha does not make the bearing of these painful experiences an end in itself.

Though we strive with great effort to get rid of suffering, we must be indifferent to the source of anguish through equanimity. Anguish cannot be mastered by anguish; anguish has to be mastered by equanimity.

Mrs. Rhys Davids has rightly pointed out that the Buddha's objection to asceticism rests on the fact that excess is *dukkha* and tapas is excess.[9] The question is raised whether happiness is to be won through suffering, and the Buddha shows that the method he advocates is not through suffering. The Buddha refers to four types of people: 1) those who torment themselves and not others, 2) those who do not torment themselves but others, 3) those who torment both themselves and others, and 4) those who do not torment themselves or others. The true Buddhist belongs to the fourth group.

THE MORAL SENSE ACCORDING TO THE BUDDHA

In the light of the Freudian criticism of the super-ego and the Buddha's own rejection of misguided religious rites, it is legitimate to ask whether Buddhism offers any positive notion of a moral sense or conscience. This is certainly found in the concepts of *hiri* (shame of evil) and *ottappa* (dread of evil). There is also great emphasis on the development of the inner self and the value of self-analysis.

HIRI-OTTAPPA

Early Buddhism certainly rejects an original sin or any concept of sin in the Christian sense. The Buddha only exhorts people to understand the nature of human motives and act wisely. The two terms *kusala* and *akusala,* referring to the 'good' and 'evil' or 'moral' and 'immoral' actions, are often rendered by the two English terms, 'wholesome' and 'unwholesome'. It is also sometimes rendered as 'skilful' and unskilful', reminding us of Aristotle's definition of virtue. Among the wholesome factors are shame of evil (*hiri*) and dread of evil (*ottappa*). But this should not be confused with remorse or guilt.

Kukucca, which can be rendered as 'uneasiness of conscience, guilt, remorse and worry', is considered unwholesome. It is associated with hateful and discontented consciousness (*dosa*) in the way that the super-ego consists of certain aggressive elements. *Kukucca* is regarded as one of the five hindrances (*nīvarana*) when combined with restlessness. *Uddhacca-kukucca* (restlessness and worry) is an obstacle to the development of the mind. Restlessness and worry are described by a simile in the Nikāyas. If a pot of water were shaken by the wind so that the water trembles, eddies and ripples, and a man were to look there for his own reflection, he would not see it. Thus restlessness and worry blind one's vision of oneself.

The other four hindrances are also explained by similes. Lust and passion (*kāmacchanda*) are compared to water mixed with variegated colours; ill-will (*vyāpāda*) is compared to a pot of water boiling and bubbling over; sloth and torpor (*hina middha*) to a pot of water covered with moss and water plants; doubt (*vicikicca*) to muddy and turbid water.[10]

According to the *Atthasālīni*, *hiri* has a subjective origin within oneself, and *ottappa* an external origin, i.e. in the impact of society. *Hiri* is based on shame and *ottappa* on dread.[11] Rhys Davids says that 'taken together they give us the emotional and conative aspect of the modern notion of conscience just as *sati* represents it on its intellectual side.'[12] *Hiri* and *ottappa* are to be cultivated as positive moral emotions. They are described as powers. He who lacks these positive emotions lacks a conscience.

DECEPTION AND GUILT

There are two types of extremes, both of which are unhealthy: deception and guilt. Many people try to deceive others consciously by pretences. Some deceive themselves by unconscious rationalisations. Deception, disguises and secrecy have been condemned by the Buddha as well as by Freud. Guilt, the other extreme, causes one to brood over the wrongs that one has done. Now this can vary from short-lived states of repentance (which may not be damaging) to uneasiness, restlessness, dejection and even pathological guilt. While conscious deception is positively evil, guilt is damaging, unwholesome and unproductive. Freud's basic criticism of current religions and moral behaviour is that they are the expression of a guilt complex.

Deception and disguise of one's real nature is condemned by the Buddha. Careful and earnest scrutiny of oneself is necessary. Throughout all the discourses of the Buddha, there is an emphasis on the axiom 'to one's own self be true'. There is no way of covering up one's faults from oneself. Even if someone tries to mask one's desires it is said, 'The

Tathāgatas and Devas see the fool who in the world walks crookedly.'[13]

The Buddha advocates honest and diligent self-analysis as a basis for healthy moral development. The only path open to an immoral man is to understand himself and bring about a transformation in his character. No amount of penance and ritual can cleanse him. Unless the immoral base of the personality of the immoral man is cleansed and rooted out, superficial religious rites are of no avail. Once a man becomes immoral, not even remorse can help him.

In admonishing both the layman and the recluse to develop a healthy moral sense, the Buddha has described the bad effects of burdening oneself with an unhealthy guilty conscience. He says that 'one who is a fool experiences threefold anguish and dejection here and now:'

> 1) If the fool is sitting in a place, like an assembly room or at crossroads where people meet, and if the people start talking about him, he thinks that he has done certain immoral acts and the people talk about it. This creates anguish and dejection in him. 2) When he sees others being punished by the king for evil deeds, he fears he will have to suffer in the same way. This makes him uneasy and creates anguish. 3) When a fool is resting on a chair or a bed, the evil deeds done by him come to his mind. 'Monks, as at eventide the shadows of the great mountain peaks rest, lie and settle on the earth, so monks, do these evil deeds that the fool has formerly done... lie and settle on him... .'[14]

The fool thinks that what is good has not been done and that he will be born in a bad place. He grieves, mourns, laments and falls into disillusionment. This sort of guilt and uneasiness is certainly the kind of restlessness that has been condemned by the Buddha. It is different from a healthy and productive sense of shame and fear (*hiri-ottappa*). Thus, both these extremes, deception and guilt, are condemned by the Buddha.

THE ORIGINS OF GUILT ACCORDING TO FREUD

Against this background of the early Buddhist conception of the roots of morality and religion, let us now view the Freudian analysis of the super-ego. The grounds on which Freud rejected pathological religious and moral behaviour are mentioned in many of his works. Freud has often been condemned for rejecting morality and religion as a whole. The fact is that Freud had to play a historical mission in exposing the pathological aspects of the 'conscience of a civilisation'.

Freud says that the long period during which the growing human being lives in dependence upon his parents leaves behind it a precipitate that forms within his ego a special agent in which his parental influence is prolonged. It has been given the name 'super-ego'. Insofar as the super-ego is differentiated from the ego or opposed to the ego, it constitutes a third force which the ego must take into account. Thus, an action by the ego is as it should be, if it satisfies simultaneously the demands of the id, the super-ego and reality. The details of the relation between the ego and the super-ego become completely intelligible if they are carried back to the child's attitude towards his parents. The parents' influence naturally includes not merely the personalities of his parents, but also the racial, national and family traditions handed on through them, as well as the immediate social circles they represent. In spite of their fundamental difference, the id and the super-ego have one thing in common – they both represent the influence of the past. The id is to a great extent the influence of heredity, the super-ego is essentially the influence of what is taken over from other people, whereas the ego is from the individual's own experience.

It is a remarkable thing that the super-ego often develops a severity for which no example has been provided by the real parents, and further, it takes the ego to task not only for its deeds but equally for its thoughts and unexecuted intentions of which it seems to have knowledge.

The hero of the Oedipus legend too, felt guilty for his actions and punished himself, although the compulsion of the oracle should have made him innocent in our judgment and his own. In the melancholic patient the super-ego becomes severe, abuses, humiliates and ill-treats his unfortunate ego. It threatens with the severest punishments. This aggressive aspect is well demonstrated in masochism.

Freud, commenting on Kant's view regarding the greatness of moral conscience within, says that where conscience is concerned, God has been guilty of a careless piece of work and though it has no doubt been within us, it has not been there from the beginning (unlike sexuality). Children are therefore essentially amoral; they have no internal inhibitions against their pleasure-seeking impulses. The role which the super-ego undertakes later in life is at first played by an external power, viz. by parental authority. The influence of the parents dominates the child by granting proofs of affection and by threats of punishment, which to the child means loss of love. This objective anxiety is the forerunner of later moral anxiety. The super-ego seems to be influenced only by the harshness and severity of the parents, their preventive and punitive functions while their loving care is not taken up by it. Apart from the activities of self-obedience and conscience the super-ego also has the function of holding up ideals, striving to attain perfection, win fame and honour, which is sometimes referred to as the ego-ideal.

When it is asked how a sense of guilt arises in anyone, the answer is given that people feel guilty (pious people call it 'sinful') when they have done something they know to be 'bad'. But how little this answer tells us! Perhaps a person who has not actually committed a bad act, but merely becomes aware of the intention to do so, may also regard himself guilty. In both cases, however, it is presupposed that wickedness has already been recognised as reprehensible, as something that ought not to be done. Freud feels that the suggestion of an original capacity for discriminating between good and evil can be rejected.

An extraneous influence is evidently at work which decides what is to be called 'good' and 'bad'. Since their own feelings would not lead men along the same path, they must have a motive for obeying that extraneous influence. It can best be designated 'the dread of losing love'. In a sense what is called guilt is obviously only the dread of losing love, i.e. 'society anxiety'.

> Consequently such people habitually permit themselves to do any bad deed that procures them something they want, if only they are sure that no authority will discover it or make them suffer for it; their anxiety relates only to the possibility of detection.[15]

The authority is internalised by the development of a super-ego. At this point the dread of discovery ceases to operate and also once for all any distinction between doing evil and wishing to do it, since nothing is hidden from the super-ego, not even thoughts.

> But the influence of the genetic derivation of these things, which causes what has been outlived and surmounted to be relived, manifests itself so that on the whole things remain as they were at the beginning.[16]

The super-ego torments the sinful ego with the same feelings of dread and watches for opportunity whereby the outer world can be made to punish it. External deprivation and adversity too, strengthen the conscience, and when some calamity befalls, he holds an inquisition within, discerns his sin, heightens the standards of his conscience, imposes abstinence on himself and punishes himself with penances. Thus Freud explains the increased sensitivity to morals in the face of ill luck. Now fate is felt to be a substitute for the agency of parents, for adversity means that one is no longer the highest power of all. Destiny is looked upon in the strictly religious sense as the expression of God's will. Thus Freud says that God functions as a magnified father. With the dread of authority, there is only the renouncing of instinctual gratification, but with the dread of the super-ego there is punishment.

Thus Freud's conception of guilt is central to his analysis of morals and religion. It is in this light that he sees a close analogy between the religious rituals and the obsessions of the neurotic. Freud also sees religion as something that issues out of man's helplessness. In the way that a helpless child clings to the parents, man isolated in a threatening world clings to his image of God which is a magnified father-figure. The derivation of a need for religion from the child's feeling of helplessness and the longing it evokes for a father seems to him incontrovertible, especially since feeling is not simply carried on from childhood days, but is kept alive perpetually by fear of what the superior power of fate will bring.

BUDDHIST MEDITATION AND PSYCHOTHERAPY

Conze says that there is very little contact or similarity between Buddhist meditation and modern psychotherapy:

> Mental health is the goal both of the practitioner of meditation and of the modern psychologist. Apart from that there is little contact or similarity between them. They differ profoundly in their definitions of mental health, in their theoretical assumptions about the structure of the mind and the purpose of human existence and in the methods which they describe for the attainment of mental health.[17]

He goes on to say that in recent years a few psychologists have shown interest in the therapeutic value of these meditations, but that little has come of it. Psychotherapy is basically the creation of Freud and it is so often associated with a pan-sexual theory of man that very few will even think of comparing psychotherapy with a spiritual system like Buddhism. However, there are many factors in a 'humanistic religion' like early Buddhism (as differentiated from an 'authoritarian religion') that Freud probably would have heartily endorsed.

Regarding Conze's claim about the disparity in the two therapeutic systems, a very stimulating answer has been given by Fromm in *Zen Buddhism and Psychoanalysis*. Fromm's analysis is of course limited to Zen Buddhism. But his discussion can be applied to the therapeutic aspects of early Buddhism too. He says that psychoanalysis is a characteristic expression of western man's spiritual crisis and an attempt to find a solution. This is explicitly so in the more recent developments of psychoanalysis in 'humanist' or 'existentialist' analysis.[18] This aim is implicitly found in Freud. Fromm adds that contrary to a widely held assumption Freud's own system transcended the concept of 'illness' and was concerned with the 'salvation' of man, rather than only with a therapy for mentally sick patients. If this is so, there are points of contact between psychotherapy and Buddhism regarding the purpose of human existence.

This fact is also seen in a remarkable change that took place within the psychoanalytic system of therapy due to a change in the kind of patients who came for treatment. 'Psychoanalysis shifted its emphasis more and more from therapy of the neurotic symptoms to therapy of difficulties in living rooted in the neurotic character.'[19] The patients who first came for treatment suffered from certain symptoms like a paralysed arm, obsessive symptoms or a washing compulsion. The difference between these patients and those who went to the regular physician for treatment was that the cause of their symptoms was mental and not organic. But there was a common pattern of cure: once the symptom was removed the patient was cured. The new kind of patient that came for treatment was not sick in the traditional sense and had no overt symptoms. These patients were not insane or considered sick by their relatives. Yet they complained about being depressed, having insomnia, not enjoying their work, etcetera. Though these people thought they suffered from this or that symptom, their complaints were only the conscious and socially recognised ways of expressing a deeper dissatisfaction. Putting his finger on the source of the malady Fromm says:

> The common suffering is the alienation from oneself, from one's fellow man, and from nature; the awareness that life runs out of one's hand like sand, and that one will die without having lived; that one lives in the midst of plenty and is yet joyless.[20]

This concept of 'alienation' can be illustrated by a typical example cited by Fromm:

> A businessman, intelligent, aggressive, successful, has come to drink more and more heavily. He turns to a psychoanalyst to be cured of his drinking. His life is completely devoted to competition and money making. Nothing else interests him. His personal relationships all serve the same goal. He is expert in making friends and gaining influence, but deep down he hates everyone he comes into contact with, his competitors, his customers, his employees. He also hates the commodity he sells. He has no particular interest in it, except as a means to make money. He is not conscious of this hate, but slowly one can recognize from his dreams and free associations that he feels like a slave to his business, his commodity, and everyone connected with it. He has no respect for himself and dulls the pain of feeling inferior and worthless by resorting to drinking. He has never been in love with anyone and satisfies his sexual desires in cheap and meaningless affairs.[21]

Now is his problem drinking? Or is his drinking only a symptom of his real problem: his failure to lead a meaningful life. Actually his problem is not his drinking but his moral failure, and this cannot be analysed in terms of the manifest symptoms. These changing visions of psychoanalysis bring it closer to a religion such as Buddhism. The psychoanalyst becomes dissatisfied with the therapy of a mere social adjustment and searches for a radical therapy that can illuminate the meaning and purpose of human existence.

This brings us logically to Conze's claim about the divergence regarding the definition of mental health. A clear insight into the Freudian position is found in a statement quoted in the book *Normality* by Daniel Offer and Melvin Sabshin:

> From an analytic point of view, there is no such animal as the 'normal' person except as an ideal—we are all relatively neurotic. The basic tenets of psychoanalysis affirm that conflict is the essence of life and that instinctual renunciation is the price of being a civilized human being. Paraphrasing Alexander Pope's phrase 'to err is human', we would say 'to be neurotic is human'.[22]

The underlying premise in this Freudian position is that all men are at least partially neurotic. And this fits in with the Buddhist axiom *sabbe puthajjanā unmattakā* (all worldlings are deranged). F.C. Redlich voices a similar sentiment regarding Freud:

> Freud also felt that absolute normality, like complete happiness, is impossible and that conflict is always present in human beings.[23]

Now the position maintained by Freud brings him quite close to early Buddhism. But there is a difference. Freud implies that complete perfection is an ideal that man can never reach. In keeping with this position, Offer and Sabshin present three basic trends regarding the definition of normality and health: 1) normality as an ideal fiction, 2) normality as optimal integration, and 3) normality as adaptation within context. The tendency to regard normality as an ideal fiction started with Freud.

Buddhism agrees with Freud regarding the universality of neurosis and the universality of unconscious conflicts, but Buddhism does not regard normality as a fiction. This ideal is hard to achieve, but it can be achieved, and it was achieved by the Buddha and some of his disciples who attained the state of *arahat* (the holy state). Freud often advocates an attainable ideal of happiness as perfect happiness cannot be attained. But the Buddha says that ultimate perfection and happiness is possible. The Buddha classifies disease into two kinds: bodily disease (*kāyiko rogo*) and mental disease (*cetasiko rogo*). We suffer from bodily diseases from time to time, but mental illness is continual until the state of arahat is attained. Thus, according to the Buddha, in a healthy mind all the selfish desires and passions are extinguished and the mind positively enjoys bliss and peace.

This brings us to the next point mentioned by Conze; the methods advocated for the attainment of mental health. In this instance, there are certainly differences, but the two systems are not so completely different ,that the Freudian system cannot gain anything from absorbing some of the techniques of Buddhist therapy. The practical and educational value of comparative studies is to stimulate such extensions of Freudian therapy. The Freudian therapy for neurosis was not so thoroughgoing as that advocated by Buddhism. Freud's despair in his inability to find a permanent solution to prevent a recurrence of the neurotic condition has great significance in the light of the radical system of therapy advocated by the Buddha.

Finally, regarding the structure of mind in the two systems, Conze thinks that there is great difference. But as has been demonstrated in our comparative study of the theory of mind and unconscious motivation, there are certain significant similarities. The similarity between the threefold desires of Buddhism (*kāma-*, *bhava* and *vibhava-taṇhā*) and the Freudian concepts of the libido, ego and the death instinct is indeed remarkable.[24] All these show that Conze's observation of the two therapeutic systems is not quite correct.

BUDDHIST MEDITATION

The early Buddhist system of therapy involves a very large field that can be described from various standpoints. Since we are interested in unconscious motivation, we will survey the Buddhist system of therapy briefly so far as it has a bearing on this theme.[25]

It is a significant fact that the Four Noble Truths—which form the essential core of early Buddhism—correspond to the basic structure of traditional Indian medicine: 1) the malady (suffering), 2) the cause of suffering according to the diagnosis (craving and ignorance), 3) treatment (the Eightfold Path) and, 4) the goal of treatment (health or nibbāna).

This basic structure brings out the therapeutic attitude that underlies the Buddha's teachings. There is both a cognitive and an emotional aspect to the cause of suffering so that it can be discussed under 'craving' and 'ignorance'. Craving (*taṇhā*) is derived from the root causes of passion (*rāga*) and hatred (*dosa*). Ignorance or lack of knowledge (*avijjā*) is basically related to another root cause, viz. *moha* (delusion). It is said in the *Saṃyutta Nikāya* that beings are 'cloaked in ignorance and tied to craving'.[26]

Thus we get two character types in whom these aspects dominate: 1) the craving temperament (*taṇhācarita*) and 2) the view temperament (*diṭṭhicarita*) or the theoriser.[27] Therapeutically, 'quiet' is advocated for the man who is excessively tied to craving and 'insight' is advocated for the man who is cloaked by ignorance. Both aspects are generally found in everyone in varying degrees. But there are character types in whom these aspects dominate and colour the whole personality. This concept of character types is given prominence in the *Visuddhimagga*. There are many possible classifications of character types. Buddhaghosa offers six basic ones: 1) greedy temperament, 2) hateful temperament, 3) deluded temperament, 4) faithful temperament, 5) intelligent temperament and 6) speculative temperament. He works out various combinations of these types and relates them to various meditations which can serve as a corrective for a particular character type. Buddhist meditation (*bhāvanā*) may be one of two kinds, viz. 1) development of tranquillity (*samatha*) also described as the development of concentration (*samādhi*), and 2) development of insight (*vipassanā*) which culminates in wisdom (*paññā*).

Sīla (morality), *samādhi* (concentration) and *paññā* (wisdom) provide the threefold basis on which the whole therapeutic structure of Buddhism stands. This threefold structure can also be presented as aspects of the Eightfold Path: 1) Right understanding, 2) Right thought, 3) Right speech, 4) Right bodily action, 5) Right livelihood, 6) Right effort, 7) Right mindfulness and 8) Right concentration. The first two come under wisdom, 3-5 under morality and 6-8 under concentration. As Francis Story remarks:

> Techniques of meditation (*bhāvanā*) in Buddhism are designed for specific ends according to the personality of the meditator and the traits it is necessary to eliminate. They are prescribed by the teacher just as treatment is given by a psychiatrist; the mode of treatment is selected with the individual requirements of the patient in view. The forty subjects of meditation, known as *Kammatthanā* (bases of action), cover every type of psychological need and every possible combination of type.[28]

This observation is quite in keeping with the spirit of this inquiry. It is said that, since the Buddha had the telepathic powers to discern the minds of others and their unconscious desires, he would always recommend a certain type of meditation as a corrective to a particular personality. Not merely could the Buddha discern the mind of another, but he could get a glimpse of the recurring patterns in one's personality through innumerable births. However, ultimately the Buddha lets each man be his own psychiatrist and then evades problematic phenomena like that of 'transference' that emerge due to excessive dependence on the analyst.

FREUDIAN PSYCHOTHERAPY

At a very early stage Freud employed what was called the 'cathartic method'. Under hypnosis certain emotionally charged memories appear in a vivid and dramatic form. This release of pent-up emotions is referred to as 'abreaction.' It is due to the recalling of memories which would not have been recalled under ordinary conditions. The inability to recall certain memories under ordinary conditions is linked up with certain traumatic events buried in the past. This theory is also connected with one of the stages in the development of the concept of the unconscious, where the unconscious is considered the realm of repressed memories and emotions.

Freud found that abreaction by itself had no permanent use. As Franz Alexander has pointed out, during this stage Freud accepted the fact that the 'Ego must face and learn to handle the repressed emotions. Thus the emphasis was on insight.' Gradually the method of free association[29] replaced the method of hypnotism. Now Freud directed his therapy not merely to reconstructing the past, but to making patients remember and above all understand it. The past had to be understood and accepted by the patients.

The phenomenon called 'transference' was discovered in a certain type of emotional relationship that arose between the analyst and the patient. In the transference the original pathogenic conflicts of the early family relationships are repeated with lesser intensity. This is what is called the 'transference neurosis'. The emotional re-enactment gradually increases the ego's capacity to face these conflicts. However, this can lead to too much dependence on the analyst and thus leads to an interminable analysis.

The question regarding the limits of analysis is directly connected with the goals of analysis. Freud first posits an ambitious definition of analysis and shows how such an ambitious concept turns out to be illusory. The ambitious goal is the attainment of absolute psychic normality. But there are three factors which make the attainment of such normality impossible: 1) the intensity of the instincts or the constitutional factor, 2) the traumatic factor, 3) the rigidity of the ego based on defence mechanisms. Freud remarks:

> [His] aim will not be to rub off every peculiarity of human character for the sake of a 'schematic normality,' nor yet to demand that a person who has been 'thoroughly analyzed' shall feel no passions and develop no internal conflicts.[30]

Thus, he rejects a goal that cannot be achieved. Commenting on his own ideal, Freud says that analysis should secure the best possible psychological conditions for the functioning of the ego. If this is the goal of analysis, then it can be achieved. He also says that whatever one's theoretical attitude is, the termination of analysis is a practical matter. Within this modest and limited ideal Freud remains an optimist, but when speaking of ultimate normality Freud remains a pessimist.

Both Freudian psychotherapy and the Buddhist system of therapy aim at breaking through the conscious layer of one's personality to the depths of the unconscious. However, Buddhism uses a spiritual and mystical dimension of experience which is not found in Freud. Though there are strong analogies between the two systems and the emphasis is on introspection, self-analysis, development of insight, etcetera, Buddhism advocates integration of personality at a higher level. By merely unravelling the origin of a personality disorder, a patient is not fully cured. The treatment has to be lasting.

Freud grappled with this question, but he could not discover a lasting solution. He said that his system was not a panacea, but that it was superior to any of the therapeutic systems so far presented. Thus the Buddhist system of therapy is more deep-rooted and advocated a more positive form of personality integration. Within the Freudian system there is a tension between descriptive clinical diagnosis and prescriptive normative therapies. Buddhist ethico-psychology cuts through the problem asserting boldly that the measure of immoral behaviour is simply the degree to which it is dominated by craving and the delusion of a selfhood. This at once gives an unchanging point of reference.[31] The advocacy of a deep-rooted therapy resting on the development of *jhānic* experience gives Buddhism a standard of absolute normality. The acceptance of the hypothesis of rebirth gives Buddhism a larger framework of reference.

These are the differences, but there are similarities which give meaning and purpose to our study. The shift from symptomatic changes to characterological changes gives a sense of depth and permanence to psychotherapy. It often happens that the therapy goes beyond the patient's expectations; he not merely recovers from the illness, but he has become an enlarged and improved person.

Freud hopes that the stimuli received during the patient's own analysis will not cease to act when the analysis is over, that the processes of ego-transformation will go on of their own accord and that all further experiences will be made use of in a newly acquired way. In fact, he says that this does happen, and insofar as it happens, it qualifies the learner who has been analysed to become an analyst. If the patient who has recovered ultimately can qualify as an analyst himself, this echoes the Buddhist theory that one becomes fully perfect when one follows and achieves the path of an arahat, the same path that the Buddha trod.

Freud also requests that every analyst should be analysed at least every five years. While this differs from the Buddhist conception of the perfected one, it is clear to what extent even the analyst has to be conscious of his own projections and prejudices.

Freud displays elements of both optimism and pessimism. As a clinician working with a practical problem, he advocates an attainable ideal of happiness and is optimistic. As a theoretician and philosopher he often betrays a pessimistic attitude. According to the Buddha the unattainable ideal of Freud is something that can be achieved. He and his disciples after him did achieve ultimate happiness and normality. In short, the Buddha claims that the 'complete mastery' of the unconscious is possible.

In conclusion, it should be said that while respecting Freud's cautious statement that he is not a prophet and that he offered no final consolation for man, the lasting value of the work of Freud lies in the fact that it certainly went beyond the narrow confines of a therapy for mentally sick patients. As MacIntyre points out:

> The scope in principle of Freudian explanation is all human behaviour; had it been less than this Freud would have been unable to draw the famous comparison between the effect of his own work and that of Copernicus.[32]

VI

THE FREUDIAN SEARCH FOR THE IDEAL THERAPEUTIC MODEL

A BUDDHIST PERSPECTIVE

Both Buddhism and the Freudian system are basically focused on the alleviation of human suffering. As Robert Thouless presents the idea:

> Freud's point of view was that of scientific medicine. Scientific medicine had one obvious characteristic in common with Buddhism, that it was concerned with the salvation of men from suffering.[1]

Thouless goes on to say that the Buddha used the principle of cause and effect to understand and make diagnosis of human suffering. Then he says:

> In the wider application of this principle of scientific causation, the aim of medical science was to discover the nature of the various diseases, their cause, the methods of their cure, and the remedies that led to their cure. This in the restricted field of organic illnesses, is a programme closely parallel to the Buddha's four truths concerning suffering.[2]

This means that the concepts of 'sickness' and 'health' in the two systems deserve a closer analysis than what was presented in the earlier editions of this work. It is most fitting that we explore in detail the intuitions of Robert Thouless, so well explicated in the 'Foreword' to the present work. It is also necessary to see to what extent Freud encountered difficulties in working out a successful therapy for the resolution of neurotic conflicts or broadly the alleviation of human suffering. A very close look at Freud's paper, 'Analysis, Terminable and Interminable' gives us some penetrating insights about Freud's understanding of the issues, as well as his difficult encounter with the perennial obstructions to working out the ideal therapeutic model.

According to the Buddha, the psychological and even the social conflicts of man are expressions of the in-built features of the human predicament. The concept of *dukkha* indicates that such conflicts and anxieties are universal, and found in everyone in different degrees. Mary Jahoda, in *Current Concepts of Mental Health,* makes a similar observation:

> If it is reasonable to assume that such conflicts are universal, we are all sick in different degrees. Actually, the difference between anyone and a psychotic may lie in the way he handles his conflicts...[3]

The Buddha describes the human proneness to incessant conflicts in this manner:

> Monks, there are to be seen beings who can admit freedom from suffering from bodily disease for one year, for two years, for three, four, five, ten, twenty... who can admit freedom from bodily disease for even a hundred years. But monks, those beings are hard to find in the world who can admit freedom from mental disease even for a moment, save in those who are liberated.[4]

Thus according to the Buddha everyone who is dominated by craving and subject to the delusion of the ego generate different degrees of conflict, anxieties, discontent and depression. Those who go to an extreme in this respect may fall into the class of psychological disorders. Of course the layman, especially, by aiming at an ideal of 'righteous and harmonious living', may live with lesser conflicts and anxieties. Thus the Buddha offers the well-adjusted, righteous and harmonious life style for the layman. Of course western concepts of therapy cannot offer a net to capture the full meaning of therapy in Buddhism, but yet these points of convergence are interesting.

In the message of the Buddha, the workable distinction between the ideal of the perfect one (*arahat*) and that of the righteous and harmonious life was quite clear and moreover these are blended in different ways. In Freud, at least in the 'Analysis, Terminable and Interminable' there is an implicit tension between the role of analysis as adjustment therapy and as a continuous life process of understanding oneself.

Sigmund Freud wrote a stimulating paper towards the latter part of his life entitled 'Analysis, Terminable and Interminable'.[5] Apart from raising some significant queries regarding the question 'Is there such a thing as a natural end to analysis?', it also contains some significant conflicts and tensions regarding the main concerns of this essay: the 'normal' and the 'abnormal', and 'sickness' and 'health'. I wish to refer to the issues of normal/abnormal and sickness/health as tensions rather than clear dualities, tensions that emerged due to Freud's ceaseless exploration of the human predicament on the one hand, and the cautious voice of science, which made him disclaim any moralistic purpose in his writings, on the other.

There were also other types of conflicts. There was a technical demand on the termination of analysis: if continuous analysis is a time-consuming business, how do we accelerate the slow progress of analysis? Can we set a fixed limit? Freud however, expressed a willingness to spend a number of years with one patient: even the wellbeing of one person, he felt, is a matter of 'ultimate concern'.[6] When the work 'Analysis, Terminable and Interminable' is placed against the wider background of Freud's other writings, it may be said that in Freud we see a kind of oscillation between a limited ideal of therapy and a more ambitious one, as well as an optimistic conception of cure and therapeutic transformation. Already in Freud's 'Studies in Hysteria', we find the celebrated passage:

> No doubt fate would find it easier than I do to relieve you of your illness. But you will be able to convince yourself that much will be gained if we succeed in transforming your hysterical misery into common unhappiness.[7]

Freud comments:

> Our aim will not be to rub off every peculiarity of human character for the sake of a schematic 'normality', nor yet to demand that the person who has been 'thoroughly

> analyzed' shall feel no passion and develop no internal conflicts. The business of analysis is to secure the best possible psychological conditions for the functions of the ego; with that it has discharged its task.[8]

From a very specific eastern perspective, I found another contrasting vision of the goals of therapy mentioned in 'Analysis, Terminable and Interminable' more interesting:

> ...but we reckon on the stimuli that he has received in his own analysis not ceasing when it ends and on the processes of remodelling the ego continuing spontaneously in the analyzed subject and making use of all subsequent experiences in this newly acquired sense. This does in fact happen, and insofar as it happens it makes the analyzed subject qualified to be an analyst himself.[9]

The path of continuous self-exploration that is mentioned here has attracted some contemporary writers, such as Anthony Storr, on the concept of 'cure'. He says quite clearly that psychoanalysis certainly offers something more than mere relief from symptoms for which they wanted to be treated; they seek the process of analysis as an end in itself. Storr says that in this manner analysis is sought not so much as treatment but more as a way of life.[10] This is the sort of dimension in which analysis as both therapeutic transformation and growth of self-knowledge offers a point of convergence for an eastern and more particularly, a Buddhist perspective.

A possible objection to my approach is that Freud grappled with the neurotic and abnormal and that we have no right to use these insights to understand the normal mind and, even more, to bring them into the Buddhist context. Though Freud was primarily interested in the mentally sick, his psychology had a broad basis. In fact, Philip Rieff, who deals at great length with the therapeutic dimensions of Freudian psychology, claims that both Freud's dictum that 'we are all somewhat hysterical' and his claim that the difference between so-called normality and neurosis is only a matter of degree comprise a central Freudian position rather than a peripheral one. In fact, we also know that Freud dealt at a very deep and intensive level with what may be called the 'pathology of normalcy', as found in his Psychopathology of Every Day Life.[11] Freud certainly went beyond the narrow confines of a therapy for mentally sick patients. As MacIntyre points out:

> The scope in principle of Freudian explanation is all human behaviour: had it been less than this Freud would have been unable to draw the famous comparison between the effect of his own work and that of Copernicus.[12]

Here again, 'Analysis, Terminable and Interminable' confirms this standpoint:

> Every normal person, in fact, is only normal on the average. His ego approximates to that of the psychotic in some part or other and to a greater or lesser extent; and the degree of its remoteness from one end of the series and of its proximity to the other will furnish us with a provisional measure of what we have so indefinitely termed an 'alteration of the ego.[13]

After this brief glimpse into our special interest in Freud's study of the termination of analysis, in the rest of this essay I will divide my discussion into three phases. First, I will present a summary of 'Analysis, Terminable and Interminable', then briefly discuss some parallels to and differences from the Buddhist concern with sickness and health, and then examine some of the Freudian dilemmas that stand in the way of a terminable analysis. I will try to analyse and understand this issue from a Buddhist position.

Before I conclude this introductory discussion, I should mention two special reasons for selecting this essay by Freud for detailed analysis. First, in spite of the conflicting strands of thought regarding the ideal of mental health, it is possible to agree with James Strachey that in this work the sceptical, pessimistic outlook dominates. This is especially so compared with the more optimistic outlook in works such as the *New Introductory Lectures*, which preceded it and the *Outline of Psychoanalysis*, which followed it. But in a rather paradoxical manner, such pessimism seems to increase our interest in schemes of therapy that go beyond the accepted patterns of scientific psychology. Perhaps, as Charles Rycroft says, 'psychoanalysis could be regarded as a semantic bridge between science and biology on the one hand and humanities on the other'.[14] The dilemmas of Freud call for a widening of the frames that we can use to plot the perennial conflicts inherent in the human situation.

The second reason, which I consider quite significant, is the insight that is available from Freud's own dilemmas regarding the crucial role of the ego in this interminable analysis. At this point, I wish to open up a line of inquiry from a Buddhist perspective and place it before you as an exercise in exploration. Apart from the complexities of psychoanalytic writings on the subject, there appears to exist a semantic thicket that has to be cleared. It is to the credit rather than discredit of Freud that he stumbled on this during the latter stages of his research and left it to future workers (including his daughter Anna Freud) to find an answer.

ANALYSIS, TERMINABLE AND INTERMINABLE

A SUMMARY

Psychoanalytic therapy, which is designed to free people from neurotic symptoms, inhibitions and abnormalities of character, is a time-consuming business. Attempts have been made to shorten the duration of analysis. Apart from the technical problem of how to accelerate the slow process of change, there is the 'more deeply interesting question': is there such a thing as a natural end to analysis?

From a practical point of view, it is easy to answer the question: 'Analysis is ended when the analyst and the patient cease to meet each other for analytic session.' Normally, such an end is reached when the patient is free from the symptoms he had and has overcome his anxieties, and the analyst feels that a certain amount of repressed material has been made conscious and intelligible and internal resistance has been conquered. At this point, 'there is no need to fear a repetition of the pathological process concerned'. The other meaning of the 'end' of analysis is a kind of absolute normality, where all the patient's repressions have been resolved and gaps in the memory filled. Freud was not only sceptical about the more ambitious ideal of psychic normality, but he came across three factors that interfered with the decisive termination of analysis.

In the early days, Freud dealt with a large number of patients who wanted to be dealt with as quickly as possible. He later dealt with a smaller number of severe cases, where the therapeutic aim was no longer the same:

> There was no question of shortening the treatment; the purpose was radically to exhaust all the possibilities of illness and to bring about a deep-going alteration of their personality.[15]

Now, there were three factors that interfered with the decisive termination of an analysis: the influence of traumatic events, the constitutional strength of instincts, and the 'alterations of ego'. As the attempt to deal with the traumatic factor had good results, the traumatic factor (as compared with the constitutional factor) was not a major obstacle. Thus here we are mainly concerned with the two other factors: the strength of instincts and the alteration of the ego.

The key question for Freud here is: 'Is it possible by means of analytic therapy to dispose of a conflict between the instinct and the ego, permanently and definitively?'[16] The terms permanently and definitively do not mean they cause the demand to disappear, but rather that there is a kind of 'taming of the ego', where the instincts are brought into complete harmony with ego.

Though the aim of analysis is thus to replace repressions that are insecure with reliable ego-syntonic control, this is not always achieved. In the defensive struggle, the ego gets dislocated and restricted. This unfavourable situation stands in the way of a permanent cure. The 'constitutional strength of instincts' adds to the difficulties. Though attempts were made to maintain the autonomy of the ego in harmony with the demands of the instincts, Freud discovered that the ego is developed from the id, and at some point the topographical distinction between the ego and the id collapses. There are other obstructions to a permanent cure, such as the 'adhesiveness of the libido' and the conflict between eros and destructiveness. These dilemmas, especially those springing from the ambiguous role of the ego in therapy, are of special interest for an eastern perspective on the question and will be discussed in the subsequent sections.

At this point, it is necessary to appreciate that, following the logic of his system, Freud honestly encountered these difficulties and stated them. It appears that the development of what may be called 'ego psychology' has not done very much to ease the situation. It is possible that ego psychology is merely moving in a vicious circle. These are built-in difficulties in the Freudian ego concept, and unless the question is approached from a different angle, as for instance from an angle found in the Buddhist tradition we may well come against a wall and a conceptual thicket.

Take the overburdened ego of the Freudian system: it is part of consciousness and control, perception and motility; it is a drive (the self-preservation drive); it is a reservoir of libido; it is the cause of repression; it conforms to reality (identical to the reality principle); it is a reaction to the drive and it constitutes the basis of character; it carries out reality testing.[17] In the final analysis, Freud discovered that the ego is developed from the id. The poor ego is at the same time, 'a precipitate of object losses' and the seat of sanity, order, and reason. It is not only that in a semantic sense it is an overworked concept, but that the inherent psychological ambiguities drove Freud into the real difficulties honestly voiced in 'Analysis, Terminable and Interminable'. The inherent ambiguities in the 'self and world' relation, 'self and other' relation, as well as the self attempting to relate to itself are meticulously worked out in the Buddhist sutras[18]

A BUDDHIST PERSPECTIVE

There have been three attempts to view Freudian psychotherapy from a Buddhist perspective that are relevant for this discussion: Erich Fromm's *Zen Buddhism and Psychoanalysis*, from a neo-Freudian standpoint; David Levin's 'Approaches to Psychotherapy', where a critique of Freud is presented from the standpoint of Tibetan Buddhism, with basic sympathies for a Jungian position; and my own *Buddhist and Freudian Psychology*.[19]

I have found Fromm's definition of wellbeing very much in line with the early Buddhist position: 'wellbeing is possible only to the degree to which one has overcome one's narcissism'.[20] Fromm says:

> Well-being means, finally, to drop one's ego, to give up greed, to cease chasing after the preservation and the aggrandizement of the ego, to be and to experience one's self in the act of being, not having, preserving, coveting, using.[21]

If the Buddhist is asked to recommend a general working norm of health and sanity, at least to be approximated in varying degrees, overcoming narcissism is one I prefer and find conducive in light of the Buddhist tradition. It may even be a point of convergence for a general religious perspective on therapy, and not merely for an eastern position. In spite of the dilemmas of ego psychology, it is a concept that makes sense to a Freudian, especially in the light of Freud's paper, 'On Narcissism'. Fromm has not merely revitalised the Freudian concept of narcissism, but he takes it beyond this and brings it close to the doctrine of the Buddha. Fromm comments: 'The awakened person of whom the Buddhist teaching speaks is the person who has overcome his narcissism, and who is therefore capable of being fully awake.'[22]

Fromm says that, quite contrary to popular assumptions, Freud's system transcends the traditional western concepts of 'illness' and 'cure'. According to Fromm, Freud's system is concerned with the 'salvation' of man rather than a mere therapy for the mentally sick:

> Psychoanalysis is a characteristic expression of Western man's spiritual crisis, and an attempt to find a solution. This is explicitly so in the more recent developments of psychoanalysis, in 'humanist' or 'existentialist' analysis. But before I discuss my own humanist concept, I want to show that quite contrary to a widely held assumption, Freud's own system transcended the concept of 'illness' and 'cure' and was concerned with the 'salvation' of man, rather than only with a therapy for mentally sick patients.[23]

For Fromm the liberation of the individual from neurotic symptoms is a task with a quasi-religious mission.

Some of these converging lines between psychotherapy and Buddhism have become relevant to the post-Freudian world, and more so in the world in which we live today. The patients who came to Freud in the early stages of his career were those who suffered from certain symptoms, such as a paralysed arm or an obsessional symptom or a washing compulsion. The difference between these patients and those who went to the regular physician for treatment was that the cause of their symptoms was not organic but mental. But there was a common pattern of cure: once the symptom was removed, the patient was cured.

The new kind of patient who came for treatment was not sick in the traditional sense and had no overt symptoms. These patients were not insane or considered sick by their relatives. Yet they complained about being depressed, not enjoying their work, and so forth. Though these people thought they suffered from certain symptoms, their apparent symptoms were perhaps socially recognised ways of grappling with their inner deadness and lack of vitality. Fromm describes the situation well:

> The common suffering is the alienation from oneself, from one's fellow men, and from nature; the awareness that life runs out of one's hand like sand, and that one will die without having lived; that one lives in the midst of plenty and is yet joyless.[24]

In spite of these converging lines between Buddhist therapy and Fromm's 'humanistic psychoanalysis', the Freudian system as such was subject to tensions between descriptive clinical diagnosis and the norms of therapeutic recommendation. The medically-oriented psychologist talks in terms of 'psychological maturity' and 'ego strength', whereas in non-medical contexts one speaks of the authenticity of moral concern and personal integrity. These dual worlds seem to separate in Freud's work due to a scientist's respect for the recognised idiom and the proper semantics of communication, but these worlds run into each other. As Freud said:

> The aim of psychoanalysis is not to tell the person what is good or bad, or what is right or wrong in a specific context, but to 'give the patient's ego freedom to decide one way or another... The medical aim is thus in substance a spiritual aim. It is to help the individual become an agent and cease being a patient; it is to liberate not to indoctrinate.[25]

THE DILEMMAS OF EGO PSYCHOLOGY AND THE BUDDHIST THEORY OF MOTIVATION

According to the psychology of early Buddhism, the mind can be considered a dynamic continuum that extends over a number of births. As such, it is composed of a conscious as well as an unconscious mind in which is contained the residue of emotionally charged memories, going back not merely to childhood but to past lives. The mind is viewed in this way as a continuum subjected to the pressure of the threefold desires of sense gratification, egoistic pursuits and self-annihilation, which have some strange affinities to the Freudian concept of the libido, ego instinct, and the death instinct. The drive for selfish pursuits, which is fed by the illusion of an indestructible ego, is the most relevant concept for the present study. The Buddha considers the ego, the seat of anxiety and the attachment to a false sense of the ego nourished by unconscious proclivities as a base for the generation of tension and unrest.

Although the ego-anxiety linkage offers an interesting point of intersection for Freudian and Buddhist therapies, the Freudian system is darkened by the ambiguities inherent in the ego concept as used by Freud.

I wish to make three specific points in the light of the Buddhist theory of motivation, very briefly outlined here. First, there are two significant uses of the term ego that have to be clearly distinguished. Sometimes it is used to describe an aspect of the personality that coordinates mental functions. It is also used in a completely different sense to convey a strong self-interest. Thus in the latter sense the word egoistical is used to refer to people with a strong ego in a negative sense. When Freud finds that the ego is rooted in the id and yet it has to control it, and the ego derives its strength from it, he creates a veritable tangle. As Freud remarks:

> When we speak of an 'archaic heritage' we are usually thinking only of the id, and we seem to assume that at the beginning of the individual's life no ego is yet in existence. But we shall not overlook the fact that id and ego are originally one; nor does it imply any mystical over-valuation of heredity if we think it credible that, even before the ego has

> come into existence, the lines of development trends and reactions which it will later exhibit are already laid down for it.[26]

It is because of this impasse that we, in the east, when we speak of personality growth, do not speak of strengthening, adding or accumulating. Rather our root metaphor is 'let go' and 'give up'. These metaphors are now gaining entry into the humanistic psychotherapies.

This is the reason that those like David Levin feel that, compared with the Buddhist approach of the analyst, the Freudian approach is coercive. What is necessary is an open, nondirective approach:

> Freudian analysis is indeed reflective. But its way of reflecting is very different from the Buddhists. The latter is like a clean mirror, or like the calm surface of a mountain lake; the former is more like an expressionist portrait to reveal the sitter's true self.[27]

The dynamic psychology of Buddhism also provides a scheme of evaluating motives that are non-egoistical, non-aggressive, springing from detachment, compassion, knowledge, etcetera. The basic springs of human motivation are analysed into three unwholesome roots: greed, hatred and ignorance, and three wholesome roots: non-greed, non-hatred, and wisdom. There is no ambiguous ego structure or a flow of energy running both ways; the ways of parting for healthy and unhealthy actions are clearly laid down, and the tricks played by the ego concept, whether they be 'conceptual' and semantic or experiential, are cautiously handled. They are not merely handled at an intellectual level, but also at the deeper levels of a 'meditative' therapy, of tranquillity meditation and insight meditation.

The second point that makes the termination of a successful analysis difficult, according to Freud, is the duality between eros and destructiveness that generates conflicts. The Buddha's analysis sheds a great amount of light on the Freudian position; the inherent conflict between the two instincts. The drive for self-preservation and for self-destruction, paradoxically, emerge from the same root of an ego illusion; they are like the two sides of the same coin. Buddha's psychological insight lay in pointing out that such apparently contradictory attitudes such as the desire to live and to die stem from the same root. Suicide for example, is paradoxically a strong form of self-love.

The enigmatic puzzle for Freud was 'how can one who is infected with such an amount of self-love consent to his own destruction?' Freud came within the very doors of an interesting solution to unravel his puzzle when he saw a link between 'wounded narcissism' (injured self-love) and the state of depression described in 'Mourning and Melancholia', but this was never integrated into his complete system as it could have been.[28] In the Buddhist context, self-destruction would be 'reactive' rather than 'appetative'. But all the same, the two forms of craving, the craving for self-preservation or egoistic pursuits and the craving for self-annihilation are not 'opposites'; they are merely the contrasting attitudes of a man who is subject to the illusion of a separate indestructible ego. Buddha describes the vagaries of ego attachment with a graphic image:

> Just like a dog, brethren, tied up by a leash to a strong stake or pillar—if he goes, he goes to that stake or pillar; if he stands, he stands close to that pillar or stake; if he lies down he lies close to that...

The pillar represents the 'ego;' the fivefold grasping group. Thus, if we take 'body' (which is one of the five grasping groups) as an example, whether we adorn the body, or like Narcissus fall in love with the reflection of one's own body in a pond, or we inflict torture on the body, we are like the dog tied to and going round the same illusory pillar: the ego.

It is unfortunate that the first expounder of the concept of narcissism in psychoanalytic theory, Sigmund Freud, could not completely get out of the spell of the strong sexual overtones of his writings. It remained a mission for Erich Fromm to revitalise the Freudian notion of narcissism:

> Narcissism is a passion the intensity of which in many individuals can only be compared with sexual desire and the desire to stay alive. In fact, many times it proves to be stronger than either. Even in the average individual in whom it does not reach such intensity, there remains a narcissistic core which appears almost indestructible.[29]

It is true that the Buddhist doctrine of egolessness offers a clue to the besetting dilemmas of the narcissistic man, but Fromm feels that it is a dimension that fits in with all the great religions of the world, east or west.

Third, the constitutional strength of instincts and the 'adhesiveness of the libido' are all accepted in the Buddhist concept in its recognition of the deep-rooted nature of craving. The Buddha does not exaggerate the role of sexuality as Freud does nor consider the duality between the life and death instinct as leading to a kind of interminable analysis. While accepting the strength of instincts, they can be tamed, redirected to sublimated goals, or even completely mastered. Although the ideal of harmonious living is sought by the householder, the recluse who has renounced the world seeks a path for the 'elimination of all conflicts'.

When Freud said that he was merely translating 'hysterical misery into common unhappiness', he was understating the potential of his own system. 'Analysis, Terminable and Interminable', though it is coloured by a heavy tinge of pessimism, paradoxically contains within itself a deeper search for the roots of human happiness. I shall conclude this analysis with the observations of Robert H. Thouless, when searching for a wider mission for psychoanalysis:

> One can speculate on the possibility of a future development of the therapy based on psychoanalysis to do more than this, to produce a radical mental reorientation that led to the complete disappearance of internal sources of unhappiness. If such a development of psychotherapy did take place, one can predict that it is likely to demand more time and energy than those of the few hours per week taken up by psychoanalysis. It is more likely to be a lifelong activity as is that of those striving for the final achievement of the Buddhist saint.[30]

APPENDIX I

SCHOPENHAUER: A LINK BETWEEN THE BUDDHA AND FREUD?[1]

> 'We have unwittingly steered our course into the harbour of Schopenhauer's philosophy.' *Sigmund Freud*

> 'Schopenhauer was influenced by Buddhism and by the Upanishads.' *Carl Jung*

THE NATURE OF INSTINCTS: BUDDHISM, SCHOPENHAUER AND FREUD

While working on a comparative study of the theory of motivation in Freud and the Buddha, the intriguing figure of Schopenhauer left an uncanny impression in our minds.[2] Schopenhauer remarks that there is 'close agreement' between his doctrine and Buddhism.[3] Freud says that Schopenhauer's concept of the unconscious 'will' is the equivalent of his theory of instincts, and thus considers the philosopher as a forerunner of psychoanalytic theory.[4] While it is possible to accept the claim that Indian thought influenced the philosopher Schopenhauer, the direct influence of Schopenhauer on Freud is a more intricate issue, especially when Freud remarks that he read Schopenhauer very late in his life. But the resemblance of some of his ideas to the thought of Schopenhauer certainly did embarrass Freud and he makes a number of attempts to clarify this issue.

The closeness of the thought of Schopenhauer to some aspects of Buddhism and the Freudian echoes of Schopenhauer seem to suggest to us the possibility of a deeper basis for the resemblance in motivational theory between Freud and the Buddha. It is the aim of this paper to suggest possible lines of inquiry and invite discussion rather than give a conclusive analysis of the problem.

In the field of scientific psychology, Freud was the first to accept the supremacy of emotions over the intellect or affection over cognition.[5] This is something that Freud shared with Schopenhauer. According to Freud, these affective processes are nourished by deep-seated instincts and the nature of these instincts is not clearly known by the individual. This again is an idea common to Freud and Schopenhauer.[6] In fact, the comparative study of the concepts of Schopenhauer, Freud and the Buddha that is attempted in this paper will be basically limited to the theory of instincts.[7]

	Buddhism		**Schopenhauer**		**Freud**
Taṇhā	*Kāma-taṇhā*	*Will to*	Sexuality	*The*	Libido
	Bhava-taṇhā	*live*	Self-preservation	*id*	Ego instinct
	Vibhava-taṇhā		Suicide		Death instinct

FREUD

Regarding the nature of instincts according to Freud, there were two stages in the development of the Freudian theory. First Freud posited two basic instincts—the sexual instinct (libido) and the ego instinct. As the word 'hunger' is used in ordinary language to represent the aims of self-preservation, so the word 'libido' is used by Freud to indicate the presence of sexual longing in man.

The popular view distinguishes between hunger and love as the representatives of the instincts that aim respectively at the preservation of the individual and at the reproduction of the species. We accept this very evident distinction, so that in psychoanalysis too, we make a distinction between the self-preservative or ego-instincts on the one hand and the sexual instincts on the other. The force by which the sexual instinct is represented in the mind we call 'libido' (sexual desire) and we regard it as something analogous to hunger, the will to power and so on, where the ego instincts are concerned.[8]

Freud, however, used the term 'sexuality' in a broad sense: it has many manifestations besides the simple connection with the genitals. Freud extended its meaning in two directions; on the one hand, to cover all bodily pleasures, and on the other hand, to cover psychological aspects like the feelings of affection and tenderness.

In the second stage, Freud postulates two contrasting drives: the eros and the death instinct (referred to by some as *thanatos*).[9] While the eros combines the sexual and the ego instincts, the death instinct conceptualises Freud's claim that in man there is an innate destructiveness or proneness to aggression, basically directed against the self (as in suicide) or deflected outward (when inflicting injury on others, the killing and destruction of objects).[10]

The base on which this theory of instincts rests is the notion of the unconscious. Freud describes three layers of the mind: the conscious, the preconscious and the unconscious. The conscious level consists of the processes which come within the normal awareness of a person at a given time. The preconscious consists of memories that could be recalled with little effort. The unconscious contains ideas, memories and images which are not accessible to the conscious mind under ordinary conditions. Thus special techniques have to be used to break through the mechanism of repression.

Freud considered the unconscious as the area of repressed memories. Later, he realised that the unconscious was not only the area of repressed memories, but the receptacle of deep instinctual desires, which try to find expression in socially acceptable ways. He accepted that even a part of the ego was unconscious. Freud described this obscure and inaccessible part of the personality as 'the id'. The little that had been learnt about it is based on the study of dreams and the formation of neurotic symptoms. We can come nearer to the id with the aid of analogies and call it a 'chaos, a cauldron full of seething excitations'.[11] The id consists of a mass of impulses, irrational and primitive, and is thus referred to as 'the reservoir of instincts'. Again, with the help of the metaphor of the iceberg, Freud has indicated his view of the mind—the visible conscious portion is extremely minute compared with the more extensive submerged depth of consciousness.

The Freudian concept of a truly dynamic unconscious, as depicted by the concept of the id, certainly puts him in line with the thought of Schopenhauer. It is this aspect of Freudian thought which attracted the attention of Heinz Hartmann:

> The concept of truly dynamic unconscious processes has a

quite different ancestry; it is, in German philosophy, found in the works of Schopenhauer and Nietzsche, and in certain romantic philosophers before them. But about this ancestry comparatively little is known, or rather little is known about the degree to which, the ways in which, this thinking might have left an imprint on Freud's work.[12]

BUDDHISM

The resemblance between the roots of motivation according to Freud and Buddhism has been dealt with in greater detail elsewhere.[13] Thus here we need only summarise the basic points relevant to the subject under discussion.

In the Early Buddhist psychology, the springs of human action are traced to six roots, which fall into two classes: moral and immoral. Of these, the immoral roots are greed (*lobha*), hatred (*dosa*) and delusion (*moha*) while the moral roots are their opposites: charity, compassionate love and wisdom. Greed has two manifestations, viz. in the form of *kāma-taṇhā* (craving for sensuous gratification) and *bhava-taṇhā* (craving for self-preservation). Hatred manifests in various types of aggression and ultimately issues forth as *vibhava-taṇhā* (craving for annihilation). Delusion is the primary root of evil, which prevents man from seeing the true nature of things.

The concept of *kāma-taṇhā* is similar to the Freudian concept of libido, *bhava-taṇhā* is similar to the Freudian notion of ego instincts and *vibhava-taṇhā* may be compared with the death instinct.

Kāma as 'sense desire' generally refers to the enjoyment of the five senses. But, in a more specific and narrow sense, *kāma* refers to sexual enjoyment as for instance in the precept concerning evil conduct with regard to sexual behaviour (*kāmesu micchācāra*). In fact, the word *'methuna'* is used to refer to sexual enjoyment in a specific way; the words *'methunasmin chanda'* for instance, refer to desires in sexual gratification. But the term *kāma* is used in a very broad manner and sexual pleasure may be one aspect of it. Thus the term *kāma-taṇhā* comes very close to Freud's pleasure principle. The Buddha quite explicitly says that it is man's nature to seek what is pleasurable and avoid that which is painful.

Kāma has two aspects: *kāma* as object (*vatthu-kāma*) and *kāma* as desire (*kilesa-kāma*). This distinction is found in the *Maha-Niddesa*, but it is related to a distinction already made in the older suttas: *pañca-kāmaguna* and *kāma-raga*. *Kilesa-kāma* may be called subjective sensuality while *vatthu-kāma* may be called objective sensuality.[14] *Pañca-kāmaguna* refers to the five types of pleasure objects obtained by the eye, ear, nose, tongue and body. *Kāma-raga* refers to the desires and passions of a sensual nature. The term *'pañca-kāmagunika-rāga'* refers to the fact that in beings there is a deep-seated proclivity for the enjoyment of the five senses.

In the final analysis, it is not the existence of sense-organs or the impact of sense-impressions that is emphasised, but the persistence of desire and lust. The eye is not the bond of objects nor are objects the bond of the eye; it is the desire and lust that arise owing to these two. Freud too makes a distinction between erotic instincts and object and considers the instincts to be more important.

According to the Buddha, unless there is the persistence of clinging (*upādāna*), excitation of the sense-organs is not sufficient to rouse the individual to activity. Clinging emerges with craving as a condition. But clinging as such works on a far deeper current and once a person clings to pleasure-giving objects, some latent tendencies (*anusayas*) have already been excited and stimulated. Fixation on pleasure-giving objects always feeds on the undercurrents of *anusayas*. In fact, all three aspects of craving mentioned above are related to the *anusayas*. The *anusaya* of sensuous craving (*kāma-rāga*) is the basis for the craving for sensuous gratification and the *anusaya* of anger (*patigha*) provides a base for the craving for annihilation. The lurking tendency to cling to existence is the *bhava-rāga anusaya* and it is related to the craving for self-preservation.

Both Freud and Schopenhauer recognised the dominating role of sexuality but Schopenhauer felt that love of life was a more basic drive.

BHAVA-TAṆHĀ

Bhava-taṇhā arises with a false conception of personality, based on the dogma of personal immortality (*sassata-diṭṭhi*). This is the belief in an ego entity existing independently of those physical and mental processes that constitute life. This entity is assumed to exist as a permanent, ever-existing thing, continuing after death. This wrong view is referred to as *diṭṭhi*. However, the ego is not merely an intellectual construction. It is fed by deeper affective processes like the desire for self-preservation, self-display, etcetera. The roots of this ego-illusion are very deep. It rests on a primitive and archaic ego-illusion, which has been functioning through countless births. It lies in the personality in the form of a dormant proclivity, described in the suttas as *bhava-rāga anusaya* and *bhava-āsava*.

Another manifestation of the ego is self-conceit (*māna*). Self-conceit takes three forms: superiority to another (*seyya māna*), equality with another (*sadisa māna*) or inferiority to another (*hīna māna*). If a person has attained fame and glory, he could suffer from an inflated sense of vanity. On the other hand, one who is beset with defeat and disappointment will suffer from a deprived ego. These analyses of ego injury and ego elation have their parallels in Freud. The Freudian concept of secondary narcissism and the Adlerian concept of inferiority complex may be compared with the Buddhist concept of *māna*. In general, it could be said that both Freud and Buddhism make a clear distinction between the desire for sense gratification and the desire for self-preservation.

Regarding the origin of the ego, Freud makes an interesting comment that the ego is first and foremost a 'body-ego'. This is similar to the Buddhist analysis of the origin of personality beliefs (*attā diṭṭhi*) in relation to corporeality. It is said that the majority who are not skilled in the doctrine, regard the body as the self. Freud also says that the ego as an organisation of mental life is derived from the primal structure of the id. This is somewhat like the relationship of the ego-illusion to *bhava-āsava*. Thus, the similarity between the ego instincts in Freud and *bhava-taṇhā* in Buddhism appear to have a deeper basis.

VIBHAVA-TAṆHĀ

The word '*vibhava*' as used in Pāli literature, has two meanings: 1) power, wealth, prosperity, 2) non-existence, cessation of life and annihilation. There seem to be two meanings of *vibhava-taṇhā* which may be connected with these two meanings of the word *vibhava*.

1) The love of the present life or craving for success and power in the present life based on the belief that there is no future state. The ego will be annihilated at death, so make the best of the present life.

2) The desire for self-annihilation accompanying the belief that there is a self-entity that is annihilated at death. This springs not from

a desire for success in the present life, but from loathing, disgust of the body and aggression. This leads to suicide and self-inflicted tortures to do away with the body. While the earlier expression of *vibhava-taṇhā* is to some extent related to sensuality the latter form basically issues from the root hate (*dosa*).

Logically, both positions are possible. It is possible for a carefree pleasure-lover to hold onto the position that death is the end of life. It is also possible for a man full of worry and anxieties to wish for the end of life even by committing suicide. The latter position is a more complex and interesting situation. Even Freud, for instance, says that so immense is the ego's self-love, we cannot conceive how the ego can consent to its own destruction. It took some time for him to accept that there is a basic aggressive aspect in the personality of man that makes the concept of a death-wish meaningful. Schopenhauer, while accepting the warlike and aggressive aspect of man, seems to consider suicide as merely another subtle expression of the will to live.

There is a crucial passage in the *Majjhima Nikāya* that gives a definite sense to the second meaning of the word *vibhava*.[15] Here, the terms *uccheda*, *vināsa* and *vibhava* are used as synonyms and thus *vibhava* clearly means 'destruction'. Though the individual attempts to get rid of the 'essential being' by destroying it, he paradoxically displays a tremendous preoccupation with the self. There is a display of undue anxiety and fear regarding one's own body (*sakkāyabhaya*) and the loathing of one's body (*sakkāyaparijeguccha*). Thus one keeps running and circling around one's body. This is compared to a dog running and circling around a post to which it is tied. Thus, those who take to suicide as an escape from intolerable conflicts are also subject to an ego-illusion, namely the annihilationist view.

According to the Buddhist theory, the thirst for annihilation expresses itself in the annihilation of the painful objects as well as one's own body. The Freudian theory is the inverse of this—the death instinct is originally directed against the self as a death-seeking urge and only secondarily deflected against the outer world. Though there is an important difference in this respect, both Freud and Buddhism recognise hatred as a dominant source of human motivation. In a later phase of Freudian theory, we get the concept of *eros*. Eros, which combines the sexual instinct and the ego instinct, is similar to the Buddhist concept of *rāga*. *Rāga* has two manifestations: *kāma-rāga* (sensual passion) and *bhava-rāga* (the lust for life). Some aspects of the death instinct may yet be compared with the concept of *vibhava-taṇhā*. However, in his later theory, the dual instincts of eros and the death instinct go beyond the limited confines of their psychological and clinical dimensions and assume, as Jones says, 'something of a transcendental significance'. They are represented as the forces of unification and separation. This metaphysical flavour is hard to find in the Buddhist theory.

The concept of unconscious motivation in Buddhism has been examined in detail elsewhere.[16] Here it should suffice to mention the relevant concepts in Buddhist psychology that help us to grasp the nature of unconscious motivation. Many scholars attempt to explain unconscious motivation in terms of concepts like the *bhavaṅga* and *ālayavijñāna*. But these concepts really do not belong to the Nikāyas of early Buddhism.

The concept of *anusayas* (latent tendencies), *asampajāna manosankārā* (dispositions of the mind of which we are not aware), *viññānasota* (the stream of consciousness) and *āsava* (influxes) help us to understand the basis of unconscious motives. We have already referred to the fact that the three aspects of craving have a deeper source in the undercurrents of the *anusayas*. The concept of *saṅkhara* refers to certain conative tendencies having both a conscious and an unconscious aspect. The *āsava* concept is close to the Freudian notion of the id.

SCHOPENHAUER

Regarding the nature of man, Schopenhauer says that 'Willing and striving is its whole being, which may be very well compared to an unquenchable thirst.'[17] The Buddhist concept of *taṇhā* could also be rendered as an unquenchable thirst. According to Schopenhauer,

> The basis of all willing is need, deficiency and thus pain. Consequently, the nature of brutes and man is subject to pain originally and through its very being. If, on the other hand, it lacks objects of desire because it is at once deprived of them by a too easy satisfaction, a terrible void and ennui comes over it.[18]

Thus man is tossed to and fro between the states of pain and satiety.[19]

This resemblance between Schopenhauer and Buddhism regarding the nature of willing has its echo in Freud. According to Philip Rieff's interpretation of the Freudian concept of instinct:

> Instinct is to him just that element which makes any response inadequate. The failure of response can be traced not merely to societal rigidities, but further back—to the ambivalent structure of instinct itself, which continually prepares the ground for conflicts.[20]

Rieff says:

> Far from being a residual idea left over from his biological training as the neo-Freudians have maintained, Freud's theory of instinct is the basis for his insight into the painful snare of contradiction in which nature and culture, individual and society, are forever fixed.[21]

Having examined the nature of will in general, it is now necessary to examine its more specific manifestations. First, it must be mentioned that for Schopenhauer 'egoism' (*principium individuationis*) is the basic mode in which the will manifests itself.[22] Schopenhauer, examining the source of egoism says that '...everyone desires everything for himself to possess, or at least to control everything, and whatever opposes it would like to destroy.'[23] This practical aspect of egoism is related to what he describes as 'theoretical egoism.' There is only one point from which the world can be seen and this is the position that a person occupies physically.[24] The individual is the supporter of the knowing subject and the knowing subject is the supporter of the world.[25] The will is objectified or given expression through this basic mode of egoism:

> ...every individual, though vanishing altogether and diminished to nothing in the boundless world, yet makes itself the centre of the world, has regard for its own existence and wellbeing before everything else; indeed from the natural standpoint, is ready to sacrifice everything else for this—is ready to annihilate the world in order to maintain its own

> self, this drop in the ocean, a little longer. This disposition is egoism, which is essential to everything in nature.[26]

The instinct of self-preservation is of course the most natural expression of the will. But Schopenhauer says that the sexual instinct is equally dominant and that, 'next to the love of life, it shows itself the strongest and most powerful of motives.'[27] He also refers to sexuality as the 'focus of the will.'[28] Schopenhauer's description of the role of the sexual impulse seems to anticipate some of the Freudian reflections on the subject:

> ...it is really the invisible central point of all action and conduct, and peeps out everywhere in spite of all veils thrown over it. It is the cause of war and the end of peace, the basis of what is serious, and the aim of the jest, the inexhaustible source of wit, the key to all allusions, and the meaning of all mysterious hints...[29]

To Schopenhauer, sexuality 'appears as a malevolent demon that strives to pervert, confuse and overthrow everything.'[30] In general, Schopenhauer gives a metaphysical picture of the universe and man; it is an expression of the will as manifested in the love of life and the impulse of sexuality:

> The parts of the body must, therefore, completely correspond to the principal desires through which the will manifests itself; they must be the visible expression of these desires. Teeth, throat, and bowels are objectified hunger, the organs of generation are objectified sexual desire; the grasping hand, the hurrying feet correspond to the more indirect desires of the will which they express.[31]

Regarding aggression, Schopenhauer discusses it mostly as the product of the conflict of individuals. The terrible side of this aggression caused by the conflict of individuals is seen in the lives of great tyrants and miscreants and in world-desolating wars. Its absurd side appears in self-conceit and vanity. The warlike nature of man so ably described by Hobbes is best seen when men are released from the bonds of law and order. This is only surpassed in actual wickedness, 'which seeks quite disinterestedly the hurt and suffering of others, without any advantage to itself.'[32] What Schopenhauer describes as wickedness is somewhat similar to the sadistic element in man described by Freud; some derive a kind of gratification by inflicting pain on others.

Regarding suicide, Schopenhauer says that it is merely another expression of the assertion of the will rather than a denial of it. 'The suicide wills life, and is only dissatisfied with the conditions under which it has presented itself to him.'[33] Suicide is a vain and foolish act as the will to live is not changed by it. That will remains unaffected by suicide, 'as the rainbow endures however fast the drops which support it for the moment may change.'[34] Schopenhauer concludes by saying the 'will to live appears just as much in suicide (Siva) as in the satisfaction of self-preservation (Vishnu) and in the sensual pleasure of procreation (Brahma)'.[35]

Schopenhauer also has a notion of an obscure depth of the mind which unknowingly influences the consciousness.[36] The distinctly conscious thoughts are merely the surface while the indistinct and obscure thoughts, feelings intermingled with disposition of the will, belong to the depth.[37] 'Consciousness is the mere surface of our mind, of which, as of the earth, we do not know the inside, but only the crust.'[38] Gardiner remarks that this statement resembles Freud's celebrated analogy of the mind as an iceberg. 'In any event, analogies certainly exist between the ways in which Schopenhauer frequently characterises the will— e.g. as 'blind incessant impulse', 'endless striving' and as 'indestructible'—and many of the terms Freud was wont to employ when talking about the nature of the unconscious'.[39]

THEIR MUTUAL INFLUENCE

Having outlined the nature of instincts according to Freud, Buddhism and Schopenhauer, we now raise the question of mutual influence. Regarding the relationship of Freud and Buddhism, we have already summed up the points of similarity; there is no problem of influence to examine, excepting the possible link through Schopenhauer. We also do not hope to examine the influence of Buddhism on Schopenhauer. In fact, Bhikkhu Nanajivako has done an excellent job in examining this question and of bringing out some significant parallels between Schopenhauer and Buddhism.[40] Our main problem in the second part of this paper is to determine the relationship between Freud and Schopenhauer against the background of Buddhist influence on Schopenhauer.

FREUD ON SCHOPENHAUER

What does Freud himself say regarding his relationship to the thought of Schopenhauer? In a number of references to Schopenhauer's philosophy, Freud mentions the similarities between his theories and some of the basic ideas of Schopenhauer. But yet he does not accept the contention that Schopenhauer influenced his psychoanalytic theories; on the contrary Freud says that he read Schopenhauer very late in his life.[41] Even if Freud did read Schopenhauer very late in his life, it is possible that the thought of Schopenhauer was a part of the intellectual climate of the time. This hypothesis is supported by L.L. Whyte in his *Unconscious Before Freud*:

> He may have been unconsciously influenced in his general attitude by Schopenhauer, Nietzsche and Dostoevsky—even if he personally read little of these writers in his early years, they were being widely read in Vienna in the last two decades of the century.[42]

There are many references to Schopenhauer in Freud's works, out of which we have selected a few. The theory of repression, the nature of unconscious processes, sexuality and the death instinct are the main topics where Freud finds certain parallels between himself and Schopenhauer:

> The theory of repression quite certainly came to me independently of any other source; I know of no outside impression which might have suggested it to me, and for a long time I imagined it to be entirely original, until Otto Rank (1911 a) showed us a passage in Schopenhauer's *World as Will and Idea*... What he says there about the struggle against accepting a distressing piece of reality coincides with my concept of repression so completely that I owe the chance of making a discovery to my not being well-read.[43]

Freud concludes by saying that he is prepared:

> To forgo all claims to priority in the many instances in which laborious psychoanalytic investigation can merely confirm the truths which the philosopher recognized by intuition.[44]

Here, Freud claims that the concept of repression was suggested by the clinical data that he examined and that it was not due to his reading of Schopenhauer. In this context it appears that we have to accept Freud at his word. It is reasonable to claim that the concept of 'repression' was suggested by the clinical material he examined. Freud's claim to a new discovery lies in transforming the cathartic procedure into a complete system of psychoanalysis, and the new factors that were added to the cathartic procedure were the theory of repression and resistance, infantile sexuality and dream interpretation.

While giving Freud due credit for these specific contributions, it seems that regarding the more general concepts like the unconscious, an indirect influence of Schopenhauer on Freud is possible. This claim can be supported by some of Freud's own statements.

In a paper entitled *A Difficulty In Psycho-analysis* (1917), Freud says that the pride of man suffered three blows: the first is the cosmological, where Copernicus pointed out that the earth was not the centre of the universe; the second is the biological, where Darwin blew up the myth of a radical difference between man and animals; and the third is the psychological, where Freud pointed out that man is not the master of his own mind. Referring to his own contribution, Freud cites two significant factors:

> That the life of our sexual instincts cannot be wholly tamed, and that mental processes are in themselves unconscious and only reach the ego and come under its control through incomplete and untrustworthy perceptions.[45]

He says that these two ideas together represent the third blow to man's pride. And he concedes to Schopenhauer the anticipation of these two profound ideas:

> It was not psycho-analysis however, let us hasten to add, which first took this step. There are famous philosophers who may be cited as forerunners—above all the great thinker Schopenhauer whose unconscious 'Will' is equivalent to the mental instincts of psycho-analysis. It was this same thinker, moreover, who in words of unforgettable impressiveness admonished mankind of the importance, still so greatly under-estimated by it, of its sexual craving.'[46]

He concludes by saying that there is, however, a difference; while the philosopher asserts this on an abstract basis, he demonstrates the same through his techniques to every individual personally.

In his *Autobiographical Study* (1925), however, he says that the assertion regarding the dominance of emotions, importance of sexuality and the mechanism of repression are not to be traced to his acquaintance with Schopenhauer's philosophy.[47]

The only concept that we have not mentioned so far is the death instinct. This is a concept that finds definite expression in his *Beyond the Pleasure Principle* (1920). By the year 1925, in his *Autobiographical Study*, he made the statement that he read Schopenhauer very late in his life. In his *A Difficulty in Psycho-analysis* (1917) Freud has already referred to 'words of unforgettable impressiveness' of Schopenhauer, implying that he had read Schopenhauer. Thus it is certain that by the time he published his *Beyond the Pleasure Principle*, he had closely read Schopenhauer. This is strengthened by the fact that he makes a specific reference to Schopenhauer's work in this book.[48] If so, did Schopenhauer influence Freud's concept of the death instinct? Freud of course says:

> We have unwittingly steered our course into the harbour of Schopenhauer's philosophy. For him death is the 'true result and to that extent the purpose of life', while the sexual instinct is the embodiment of the will to live.[49]

As early as 1913, Freud refers in his *Totem and Taboo*, to Schopenhauer's preoccupation with the problem of death. The concept of death instinct is considered one of the most speculative aspects of Freud. It is at this point that Freud makes the reference to the '*nirvāna* principle'[50] inviting Rieff's comment that there is 'something oriental in the Freudian ethic.'[51]

As Freud refers to the '*nirvāna* principle' as an aspect of the death instinct, the concept of death instinct needs careful analysis. The concept of *nirvāna* has a key place in Schopenhauer; it is also the ultimate ideal of the Buddhist. Ernest Jones points out that Freud was influenced by Fechner who in turn was influenced by Buddhism. Regarding the *nirvāna* principle Jones says:

> Dorer has plausibly suggested that it derives from the quietist teaching of Buddhism which is known to have greatly influenced Fechner.[52]

Thus in the case of the *nirvāna* principle, Freud had some contact with Buddhism via an indirect route; Fechner and Schopenhauer. Yet *nirvāna* is not an expression of the death instinct, according to the Buddhist. Freud says that the 'pleasure principle represents the demands of the libido' and 'The *nirvāna* principle expresses the trend of the death instinct.'[53] It is *vibhava-taṇhā* rather than *nirvāna* that can be compared with the death instinct of Freud.

However, as Flugel has shown, there are six strands of meaning that come under the Freudian concept of the death instinct.[54] 1) The universal tendency of living things to suffer dissolution and die, 2) the tendency to achieve and maintain equilibrium in the inorganic and organic world, 3) the tendency to reduce or abolish tension, 4) the repetition compulsion and the restoration of earlier states, 5) source of aggression aims at annihilation of self, redirected outwards as hostility to others, and 6) the death instinct as contrasted with life instinct; the former integrating and uniting and the latter separating and disintegrating.

Of these, point 5) can be compared with *vibhava-taṇhā*. The difference is that the death instinct is originally directed against the self, whereas the Buddhist considers that aggression is usually directed outwards, and only later directed against oneself. However, both systems consider hatred and aggression as a primary base of motivation. It is in fact in his later works like the *Civilization and Its Discontents* that Freud turned his attention to the outward expression of the death instinct; to aggressiveness and destructiveness.[55] Schopenhauer also lays emphasis on the conflict between individuals and the warlike nature of men set free from the bonds of law.

Point 1) can be compared with the Buddhist doctrine of *anicca*. Schopenhauer too refers to the endless change and dissolution in things. Point 3) may be compared to the concept of craving in Buddhism and Schopenhauer, while 2) is similar to 3). Point 3) refers to the physiological and psychological aspects of desire, while point 2) refers to a more general pattern in the universe, both in the organic and inorganic world. However, it may be confusing to equate this principle of equilibrium with the *nirvāna* of the Buddhist. The concept of equilibrium can conceptualise some aspects of *nirvāna,* a state free from tension and conflict. On the other hand, as an expression of the death instinct it can be very misleading. *Nirvāna* cannot be described as an inorganic state of rest or a state of pure quiescence. *Nirvāna* has been described in positive terms like the concepts of perfect health, knowledge, insight, etcetera. It is the culmination of one's spiritual growth and not merely the annihilation of instincts.

Schopenhauer emphasised the negative aspects like the denial of the will and thus perhaps indirectly contributed to strengthening the view that *nirvāna* is annihilation. The concept of repetitive compulsion in point 4) has a parallel in the Buddhist concept of *saṅkhara*, translated as 'karmic formation', 'conative dispositions', etcetera. Schopenhauer's concept of 'will' too contains the idea of repetition as an aspect of its meaning. Regarding 6) Schopenhauer expresses a similar idea: 'generation and death are essentially correlatives, which reciprocally neutralise and annul each other.'[56] An exact correlative of this idea is not found in Buddhism.

In general, it could be said that the concept of death instinct with all its diverse strands of meaning, refers to some puzzling aspects of man's experience. And in this, Freud is attempting to state the nature of a dilemma rather than present a straightforward solution. Not only has he steered his course into the harbour of Schopenhauer's philosophy, but at this point his thinking appears to be nourished by a drop of alien blood (via the route of Fechner and Schopenhauer).

Apart from Freud, Jung is another psychoanalyst who refers to the philosophy of Schopenhauer in most of his works. He has made a study of both Schopenhauer and Buddhist thought and quite clearly says that Schopenhauer was influenced by Buddhism.[57] Though Jung differed from both Schopenhauer and Buddhism regarding certain facts, he certainly attempts to use Schopenhauer as a bridge between Buddhism and his version of psychoanalysis. An interesting example cited by him is the common etymological root of the Latin *libido* and Sanskrit *lobha*. In fact, *lobha* (greed) along with *dosa* (hatred) and *moha* (delusion) are the three roots of motivation according to the Buddha.

In spite of the somewhat obscure and speculative thinking that Jung often displays, he has struck an interesting line of thought by working his ideas, through Schopenhauer, back to Indian thought. All this seems to suggest that behind 'the philosophic climate he (Freud) shared with figures like Schopenhauer and Nietzsche'[58] there are haunting shadows of Indian thought.

TENTATIVE CONCLUSIONS

1) Freud did not knowingly make use of Schopenhauer's ideas as hypotheses for organising his clinical data. This is especially true of some of his specific and limited concepts like repression, Oedipus-complex, infantile sexuality, transference, etcetera.
2) But regarding the more general concepts like the unconscious, libido and death instinct, the possibility of indirect influence cannot be denied. There were others who read Schopenhauer and his ideas belong to the intellectual climate of the time.
3) At some point in his life he did read Schopenhauer closely. In his paper, *A Difficulty in Psycho-analysis* (1917), he refers to Schopenhauer's 'words of unforgettable impressiveness'. In *Beyond the Pleasure Principle* (1920) Freud makes specific references to Schopenhauer's work.
4) Taking into account both indirect influence and some kind of direct influence (after he read Schopenhauer), we could do no better than sum up in the words of R.S. Peters who says of Freud: 'Schopenhauer peered wanly through some of his constructs'.[59]
5) The close agreement between Buddhism and Schopenhauer is evident; some degree of influence of Buddhist and Upanishadic thought on Schopenhauer can be established.
6) Thus it appears that in the philosophy of Schopenhauer, may be present a link between Buddhism and Freud.

APPENDIX II

DOCTRINAL BUDDHISM AND HEALING RITUALS

> 'The analogies between ancient myths and stories that appear in the dreams of modern patients are neither trivial nor accidental. They exist because the unconscious mind of modern man preserves the symbol-making capacity that once found expression in the beliefs and the rituals of the primitive. And that capacity still plays a role of vital psychic importance.' *Man and His Symbols.*[1]

This paper has two main objectives: to examine the therapeutic basis of doctrinal Buddhism in relation to the healing rites of Sri Lanka and to raise the question of whether the psychology of Jung rather than of Freud helps us to grasp the mechanism that pervades the healing rituals.

Why are we interested in these two issues? Our own research into the psychology of Buddhism in the past was focused on a comparative study of Freud and Buddhism.[2] As Carl Jung has displayed a dominant interest in Eastern religions, a natural question one could raise is whether the psychological insights of Jung throw light on any facets of doctrinal Buddhism.

Thinking on these lines it struck us that the later expression of Buddhism through the vehicles of art, literature, myths and symbols should provide an interesting field for a Jungian study. A Jungian analysis of religion appeared to be more meaningful in the light of the later developments of Buddhism and the compromises made with the folk culture.

Another factor that emphasises the value of an exploration into the therapeutic basis of healing rituals is that during recent times there has been considerable interest in such 'primitive psychiatry'. Accounts of illness and healing in rural society which have apparently little in common with psychiatric healing are receiving the careful attention of psychologists and anthropologists today:

> The Shaman, like the physician, tries to cure the patient by correcting the causes of illness. In line with his culture's concept of disease, this cure may involve not only the administration of therapeutic agents but provision of means for confession, atonement, restoration into the good graces of the family and tribe, and intercession with the spirit world. The Shaman's role may thus involve aspects of the roles of physician, magician, priest, moral arbiter, representative of the group's world-view, and agent of social control.[3]

Thus we hope to compare the therapeutic framework of the Buddhist cure for suffering and anxiety with that of the healing rituals.

If we accept the distinction between the 'cognitive' and the 'symbolic' as two modes of mental activity, doctrinal Buddhism is presented in the cognitive mode whereas the healing rituals are expressed through the symbolic mode.[4] In spite of the fact that Freud was a pioneer in the exploration into dream symbols, the god of Freudian psychology was *logos* (reason).

While the comparison of the Buddhist and Freudian psychology was made through the medium of the cognitive mode, there is certainly room for a fascinating study, a Jungian study of Buddhism both with reference to the doctrine as well as its expression in culture, myths and rituals. While it is not intended to undertake a task of such a magnitude in a short paper, we believe that some student of the anthropology of religions will undertake this task in the near future. Our observations here will be limited to an analysis of the therapeutic potential of doctrinal Buddhism in relation to the healing rituals of Sri Lanka.

FOLK RELIGION AND BUDDHISM

Though both the therapeutic aspects of the psychology of Buddhism as well as the cathartic value of the healing rituals have received the attention of scholars as independent subjects for serious study, a comparative study of their respective goals of therapy and the techniques of cure have received scant attention. In some recent sociological studies of the healing rituals queries have been raised and pointers made towards some possible lines of convergence as well as divergence.[5]

The psychology of Buddhism offers a clear analysis of the problem of human suffering and the recommendation of a way out of it. However, while doctrinal Buddhism provided an answer for human suffering and cosmic anxiety, folk beliefs and rituals helped them to deal with the trials and tribulations of daily life. When people were faced with problems like the failure of a crop, famine, disease and mental sickness they often sought the aid of rituals, ceremonies and certain magical devices. Our interest in this paper is in mental sickness and it may be said that in this case the cure offered by western medicine or *ayurveda* did not conflict with the use of healing rituals. The diverse causes for mental sickness like the medical, *ayurvedic*, magical and the demonological are often accommodated within one belief system. The focus of this paper is of course not the relationship between these healing rituals and the other alternatives open to people, but rather the relationship of these healing rituals to the meaning and cure for human suffering as found in the dialogues of the Buddha.

What exactly is the general relationship between the essential ingredients of doctrinal Buddhism and the popular practices of the rituals in the folk religion? Some feel that the popular rituals and the magical practices go counter to the message of the Buddha, while others feel that without any violent contradiction, these practices help the Buddhist to survive the crises of daily life. It appears to us that while some facets of the folk religion, like the use of magic to harm people, unmistakably go counter to the spirit of doctrinal Buddhism, the concepts of 'demonic possession' and 'ritual cure' call for a serious study by students interested in the therapeutic potential of doctrinal Buddhism.

Perhaps some of the healing rituals facilitate a symbolic encounter with facets of human suffering and anxiety which are dealt with in a more prosaic and rational manner in the discourses of the Buddha. If such a deepening and illumination of human suffering is found in some facets of ritual cure, the aesthetic and the therapeutic dimension of these rituals need to be understood from the standpoint of doctrinal Buddhism. It must be mentioned that while our observations are limited to the rituals in Sri Lanka, there are other countries like Thailand and

Burma, where the doctrine of Theravāda prevails like in Sri Lanka, but the healing rituals differ.[6]

There is one more important issue before we get to the main subject; the ontology of demonic existence. In the ritual context, the demons may function at a symbolic level, but the actual existence of spirits and demons is referred to in the suttas. There are references in the dialogues of the Buddha to the existence of evil spirits and demons as well as the heavenly beings and radiant ones. The *Ātānā Suttta* is especially recited to protect people from evil spirits and demons. Rhys Davids says the recitation of something true (*saccakiriya*) has the power to heal. The spirits are dealt with the suffusion of amity rather than enmity:

> The profusion of amity, according to Buddhist doctrine, was no mere matter of pretty speech. It was to accompany and express a psychic suffusion of the hostile man or beast or spirit with benign, fraternal emotion—with metta.[7]

Even in the ritual context, though the demons are the symbols of attachment, lust and frustration, they are converted into more human forms, confronted and tamed. It has even been pointed out that there is a process of movement from excessive craving (represented initially by the demons) to renunciation (taming of the demons).[8]

Perhaps what exactly takes place in this process of transformation is not an existential change in the demon, but merely the way in which we perceive them.[9] Thus it seems that there is at least one central point on which the healing ceremonies as forms of 'psycho-drama' offer an interesting extension of doctrinal Buddhism: the demons present themselves as 'images of excess and craving'.[10] But while both doctrinal Buddhism and the healing rituals deal with the springs of suffering: greed (*lobha*) and hatred (*dosa*), Buddhism does not limit itself to the affective roots of greed and hatred but also the cognitive spring of delusion.

In the final analysis the psychology of doctrinal Buddhism concentrates not merely on the roots of greed and ill-will but the contradictions emerging from the attachment to the ego. It may be possible to articulate this difference in the technical language of the psychology of therapy by saying that the healing rituals are a form of 'symbol therapy' while doctrinal Buddhism is a form of 'cognitive therapy'.

THE JUNGIAN APPROACH AND SYMBOL THERAPY

Jung remarked that he was not content to equate man's creative imagination to infantile wishes like Freud. The problems of life and its anxieties and tensions may be articulated and confronted at a deeper psychic layer through myths, symbols and 'archetypes,' or to use Jungian terminology, at the level of man's collective unconscious:

> ...the analogies between ancient myths and stories that appear in the dreams of modern patients are neither trivial nor accidental. They exist because the unconscious mind of modern man preserves the symbol-making capacity that once found expression in the beliefs and rituals of the primitive. And that capacity still plays a role of vital psychic importance.[11]

Jung divided the unconscious into two parts: the 'personal unconscious' consisting of the individual's forgotten and repressed memories and the 'collective unconscious' shared by all men which is derived from his ancestors. An individual's personal unconscious can be explained in terms of his personal history and the web of emotions, and ideas thus repressed were referred to by the term 'complexes'. But these complexes of the personal unconscious develop in terms of the basic elements of the collective unconscious called the 'archetypes' by Jung. The collective unconscious is a deeper stratum of the unconscious than the personal unconscious; 'it is the unknown material from which our consciousness emerges'.[12]

The tendency to apprehend and experience life in a certain manner conditioned by our past history is described as 'archetypal' by Jung. These 'pre-existent forms of apprehension' are unconscious but we become aware of them through certain typical images which recur in the psyche. Some of the most dominant archetypes are *anima* (inherited image of woman), *animus* (inherited image of man), mother earth, wise man and the devil, etcetera. Thus the widespread recurrence of the same symbols, myths and stories across different cultures and religions interested Jung.

These 'primordial images' can appear through dreams, fantasies, phobias as well as creative literary work. A person can be dominated and possessed by these archetypes as for instance, when he is possessed by a demon.

Jung also uses the term 'shadow' to refer to the dark, repressed and uncivilised desires of man and the term 'persona' to refer to the manner in which one relates oneself to the world. Persona is the socially accepted mask imposed on the person behind which is found the real man. In therapeutic contexts, whether it be a healing ritual or a psychiatric session this mask is unmasked.

We know that unlike the psychiatric encounters, the healing ritual is a communal or a social event and Jung would say that communal participation is possible because of the collective unconscious that cuts across the people who witness the ritual ; the patient, the dancers etcetera.

In the light of this brief resume of Jungian psychology it should be possible to understand what Halverson meant when he referred to the pattern of the *sanniyakuma* as meaningful in the light of Jungian Symbol therapy:

> Indeed, a Jungian analyst would recognize immediately most of the symbolic figures of the ritual as familiar archetypal images of the unconscious... .[13]

THE PROBLEM OF HUMAN SUFFERING

The Buddha was basically concerned with the problem of human suffering summarily described by the Pāli word *dukkha* (and the Sinhala word *duka*). Disease, death, sorrow, lamentation, pain and grief are all facets of *dukkha* and in a deeper sense birth is a facet of *dukkha*. To be joined with the unpleasant, to be separated from the pleasant, and the failure to get what one wants is also suffering. In short, clinging to the five groups of mental and physical qualities that go to make up the individual is suffering.

In translating the Pāli word *dukkha* it is not possible to find one simple word that will compress all the aspects of its meaning. Starting with specific and concrete instances of physical pain and bodily ailments, we discern a broadening group of more abstract meanings: mental sorrow, frustration, conflict, insecurity and anxiety. Then we come to even broader concepts like unsatisfactoriness, disharmony, emptiness and insubstantiality. The genesis of this human predicament tied to pain and suffering is traced to the deep-rooted bases of greed, ill-will and the contradictions emerging from the attachment to the ego.

If we are to use the language of the folk ritual we may say that the demons of greed, rage and egotism cause human misery. Greed takes the dual form of the desire for sensuous gratification and selfish pursuits and ill-will is the base of the destructive urge in man. These desires work both at the conscious and the unconscious level. There are also the healthy bases of human action which evoke liberality, kindness and wisdom. The person who wants to break through the vicious circle of pain and pleasure has to develop the healthy bases of human activity. As this is an arduous task, some accept the ideal of renunciation and become monks, while the others who make a compromise with life, practise the virtuous life advocated by the Buddha within the bounds of the layman's social ethic and spiritual development.

A solution to a problem of human suffering such as this is certainly an ethically and psychologically oriented system of therapy. It leaves out by its very nature the use of rituals, the belief in mysterious powers and magic. The fact that with the passage of time these very components entered into the daily life of the villager has been pointed out by scholars who made a close study of religions in their popular form.

Folk religion is based on a belief in the supernatural and the efficacy of prayers and rituals. But if so, how did these mechanisms sustain the affective dimension of village life? Some scholars feel that unlike Hinduism, Buddhism did not prescribe any specific ritual and that the folk religion found it easy to fill the gap:

> It provided the layman with the means of solving his practical problems—that is, it gave him ceremonies of ensuring the success of his crop, it showed him how to propitiate the deities that cause disease and famine, and it opened up ways of gaining favours from the powers that control the elements. Its priests interceded between man and the unseen agencies, and performed benediction rites for him in the crises of his daily life.[14]

It has also been observed that instead of absorbing non-Buddhist beliefs and practices and thus tarnishing the original doctrine, Buddhism came to a different kind of compromise with the folk religion: the gods and demons of the folk religion became instruments to deal with practical problems and in fact they were subservient to the Buddha in performing these tasks. This is perhaps not the sole answer to the relation between doctrinal and popular Buddhism (as doctrinal Buddhism did get distorted in some way in making this compromise with the folk religion). But this analysis points out distinctly how the doctrine of the Buddha sustained the life of the villager without coming into any violent conflict with the benediction rites and the curing rituals that he practised.

THE HEALING RITUALS

It is not our purpose here to pursue in detail the relationship between doctrinal Buddhism and the folk religion as such, but focus attention on the therapeutic features of 'ritual cure' against the background of the doctrine of the Buddha.

The first point that has to be mentioned is that there is a great deal of symbolism in these healing rituals. If we take for instance the ritual dance of the *sanni* demons it will be seen that the 'concept of the demonic' has a symbolic role to play. The concept of the demonic helps the people to symbolise and dramatise the emerging passions of greed, rage, terror and anxiety. The demons possess the human beings because humans have greed, anger and attachment. The demonic in the ritual situation symbolises these passions in man as the concept of *mara* in doctrinal Buddhism represents the forces of evil which obstruct the man bent on seeking contentment and serenity.

It may be said that doctrinal Buddhism is concerned with the basic context of the suffering human being in a wide cosmic setting which stands in contrast with the role of folk rituals dealing with famine, misfortune, sickness and mental instability. Though the range of doctrinal Buddhism in this context is both wider and deeper than that of folk religion, the points at which they cut across the question of mental sickness should be interesting. In fact, a recent researcher in this field has made an interesting observation:

> Doctrinal Buddhism, as I have shown, places great emphasis on the problem of suffering, and curing rituals deal with suffering in everyday life. It seems reasonable to suspect that there are 'deeper affinities' (Geertz) between these two expressions of the problem of suffering than are apparent from a hierarchical rendering of their relationship. This is particularly likely when we consider that there is less clear-cut contradiction between Buddhism and practical religion than is sometimes assumed in delineating the differences between them.[15]

The use of symbolism, imagery and metaphor form a part of the aesthetic dimension in which the doctrine of the Buddha relating to the problem of human suffering is presented. Dramatisation or literary presentations of the doctrine supplement the analytical mode through which the doctrine is presented. But the diagnosis and remedial measures advocated by the Buddha are a systematic and methodical approach to the development of mental culture. It is in this context that any comparison with folk rituals should be made. Assuming that the symbolisation of psychological conflicts enriched by Buddhist terminology offers an interesting point of convergence, what can we say about the other elements in the healing rituals?

CATHARSIS

The cathartic function of these healing rituals has been commented on by those who have made a close study of them. Certain demons are capable of causing particular ailments and in many cases it is possible to identify the demon that has to be exorcised. These demons are attracted by blood, faeces, oily food, sex, lonely places and the power of sorcery etcetera. The demons symbolise human greed and attachment and have the power to arouse a sense of terror in people.

In the ritual situation these awe-inspiring beings are brought down to earth in human forms. They are 'stripped of their mythological trappings' and subjected to jokes, humour and obscenity.[16] It has also been observed that we do not meet them only as human beings but as a part of ourselves. This process of converting the 'demonic' into the 'ludicrous' is not merely an encounter with the demonic within one's own dark interior, but perhaps a way of laughing at oneself.

Can this kind of 'catharsis' be accommodated within the authentic fold of doctrinal Buddhism? The concept of catharsis itself has a number of components. Aristotle used the concept to describe the purification of the emotions: this could mean that emotional tensions are lessened by expressing them in aesthetic experience or refined by sharing in emotions universalised and artistically portrayed. In the psychoanalytic context, there is a release of tension by reliving past incidents (abreaction). Catharsis in the context of folk belief could mean that uninhibited expressive behaviour in one situation reduces the need for it in similar situations.[17]

There is nothing peculiarly Buddhist about the release of pent-up emotions. But the attempt to master tensions and anxieties by breaking through layers of repression, bringing them into the open by presenting them in a universalised artistic or religious idiom should be of interest to the Buddhist. Tranquillity is an ideal of one form of Buddhist meditation, but it is not preceded by a kind of 'bursting out', a storm before the calm. In the final analysis, the therapeutic aim of doctrinal Buddhism is to develop self-analysis, self-knowledge and insight. Insights refer to one's own nature, the perception of other persons and the nature of the world.

If a patient who takes part in a ritual emerges out of it with a sense of relief but 'knows not why', there is no development of self-knowledge. It is of course possible that the audience that witnesses the ritual derives a higher form of catharsis by re-enacting their own conflicts plus the obtaining of an insight both regarding themselves and the patient. We of course know that the kind of atmosphere generated by the chanting of *pirith* has a tranquillising effect, and that some of the musical components of the healing rituals have a tranquillising effect on the patient. But if the concept of 'ritual cure' implies that there is emotional relief without personal insight, here perhaps is a line of demarcation between the therapy of doctrinal Buddhism and that of the healing rituals.

Another problem relevant to the issue under discussion is the concept of 'personal responsibility' in relation to the patient. The fact that the cause for illness is accountable in terms of demonic possession does not make the patient committed or responsible for the illness. It has even been observed that the process by which mental sickness is centred on supernatural causation rather than a sense of personal responsibility makes way for quick recovery: when the 'self' remains unchanged it is easy for a person to shed the sick role quickly.[18]

This facet of 'ritual cure' may conflict with the concept of moral responsibility that runs through the Buddhist scriptures:

> 'Tis by self that evil is done, 'tis by self
> One comes to grief; 'tis by self that evil is left
> Undone; 'tis by self that one is purified;
> The pure, the impure, both are of the self.[19]

The answer that may be given to this query is that hidden facets of the self are brought out by the symbolic identification with the demonic. It may be also said that it is difficult to apply the notion of responsibility to abnormal and deranged minds. Finally, society also works out its own mechanisms of coming to terms with aberrant behaviour in a humane way, and long before the emergence of psychiatry and healing rituals played this role.

OBSESSIVE ACTIONS AND RELIGIOUS PRACTICES: THE FREUDIAN CRITIQUE

Sigmund Freud remarks that there is a resemblance between 'neurotic ceremonials and the sacred acts of religious ritual'.[20] Freud made a comparison of the ceremonies followed by obsessive neurotics and those of religious practices and said that both were fed by an inner compulsion. In spite of the fact that one was done in privacy and the other in the larger community he thought the resemblance was important. They spring from a certain sense of guilt and fear and are designed both to keep out temptations together with possible punishment. While sexual impulses dominate in obsessive neurosis, selfish and aggressive impulses have to be dealt with in religion. Freud came to the conclusion that obsessive neurosis was the pathological counterpart of religion.

It is of course not necessary to accept the Freudian analysis completely and reject the health-giving healing rituals as a kind of obsessive neurosis. But the question is important as the Buddha himself criticised some misguided religious cults and rituals of his time and brought them under the term, 'rite and ritual clinging' (*sīlabbata-parāmāsa*). The term *parāmāsa* suggests that one clings to these rituals with a feeling of compulsion rather than a judicious understanding of their function; in the Buddhist context it came to mean the man who is attached to the merely outer ceremonial aspect of rules rather than their internal meaning. Religious fetishes like bathing in the river, wearing hides and penances would fall into this category. If the healing ritual provides through its symbolism an opportunity for a deeper encounter with one's anxieties rather than an external purification ceremony for washing away sins, it need not be considered as an expression of 'rites and ritual clinging'. In fact, the Buddha has said that even 'clinging to the Dhamma' is an obstruction to one's spiritual development. A raft is only for crossing the river; if someone carries it on his head after crossing, he does not understand the purpose for which the raft is intended; and so it is with the Dhamma.

Some of the religious fetishes mentioned by Freud, like the instance of hand-washing, are expressions of obsessions and compulsions. The Buddha too exposed the vacuity of forms of purification which were merely external. Doctrinal Buddhism encourages man to develop a healthy sense of moral dread and shame (*hiri-ottappa*) but uneasiness of conscience, remorse and worry are an obstruction for spiritual development. Guilt-laden rituals and the self-punishing ascetics violate the spirit of the healthy sense of dread advocated by the Buddha. To use the vocabulary of Kleinian psychology, Buddhism can accommodate a concept of 'reparative guilt' rather than one of 'persecutory guilt'. Doctrinal Buddhism did not encourage the development of a guilt-complex or rituals to deal with them:

> In the place of priestly rituals he offered a radical inward purification of the springs from which outer evils arise: attachment, aversion, spiritual blindness. He was as realistic as St. Paul or Freud in recognizing the egocentric, lustful, hostile and grasping proclivities of unawakened man; he set forth a way to uproot them...and founded a religion which in general seems to have produced far fewer neurotic guilt feelings than has Judaism or Christianity.[21]

SOME POSITIVE THOUGHTS

Now that we have weighed the *pros* and *cons* regarding the case for healing rituals in terms of doctrinal Buddhism, we would like to conclude this analysis with some positive thoughts at a deeper level of understanding the Buddhist doctrine as well as the healing rituals. An entry into this dimension of thinking may be made by an analysis of the meaning of *dukkha* with which we started our exposition of Buddhism.[22]

A deeper grasp of the *dukkha* concept involves a 'perception of incongruities' and the catharsis in the ritual context is generated by a concept of the ludicrous—placing the fearful in a playful setting. Though laughter as such does not figure prominently in the teachings of the Buddha, there is a deep sense of the ludicrous embedded in the doctrine of the Buddha. This is a dimension of experience that has entered the Zen Buddhist tradition.

Dukkha in this context may be rendered as tragi-comedy—the discrepancy between my self which I automatically assume to be permanent, and the only too manifestly impermanent things which I strive to possess in the temporal object. The situation is at once both *comic* and *tragic*. Here both tragedy and comedy are ways of apprehending contradictions:

> There are little cracks and fissures in our complacent serious-minded existence, and the reason why we laugh at them is to keep them at a distance, to charm them, to exorcize them, to neutralize them.[23]

When we laugh at a comedy or weep at a tragedy, what we are doing is busying ourselves repairing all the little crevices that have appeared in our familiar world in the course of the day.[24] This profound sense of the ludicrous has gone along with its Buddhist inspiration to the folk poetry of the villagers. To cite one instance in *Aspects of Sinhalese Culture*:[25]

> Tired, carrying a pingo of pots and pans
> At an ambalama I rested.
> The pots and pans a bull did smash
> At which I laughed and laughed.

On the day before Sinhalese New Year a village potter was carrying a *pingo* of pots and pans either as a present or for sale. Being tired, he entered a dilapidated *ambalama* to rest. A bull resting in a corner of the *ambalama* rushed out in fright, smashing the pots and pans. On seeing the havoc caused he says, 'I laughed and laughed.'[26] The word 'pottery' is a proverbial metaphor for impermanence, and it is often used in the Buddhist texts as a metaphor. Like the bull, death will smash the worldly life of any man. The folk poetry of the Sinhalese is rich in such Buddhist insights presented in a humorous vein. The ability to look at life with a sense of equanimity provides the Buddhist a rich base for the development of a profound sense of humour and irony. Such philosophical insights into the nature of human suffering may be found in the doctrine, healing rituals and folk poetry.

THE GAP BETWEEN THE HEALING RITUALS AND DOCTRINAL BUDDHISM

While it is possible to see interesting points of convergence as we pointed out between the healing rituals and doctrinal Buddhism, basically the healing rituals are a form of Jungian symbol therapy while Buddhist therapy will not fit into such a description. Halverson commenting on the 'Dynamics of Exorcism' in the *Sinhalese Sanniyakuma* says that the experience of cure undergone by the patient is symbolic rather than cognitive:

> Yet whatever he experiences, it can be hardly at the level of cognition; that level of the ritual is at very best slight. The symbolism, on the contrary, is extremely rich and pervasive. The close attention given by the patient is perforce directed to the pre-cognitive symbols.[27]

The patient does not translate the symbolic into cognitive terms, rather 'the symbolic patterns of the ritual correspond to and activate parallel patterns in the patient's unconscious mind on a principle of homology.'[28] Thus the kind of therapy found in the healing rituals is close to Jungian symbol therapy.

The Freudian 'id', the Jungian 'shadow' and the Buddhist *āsavas* all depict the alien, primitive and irrational in man. But while Jung adopts a symbolic mode of confrontation with the irrational, Buddhism offers a cognitive mode of confrontation with the irrational. These basic modes of therapeutic confrontation may supplement each other.

FOOTNOTES

FOREWORD

[1] Thouless, *Conventionalization and Assimilation in Religious Movements as Problems in Social Psychology, with special reference to the development of Buddhism and Christianity*, 1940.

[2] Muller, 'The Foundation of the Kingdom of Righteousness' (*Dhamma-Cakkappavattana Sutta*), *Sacred Books of the East*, XI, Ed. Oxford.

[3] Wells, *God the Invisible King*.

[4] Stevenson, *Twenty Cases Suggestive of Reincarnation*, 1966.

PRELUDE

[1] Fromm, *The Art of Listening*, 1994, p. 180.

[2] Safran, quoted by Unno, *Buddhism and Psychotherapy: Across Cultures*, 2006, p. 1.

[3] Aronson, *Buddhist Practice on Western Grounds*, 2004, p. 56.

[4] Engler, 'Promises and Perils of the Spiritual Path', Unno, ed. ibid., 2006, p. 17.

[5] Epstein, *Going to Pieces Without Falling Apart*, 2008, p. 14.

[6] Epstein, 'Psychotherapy Without the Self: A Buddhist Perspective,' Safran, ed., *Psychoanalysis and Buddhism: An unfolding Dialogue*, 2007, p. 15.

[7] op cit, 22.

[8] de Silva, *An Introduction to Mindfulness-Based Counselling*, 2008, pp. 128-131.

[9] Rubin, *Psychoanalytic and Buddhist Conceptions of Self*, 1996, p. 66, also cited in de Silva, ibid., 2008, pp. 121-134.

[10] Kumar, *Grieving Mindfully*, 2005, p. 9.

[11] Ladner, *The Lost Art of Compassion*, 2004, p. xv.

[12] de Silva, ibid., 2008, p. 82-98.
[13] Lutz, 'Need, Nurturance and Emotions On a Pacific Atoll', Marks & Ames, eds. *Emotions in Asian Thought*, p. 1995.
[14] Engler, ibid., 2006, p. 26.
[15] Oatley, *Emotions: A Brief History*, 2004, p. 53.
[16] Epstein, ibid., 2007, p. 5.
[17] op cit, p. 6.
[18] James, *Principles of Psychology*, 1963, p. 51.
[19] de Silva, ibid., 1992, p. 119 & Fromm, *The Heart of Man*, 1964, p. 88.
[20] de Silva, ibid., 1992, 148 & Flugel, ibid, 1955, p. 140.
[21] de Silva, ibid., 2005, p. 94-97.

CHAPTER ONE
[1] Soma Thera, *Kālāma Sutta*, 1959.
[2] Fromm, *Psychoanalysis and Religion*, 1961, p. 38.
[3] S.E. Vol. XXI.
[4] Rieff, *Freud: The Mind of the Moralist*, 1959, p. 1.
[5] Fromm, *Beyond the Chains of Illusion, My Encounter with Marx and Freud*, 1962, p. 17.
[6] MacIntyre, *The Unconscious: A Conceptual Analysis*, 1958, p. 93.
[7] Fromm, Suzuki & Martino, *Zen Buddhism and Psychoanalyis*, 1960, p. 80
[8] Auden, *The Age of Anxiety: a baroque eclogue*, 1947.
[9] Eliot, *The Wasteland*, 1992.
[10] S.E. Vol. XXI.
[11] Sartre, *Nausea*, 1959
[12] de Silva, 'Buddhism and the Tragic Sense of Life', *University of Ceylon Review*, Vol. 25, Ceylon.
[13] Fromm, Suzuki & de Martino, ibid., pp. 77-141.

CHAPTER TWO
[1] See Section on *viññāna*, chapter two.
[2] Nyanatiloka Thera, *Guide through the Abhidhammapitaka*, Ch. VII, 1957.
[3] Anuruddha, *Compendium of Philosophy*, (*Abhidhammattha-Saṅghaha*), 1963.
[4] Flugel, *Studies in Feeling and Desire*, 1955, p. 49.
[5] Jayasuriya, *The Psychology and Philosophy of Buddhism*, p. 16.

[6] Sarachchandra, *Buddhist Psychology of Perception*, 1958, p. 3.
[7] S.I., p. 15.
[8] D. II, 337-339.
[9] Jayatilleke, *Buddhism and Science*, 1958, p. 3.
[10] ibid.
[11] Sarachchandra, ibid., p. 20.
[12] D. II, 62, 63; S II, 6,8,12; S III, 102.
[13] Sarachchandra, ibid., p. 20.
[14] op cit.
[15] op cit, pp. 15-21.
[16] Wijesekera, 'Vitalism and Becoming: a Comparative Study,' *Ceylon University Review*, Vol. I, No. 1, pp. 49-58.
[17] D. II, 62.
[18] Wijesekera, ibid.
[19] D. II, 62.
[20] M. II, 262.
[21] Broad, *The Mind and its Place in Nature*, 1929, p. 551.
[22] S. II, 11.
[23] S. II, 12
[24] D. III, 105.
[25] M. I, 69.
[26] S. II, 217.
[27] Jayatilleke, *Early Buddhist Theory of Knowledge*, p. 438.
[28] Jayatilleke, *Survival and Karma*.
[29] M. I, 190.
[30] ibid.
[31] Sarachchandra, ibid. p. 4.
[32] M. III, 281.
[33] Wijesekera, 'The Concept of *Viññāna* in Theravāda Buddhism', *Journal of the American Oriental Society*, July-September 1964.
[34] M. III, 196.
[35] ibid.
36 S. III, 9.
[37] S. II, 11.
[38] Nyanatiloka Thera, *Buddhist Dictionary: Manual of Terms and Doctrines*, 1956, p. 148.
[39] M. I, 206.

[40] Nyanatiloka Thera, ibid., p. 148.
[41] M.I, 301.
[42] Rhys Davids and Stede, *Pāli Text Society's Pāli-English Dictionary*, p. 122.
[43] M. I, XXV.
[44] ibid.
[45] Jayatilleke, 'Some Problems of Translation', *Ceylon University Review*, Volumes, 7 and 8.
[46] S. III, 60.
[47] Rhys Davids and Stede, ibid., VIII, p. 123.
[48] Nyanatiloka Thera, ibid., p. 148.
[49] D. III, 218.
[50] S. II, 82.
[51] Anuruddha, *Compendium of Philosophy*, (*Abhidhammattha-Saṅgaha*), p.274.
[52] op cit.
[53] op cit.
[54] A. I, III.
[55] Anuruddha, ibid., p. 274.
[56] Mrs. Rhys Davids, ed. and trans., *Buddhist Psychological Ethics* (*Dhamma Sangani*), 1900, p. 34, n. 1.
[57] Jayatilleke, 'Some Problems of Translation,' *University of Ceylon Review*, Volume 7, p. 216.
[58] Flugel, *Studies in Feeling and Desire*, 1955, p. 49.
[59] Mrs. Rhys Davids, ibid., p. 6.
[60] Buddhaghosa, *The Expositor* (*Atthasālinī*), 1958, p. 145.
[61] M. I, 397-398.
[62] M. I, 398 (see translator's notes 3-9).
[63] M. I, 303.
[64] Nyanatiloka Thera, ibid, 1956, p. 94.
[65] lugel, ibid., p. 61.
[66] Buddhaghosa, *The Path of Purification* (*Visuddhimagga*), p. 656.
[67] Kaccayana Thera, *Netti-ppakaranam*, p. 124.
[68] Mrs. Rhys Davids, ibid., p. 7, n. 2.
[69] Jayasuriya, *The Psychology and Philosophy of Buddhism*, 1963, p. 69, n. 2.
[70] M. I, 293.
[71] Buddhaghosa, ibid., p. 146.
[72] ibid.
[73] M. I, 41, 160.

[74] S.E. Vol. XXIII: an outline of psychoanalysis.
[75] J. C. Flugel, ibid., p. 79.
[76] Hook, ed., *Psychoanalysis, Scientific Method and Philosophy*, 1959, I:I.
[77] op cit.
[78] op cit.
[79] S.E. Volume XXIII, p. 145, author's emphasis.
[80] op cit.
[81] S.E. Vol. XXII, p. 74.
[82] op cit, p. 73, author's emphasis.
[83] S.E. Vol. XIX.
[84] Peters, *The Concept of Motivation*, 1958.
[85] S.E. Vol. XII.
[86] Peters, ibid., p. 69.
[87] MacIntyre, *The Unconscious: A Conceptual Analysis*, 1958.
[88] op cit, p. 90.
[89] op cit, p. 93.
[90] Mrs. Rhys Davids, ibid.
[91] See chapter four.
[92] Ledi Sayadaw, *The Manual of Insight*, 1961, p. 80.
[93] Taylor, *Dynamic and Abnormal Psychology*, 1954, p. 2.
[94] Jayasuriya, *The Psychology and Philosophy of Buddhism*, 1963, p. 100.
[95] de Silva, *An Analysis of Some Psychological Concepts in Early Buddhism*, 1965, p. 6.
[96] Rieff, *Freud: The Mind of the Moralist*, 1959.
[97] Nimalasuriya, *The Buddha as a Healer*, 1960, p. 25.
[98] Jayatilleke, *Buddhism and Peace*, 1962, p. 12.
[99] Fromm, Suzuki & de Martino, ibid., p. 81.
[100] op cit, p. 84.
[101] Jones, *The Life and Work of Sigmund Freud*, Vol. I, 1957, p. 320.
[102] Rieff, ibid., p. 317.
[103] Chandavimala Thero, *Cittopakleśa Dīpani* (*An Analysis of Defilers of Mind*), 1961.

CHAPTER THREE

[1] MacIntyre, *The Unconscious: A Conceptual Analysis*, 1958, pp. 29-32.
[2] op cit, p. 29.

[3] Freud, *Collected Papers, Volume IV*, 1949, pp. 26-27.
[4] Wolman, editor, *Scientific Psychology*, 1965, p. 377.
[5] MacIntyre, ibid., p. 25.
[6] Chapter three. See references to Jung's *Collective Unconscious and the ālayavijñāna.*
[7] S.E. Vol. XIV.
[8] S.E. Vol. XIX.
[9] Gill, 'Topography and Systems in Psychoanalytic theory', *Psychological Issues*, p. 128.
[10] op cit.
[11] See S.E. 7 Vol. XIX for a development of this theme.
[12] English & English. *English Dictionary of Psychological and Psychoanalytical Terms.*
[13] op cit.
[14] Badget, ed., *Subconscious Phenomena*, pp. 9-15.
[15] S.E. Vol. II.
[16] S.E. Vol. XVI, p. 296.
[17] Miller, *Unconsciousness*, pp. 22-24.
[18] op cit, p. 26.
[19] op cit, p. 41.
[20] Levitt, editor, *Readings in Psychoanalytic Psychology*, 1:3, 1959, p. 31 & Hook, *Psychoanalysis, Scientific Method and Philosophy*, 1959, p. 284.
[21] Levitt, ed. ibid., p. 284.
[22] Hook, ibid., p. 284.
[23] MacIntyre, ibid., 1958.
[24] op cit, p. 43.
[25] op cit, p. 57.
[26] Broad, *The Mind and its Place in Nature*, 1929, pp. 363-364.
[27] op cit., p. 367.
[28] Beck, 'Conscious and Unconscious Motives', *Mind*, 1966, pp. 155-179.
[29] A. II, 79.
[30] Sarachchandra, *The Buddhist Psychology of Perception*, 1958, p. 75.
[31] op cit, p. 91.
[32] op cit, p. 96.
[33] op cit, p. 19.
[34] op cit, p. 78.
[35] Anuruddha, *Compendium of Philosophy*, 1963, p. 266.

[36] op cit.
[37] Nyanatiloka Thera, *Buddhist Dictionary: Manual of Terms and Doctrines*, 1956, p. 29.
[38] ibid., p. 29-30.
[39] Sarachchandra, *The Buddhist Psychology of Perception*, 1958, p. 49 & Buddhaghosa, *The Path of Purification* (*Visuddhimagga*), 1964, p. 515
[40] op cit, p. 75.
[41] D. III, 105.
[42] Jayatilleke, 'Some Problems of Translation and Interpretation,' *University of Ceylon Review*, Vol. 7, p. 216 & Jayatilleke, 'Buddhism and Peace, ' *Wheel Publication*, Kandy, Ceylon, 1962, p. 12. Jayatilleke has taken a different line of interpretation in his later writings. 'It is also said of a living person that part of his "stream of consciousness" (*viññāna-sota*) is present in this world (*idha-loke patiṭṭhitaṃ*) and part in the world beyond (*para-loke patiṭṭhitaṃ*) without a sharp division into two parts (*ubhayato abbochinnaṃ*)' D. III. 105. This means that a man's stream of consciousness has a conscious and an unconscious component. Our conscious mental activity gradually gets into this unconscious and accumulates in it, continuing to influence our conscious behaviour.' 'The Buddhist Analysis of Mind', *Unpublished Paper*, 1968. Even this interpretation accepts the existence of an unconscious.
[43] Jayatilleke, ibid., p. 216.
[44] A. II. 158; S. II 36-41.
[45] Rhys Davids and Stede, *The Pāli Text Society's Pāli-English Dictionary*.
[46] S. III, 130.
[47] Nyanatiloka Thera, *Guide Through the Abhidhamma-Piṭaka*, 1957, p. 104.
[48] D. III, 254.
[49] M.I., 303.
[50] M.I., 433.
[51] Buddhaghosa, ibid., I: 5.
[52] Sayadaw, *Manual of Insight*, 1961, p. 80.
[53] op cit., p. 81.
[54] Buddhaghosa, ibid., I:5, A. I. 233.
[55] Jayasuriya, *The Psychology and Philosophy of Buddhism*, p. 108.
[56] Conze, *Buddhist Thought in India*, 1962, p. 132.
[57] M. I., trans. I.B. Horner, *P.T.S.*, London, 1954, P. XXIII.

[58] Mrs. Rhys Davids, *Buddhist Psychological Ethics* (*Dhamma Sangani*), 1900, p. 291.
[59] Buddhaghosa, *The Expositor* (*Atthasālinī*), 1958, p. 63.
[60] Chandavimala Thera, *Cittopaklesa Dipani: An Analysis of the Defilers of the Mind*, 1961.
[61] Buddhaghosa, ibid., p. 257.
[62] Chandavimala Thera, ibid., p. 163.
[63] op cit, p. 174.
[64] Smart, *Doctrine and Argument in Indian Philosophy*, 1964, p. 58.
[65] Jung, *Two Essays in Analytic Psychology*, 1965, p. 313, n. 15.
[66] de Silva, *An Analysis of Some Psychological Concepts in Freud and Early Buddhism*, 1965, p. 172.
[67] Conze, ibid., p. 133.
[68] Rahula, 'Ālayavijñāna' (Store Consciousness)', 1964, p. 57.
[69] op cit., p. 56.
[70] op cit., p. 56, n. 5.
[71] Suzuki, *Studies in the Lankavatara Sutra*, 1930, pp. 179-180.
[72] Sarachchandra, *The Buddhist Psychology of Perception*, 1958, p. 94.
[73] Suzuki, ibid., pp. 179-180.
[74] op cit, p. 258.
[75] Fromm, Suzuki & de Martino, ibid., p. 97.
[76] op cit, p. 108.
[77] op cit, p. 109.
[78] Horner, trans. *The Book of the Discipline* (*Vinaya-Piṭaka*), 1949, I:III:112.
[79] Sarachchandra, ibid. & Anurudha, *Compendium of Philosophy* (*Abhidhammattha-Saṅgaha*), 1963.
[80] Mrs. Rhys Davids, trans. *The Questions of King Milinda* (*Milinda Panha*), S. B. E., Vol. 36, p. 298.
[81] Horner, ibid., III: 112.
[82] Beck, 'Conscious and Unconscious Motives', *Mind*, 1966, pp. 155-179.
[83] M. III, 2.
[84] de Silva, ibid.
[85] Rieff, *Freud: The Mind of the Moralist*, 1959, p. 392.
[86] S.E. Vol. II, p. 305.
[87] S.E. Vol. XXIII, pp. 216-253.
[88] S.E. Vol. XXI, p. 86.

CHAPTER FOUR

[1] Atkinson, *An Introduction to Motivation*, 1964, p. 1.
[2] op cit.
[3] Peters, *The Concept of Motivation*, 1958, p.3.
[4] op cit, p. 1.
[5] op cit, p. 3.
[6] S.E. Vol. XIV.
[7] Rapaport, 'On the Psychoanalytic Theory of Motivation', *Nebraska symposium on Motivation*, 1960, p. 191.
[8] op cit.
[9] S.E. Vol. VII.
[10] S.E. Vol. XIV.
[11] op cit.
[12] op cit.
[13] S.E. Vol. XVIII.
[14] Rapaport, ibid., p. 196.
[15] Jayatilleke, *Early Buddhist Theory of Knowledge*, 1963, p. 126. & Nyanatiloka Thera, *Guide Through the Abhidhammapitaka*, p. 117.
[16] op cit, p. 118.
[17] Jones, *The Life and Work of Freud*, Vol. II, 1963, p. 283.
[18] S.E. Vol. XVIII, p. 137.
[19] Rickman, *A General Selection From the Works of Freud*, 1953, p. 205.
[20] S.E. Vol. XXIII, p. 148.
[21] Freud, *A General Introduction to Psychoanalysis*, 1960, p. 365.
[22] S.E. Vol. VII, p. 148.
[23] op cit, p. 149.
[24] op cit, p. 156.
[25] Rickman, ibid., p. 28.
[26] Freud, ibid., p. 323.
[27] op cit, p. 341.
[28] op cit, p. 342.
[29] Suttie, *Origins of Love and Hate*, 1935.
[30] S.E. Vol. XXI, p. 196.
[31] S.E. Vol. XVIII, p. 103.
[32] Freud, *Collected Papers*, p. 165.
[33] Rieff, *Freud: The Mind of the Moralist*, p. 165.

[34] op cit, p. 327.
[35] op cit, p. 31.
[36] op cit, p. 34.
[37] op cit, p. 158.
[38] A. IV, 53-54.
[39] S .IV, 9.
[40] M. I, 397.
[41] op cit, 303.
[42] op cit, 506.
[43] op cit, 303-304.
[44] A. I, 80.
[45] A commentary on the *Kamasutta* in the *Sutta Nipata.*
[46] Nyanatiloka, *Dictionary of Buddhist Terms*, 1956, p. 190.
[47] S. IV, 60.
[48] op cit, p. 68.
[49] S.E. Vol. VII, p. 148.
[50] D. II, 59.
[51] M. I, 73.
[52] D. III, 180.
[53] A. V, 176.
[54] M. I. 88.
[55] Freud, *Civilization and Its Discontents*, 1957, p. 22.
[56] M. I. 85.
[57] op cit, 132.
[58] A. IV. 53-54.
[59] op cit.
[60] A. IV. 195.
[61] A. I, 1.
[62] A. III, 95.
[63] Rickman ed., *A General Selection From the Works of Sigmund Freud*, 1953, p. 205.
[64] A father-centred or a mother-centred attachment of an erotic nature. Intense attachment to the parent of the opposite sex and antagonism against the parent of the same sex.
[65] Suttie, ibid.
[66] Fromm, *Art of Loving*, 1962, p. 13.
[67] Reik, *Of Love and Lust*, 1959.

[68] Fromm, ibid., p. 13.
[69] op cit, p. 85.
[70] D. III, Sutta 31.
[71] A. III, 226.
[72] *Sutta-Nipata*, 36.
[73] ibid., verse 37.
[74] S. IV, 326-329.
[75] *Dhammapada*, 213.
[76] A. IV, 328.
[77] op cit, 340-343.
[78] Wijesekera, *Three Signata*, 1960, pp. 9-10.
[79] See p.
[80] See p.
[81] S.E. Vol. VII, p. 156.
[82] op cit.
[83] S.E. Vol. XXII, p. 74.
[84] op cit.
[85] M. I. 433.
[86] S.E. Vol. XIX, p. 18.
[87] Fromm, *The Heart of Man*, p. 62.
[88] A very clear analysis of the concept of the ego is found in his ego and the id, S.E. Vol. XIX, p. 25.
[89] S.E. Vol. XIX, p. 25.
[90] op cit, p. 27.
[91] Freud, *Civilization and Its Discontents*, p. 12.
[92] ibid., p. 10.
[93] S.E. Vol. XIV.
[94] op cit, p. 73.
[95] op cit, pp. 73-74.
[96] op cit, p. 88.
[97] op cit, pp. 90-91.
[98] Freud, *A General Introduction to Psychoanalysis*, 1960, p. 424.
[99] This aspect has been discussed by Adler in his concept of the inferiority complex.
[100] S.E. Vol. XX.
[101] Anna Freud, *The Ego and the Mechanism of Defence*, 1946.
[102] Fromm, *The Heart of Man*, 1964, p. 88.

[103] op cit.
[104] See p.
[105] Nyanaponika, *Anatta and Nibbana*, 1959, pp. 2-4.
[106] op cit., p. 2.
[107] Unamuno, *The Tragic Sense of Life*, 1921.
[108] Freud, *Future of an Illusion*, S.E. Vol. XXI.
[109] Nyanaponika, ibid., p. 3.
[110] S. III, 2-4.
[111] Freud, 'Analysis Terminable and Interminable,' *Collected Papers*, Vol. V.
[112] The notion of the collective unconscious has also been developed by Jung.
[113] Freud, *Moses and Monotheism*, 1955, p. 127.
[114] A. III, 356-359.
[115] See also Freud's *Mourning and Melancholia*, S.E. Vol. XIV.
[116] Fromm, *Psychoanalysis and Religion*, 1959.
[117] M. I. Sutta 30.
[118] S. III, 235.
[119] S. I, 221-222, S. II, 29
[120] S. I, 222.
[121] S. II, 29.
[122] A. I, 148.
[123] S.E. Vol. XIV, p. 249.
[124] op cit, p. 251.
[125] op cit, p. 252.
[126] op cit, p. 252.
[127] Reik, *Masochism in Modern Man*, 1941, p. 234.
[128] The five lower fetters are personality-belief, sceptical doubt, clinging to mere rules and rituals, sensuous craving and ill-will.
[129] Jones, *Life and Work of Freud*, 1963, p. 340.
[130] ibid.
[131] Flugel, *Studies in Feeling and Desire*, 1955, p. 99.
[132] Ernest Jones, ibid., p. 302.
[133] S.E. Vol. XIV, p. 252.
[134] S.E. Vol. XVIII.
[135] op cit, p. 15.
[136] op cit, p. 22.
[137] op cit, p. 53.

[138] op cit, p. 54.
[139] op cit.
[140] Jones, ibid., p. 266.
[141] Flugel, *Man, Morals and Society*, 1955, p. 125.
[142] ibid., p. 97.
[143] S. II, 12.
[144] *P.T.S. Pali English Dictionary*, 1952.
[145] ibid.
[146] D. II, p. 340, Note I.
[147] Mrs. Rhys Davids, *Manual of Buddhism for Advanced Students*, 1932.
[148] A. IV, 97.
[149] M. III, Sutta 102.
[150] M. III, 232-233.
[151] *Udana*, 32.
[152] Roubiczek, *Thinking in Opposites*, 1952, p. 72.
[153] op cit, p. 72.
[154] op cit.
[155] M. I, 140.
[156] See the section on the death instinct.
[157] M. I, 141.
[158] M. Sutta 75.
[159] D. II, 307.
[160] Milinda Panha, Part I, 44, *Sacred Books of the East*, Vol. XXXV, 1890.
[161] D. II, 331.
[162] Quoted by Poussin, E.R.E. Vol. XXI, p. 25.
[163] M. I, 10.
[164] *It*. 49.
[165] M. I, 137.
[166] Poussin, E.R.E., Vol. XII, p. 25.
[167] *Milinda Panha*, Part I:73.
[168] Flugel, ibid., p. 59.
[169] Freud, *Beyond the Pleasure Principle*, S.E. Vol. XVIII.
[170] M. III, 232-233.
[172] Nyanamoli, *Three Cardinal Discourses of the Buddha*, 1960, p. 19.
[173] Freud, *A Critical Evaluation of His Theories*, 1962, p. 74, author's emphasis.
[174] Freud, *Collected Papers*, Vol. V.

CHAPTER FIVE

[1] E.R.E., Vol. II, p. 71.
[2] Fromm, *Psychoanalysis and Religion*, 1961.
[3] Flugel, *Man, Morals and Society*, 1955, p. 40.
[4] S. IV, 118.
[5] M. I, 36.
[6] S. I, 169.
[7] E.R.E. Vol. XIII, p. 25.
[8] M. II, 214.
[9] E.R.E. Vol. II, p. 70.
[10] A. III, 230.
[11] Buddhaghosa, *The Expositor* (*Atthasalini*), p. 165.
[12] Mrs. Rhys Davids, ed. and trans. *Buddhist Psychological Ethics*, 1900, p. 20, n. 1.
[13] A. I, 149.
[14] M. III, 164.
[15] Freud, *Civilization and its Discontents*, 1957, pp. 107-108.
[16] op cit, p. 108.
[17] Conze, *Buddhist Meditation*, 1965, pp. 37-38.
[18] Fromm, Suzuki & de Martino, *Zen Buddhism and Psychoanalysis*, pp. 80-81.
[19] Fromm, ibid.
[20] Fromm, Suzuki & de Martino, ibid., 1960, p. 86.
[21] Fromm, ibid., p. 72.
[22] Offer & Sabshin, *Normality*.
[23] Leighton, Clansen & Wilson, eds, *Explorations in Social Psychiatry*, 1957, p. 144, n. 5.
[24] See chapter four.
[25] Vajiranana Thera, *Buddhist Meditation*, 1962.
[26] Conze, ibid.
[27] S. II, 178.
[28] Kaccayana Thera, *Netti-pakaranam*, 1962, p. 170.
[29] Ananda Nimalasuriya, ed., *The Buddha as a Healer*, 1960, p. 23.
[30] Thompson, *An Outline of Psychoanalysis*, 1955, p. 436.
[31] S.E. Vol. XXIII, p. 250.
[32] Ananda Nimalasuriya, ibid., p. 21.
[33] MacIntyre, *The Unconscious*, 1962, p. 25.

CHAPTER SIX

[1] See Foreword to the present work.

[2] op cit, p. viii.

[3] Jahoda, *Current Concepts of Mental Health*, 1959, p. 13.

[4] *Gradual Sayings* II, 143.

[5] Freud, 'Analysis Terminable and Interminable', *The Standard Edition of the Complete Psychological Works of Sigmund Freud*, 1966, p. 216-53.

[6] Fromm, Suzuki & de Martino, *ibid.*, pp. 77-142.

[7] Freud, 'Studies in Hysteria', *The Standard Edition*, Vol. 2, p. 305.

[8] Freud, ibid., p. 250.

[9] op cit, p. 249.

[10] Storr, 'The Concept of Cure', *Psychoanalysis Observed*, 1966, p. 53.

[11] Freud, 'The Psychopathology of Everyday Life', *The Standard Edition*, Vol. 6, 278.

[12] MacIntyre, *The Unconscious*, p. 25.

[13] Freud, ibid., p. 35.

[14] Rycroft, 'Causes and Meaning', *Psychoanalysis Observed*, 1966, p. 21.

[15] Freud, ibid., p. 224.

[16] op cit, p. 224.

[17] Wyss, *Depth Psychology: A Critical History*, 1966, p. 121.

[18] A more fruitful connection between Buddhism and Freudian analysis might begin with Freud's paper, 'On Narcissism: An Introduction', *The Standard Edition*, 14, 73-102, which is a great contribution. See my discussion of the Freudian notion of 'narcissism' in the light of the ego concept in early Buddhism, in de Silva, *Buddhism and Freudian Psychology*, Colombo, Sri Lanka, Lake House Investments, 1978, pp. 127-32. (The first edition of the present work.)

19 Fromm's 'Zen Buddhism and Psychoanalysis', David Levin's 'Approaches to Psychotherapy: Freud, Jung and Tibetan Buddhism', in Valle, ed. *The Metaphors of Consciousness*, 1981, pp. 243-274.

[20] Fromm, 'Zen Buddhism and Psychoanalysis', p. 91.

[21] op cit, p. 92.

[22] Fromm, *The Heart of Man*, 1964, p. 88.

[23] Fromm, 'Zen Buddhism and Psychoanalysis', pp. 80-81.

[24] op cit, p. 86.

[25] Fingarette, *Self-Deception*, 1969, p. 142.

[26] Freud, ibid., p. 240.

[27] Levin, 'Approaches to Psychotherapy', p. 225.
[28] Freud, 'Mourning and Melancholia', *The Standard Edition*, 14, pp. 243-258.
[29] Fromm, *The Heart of Man*, p. 72.
[30] Thouless, Foreword, *Buddhist and Freudian Psychology*.

APPENDIX I
[1] Reprinted from the *Ceylon Journal of the Humanities*.
[2] de Silva, 'An Analysis of Some Psychological Concepts in Early Buddhism and Freud', p. 5. Also see de Silva, 'A study of Motivational Theory in Early Buddhism with Special Reference to the Psychology of Freud,' 1967.
[3] Schopenhauer, *World as Will and Idea*, 1909, p. 371.
[4] Bikkhu Nanajivako has examined the similarities between the philosophy of Schopenhauer and Buddhism and demonstrates quite clearly the influence of Buddhism on Schopenhauer; See Bhikkhu Nanajivako, *Schopenhauer and Buddhism*, 1970.
[5] Freud, *The Standard Edition of the Complete Psychological Works of Sigmund Freud*, 24 Vols, Vol. 14, 1953, pp. 143-144.
[6] Rieff, *Freud: The Mind of the Moralist*, 1961, p. 54.
[7] Gardiner, *Schopenhauer*, 1963, p. 176.
[8] The chart summarises the basic points of resemblance only with reference to the nature of instincts. As this inquiry is basically focused on this problem other possible subjects for comparative examination (e.g. the nature of religion) will not be discussed here.
[9] S.E. Vol. 17, p. 137.
[10] Jones, *The Life and Work of Sigmund Freud*, 3 vols. vol. 3, 1963, p. 273.
[11] S.E. Vol. 22, p. 73.
[12] Hartmann, *Essays on Ego, Psychology*, 1964, p. 274.
[13] de Silva, 'An Analysis of Some Psychological Concepts in Early Buddhism and Freud,' 1966.
[14] Nyanatiloka Thera, *Buddhist Dictionary*, 1956, p. 68.
[15] M. 232-233.
[16] de Silva, 'A Study of Motivational Theory in Early Buddhism with Special Reference to the Psychology of Freud,' 1967.
[17] Schopenhauer, ibid., p. 402.

[18] op cit.
[19] Mann, *Schopenhauer*, 1939, p. 10.
[20] Rieff, ibid., p. 32.
[21] ibid., p. 35.
[22] Gardiner, ibid., p. 266.
[23] Schopenhauer, ibid., p. 427.
[24] Gardiner, ibid., p. 264.
[25] Schopenhauer, ibid., p. 428.
[26] op cit.
[27] Schopenhauer, Vol. 3, p. 339.
[28] op cit, p. 380.
[29] op cit, p. 313.
[30] op cit, p. 339.
[31] Schopenhauer, Vol. 1, p. 141.
[32] op cit, p. 429.
[33] op cit, p. 515.
[34] op cit.
[35] op cit.
[36] Schopenhauer, Vol. 2, p. 328.
[37] op cit, p. 327
[38] op cit, p. 328.
[39] Gardiner, ibid., pp. 176-177.
[40] Bhikkhu Nanajivako, *Schopenhauer and Buddhism*, 1970.
[41] S.E. Vol. 20, pp. 59-60. Freud says that Nietzche is another philosopher whose ideas had some resemblance to his psychology: precisely for this reason, Freud claims that he refrained from reading Nietzche.
[42] Whyte, *The Unconscious Before Freud*, 1962, p. 157.
[43] S.E. Vol. 14, p. 15.
[44] ibid., p. 16.
[45] S.E. Vol. 17, pp. 143-144.
[46] ibid., emphasis mine.
[47] S.E. Vol. 20, p. 59.
[87] S.E. Vol. 18, p. 50; also cf. p. 101.
[49] ibid., pp. 49-50.
[50] ibid., p. 56.
[51] Rieff, ibid., p. 376.

[52] Jones, ibid., Vol. 3, p. 20.
[53] S.E. Vol. 19, p. 160.
[54] Flugel, *Studies in Feeling and Desire*, 1955, pp. 96-97.
[55] S.E. Vol. 19, pp. 157-158, n. 2.
[56] Schopenhauer, Vol. 1, p. 355.
[57] Jung, *Collected Works*, 1958, p. 481.
[58] Walker Puner, *Freud*, 1949, p. 162. The word 'Freud' within parenthesis has been inserted by the author.
[59] Peters, ed. *Brett's History of Psychology*, 1962, p. 717.

APPENDIX II

[1] Henderson, 'Ancient Myths and Modern Man,' in *Man and His Symbols*, 1964, p. 107.
[2] See pp. 1-29.
[3] Kiev ed., *Magic, Faith and Healing*, 1964.
[4] Halverson, 'Dynamics of Exorcism: The Sinhalese Sanniyakuma', *History of Religions*, Vol. 10, pp. 358-359.
[5] Amerasinghe, *Laughter as Cure: Joking and Exorcism in a Sinhalese Curing Ritual*, 1973.
[6] Thambiah, *Buddhism and the Spirit Cults in North-East Thailand*, 1970, pp. 327-337.
[7] *Dialogues of the Buddha*, Part III, pp. 185-187.
[8] Amerasinghe, ibid.
[9] op cit.
[10] op cit.
[11] Henderson, 'ibid., p. 107.
[12] Fordham, *An Introduction to Jung's Psychology*, 1954, p. 23.
[13] Amerasinghe, ibid., p. 35.
[14] Sarachchandra, *The Folk Drama of Ceylon*, 968, p. 2.
[15] Amerasinghe, ibid.
[16] Obeyesekera, 'The Ritual Drama of the Sanni Demons', *Comparative Studies in Sociology and History*, 1969.
[17] English & English, *A Comprehensive Dictionary of Psychoanalytical and Psychological Terms*, 1958.
[18] Waxler, 'Culture and Mental Illness: A Social Labelling Perspective', *Journal of Nervous and Mental Disease*, 1974, Vol. 159, pp. 379-395.

[19] *Dhammapada*, 165.
[20] Freud, 'Obsessive Actions and Religious Practices', *Complete Works of Freud*.
[21] Havens, 'Dynamics of Confession', *Wijesekera Felicitation Volume*, 1970, pp. 20-27.
[22] See p. 4.
[23] Personal notes from the *Unpublished Letters of Ven. Nanavira*.
[24] op cit.
[25] Wickramasinghe, *Aspects of Sinhalese Culture*, 1973, pp. 38-41.
[26] op cit.
[27] Amerasinghe, ibid., p. 349.
[28] op cit.

BIBLIOGRAPHY

PRIMARY SOURCES

PĀLI TEXTS AND TRANSLATIONS ON BUDDHISM

Anguttara Nikāya, ed. H. Morris and H. Hardy. Vols. I-V. P.T.S. London, 1932-1936.

Gradual Sayings (trans.), Vols. I, II and V. translated by Woodward; Vols. III and IV translated by E. H. Hare, 1932-1936.

Buddhist Psychological Ethics, (trans of *Dhammasangani*), translated and edited by Rhys Davids, London, 1900.

Dhammapada, Pāli text and translation, P.T.S. London, edited and translated by Mrs. Rhys Davids, 1931.

Dīgha Nikāya, ed. T. W. Rhys Davids and J. Estlin Carpenter, vols. I, II and III, P.T.S. London, 1908-1911.

Dialogues of the Buddha, Part I translated by T. W. Rhys Davids; Part II and III translated by T. W. and C. A. F. Rhys Davids, P.T.S. London, 1956-1957.

The Expositor, (trans, of *Atthasālini*), two volumes, translated by Mrs. Rhys Davids, 1920-1921.

Itivuttaka, ed. E. Windisch. P.T.S. London, 1889.

As It Was Said, (trans.) Woodward, London, 1888-1889.

Majjhima-Nikāya, vols. I, II and III., ed. V. Trenkner and R. Chalmers. P.T.S. London, 1948-51.

Middle Length Sayings, (trans.) vol. I, II and III, translated by I. B. Horner. P.T.S. London, 1954-1959.

Saṃyutta Nikāya, vol. 1-4., ed. L. Freer. P.T.S. London, 1884-1898.

Kindred Sayings, (trans.) Part I and II, translated by Mrs. Rhys Davids. Part III, IV and V translated by Woodward, 1917-1956.

The Path of Purification, (trans. of *Visuddhimagga*). Translated by Nanamoli. Ceylon, 1964.

The Questions of King Milinda, (trans. of *Milinda Pañha*), S.B.E. Vol. XXXV and XXXVI, translated by Mrs. Rhys Davids, Oxford, 1980.

WORKS BY SIGMUND FREUD

The standard edition of the complete psychological works of Sigmund Freud, translated from German under the general editorship of James Strachey, Hogarth Press, London, 1953.

Vol. 1. *Pre-Analytic publications and unpublished drafts.*

Vol. 2. *Studies on Hysteria*, J. Breuer and S. Freud.

Vol. 3. *Early Psycho-Analytic publication.*

Vol. 4. *The Interpretation of Dreams (Part I).*

Vol. 5. ibid., (Part II).

Vol. 6. *The Psychopathology of Every Day Life.*

Vol. 7. *A Case of Hysteria: Three Essays on Sexuality and Other Works.*

Vol. 8. *Jokes and Their Relation to the Unconscious.*

Vol. 9. *Jensen's 'Grandiva' and other works.*

Vol. 10. *Two Case Histories (Little Hans and The Rat Man).*

Vol. 11. *Five Lectures on Psycho-Analysis: Leonardo da Vinci, and other works.*

Vol. 12. *The Case of Schrober, papers on technique and other works.*

Vol. 13. *Totem and Taboo and other works.*

Vol. 14. *On the history of the psycho-analytic movement.*

Vol. 15. *Introductory lectures on Psycho-Analysis, I.*

Vol. 16. ibid. II.

Vol. 17. *An Infantile Neurosis and other works.*

Vol. 18. *Beyond the Pleasure Principle. Group psychology and other works.*

Vol. 19. *The Ego and the Id and other works.*

Vol. 20. *An Autobiographical Study: Inhibition, symptoms and anxiety, the question of lay analysis and other works.*

Vol. 21. *The Future of an Illusion, Civilization and its Discontents, other works.*

Vol. 22. *New Introductory lectures and other works.*

Vol. 23. *Moses and Monotheism, outline of psycho-analysis and other works.*

SECONDARY SOURCES

WORKS ON BUDDHISM

Anaruddha, *Compendium of Philosophy* (Adhidhammattha-Sangaha), translated by S.Z. Aung and edited by Mrs. Rhys Davids, P.T.S. London, 1963.

Chandravimala Thera. *Cittopakleśa Dīpani* (An Analysis of the Defilers

of the Mind), a work in Sinhalese, Anula Printers, Ceylon, 1961.
Conze, E., *Buddhist Thought in India*, Allen and Unwin, 1962.
Conze, E., *Buddhist Meditation*, Allen and Unwin, London, 1956.
Jayatilleke, K.N., *Buddhism and Peace*, Wheel Publication, Kandy, Ceylon, 1962.
Jayatilleke, K.N., *Buddhism and Science*, Wheel Publication, Kandy, Ceylon, 1958.
Jayatilleke, K.N., *Early Buddhist Theory of Knowledge*, Allen and Unwin, London, 1963.
Jayatilleke, K.N. 'Some Problems of Translation', *Ceylon University Review*, Vol. 7 and 8.
Jayatilleke, K.N. *Survival and Karma*, Wheel Publications, Kandy, 1969.
Jayasuriya, W.F. *The Psychology and Philosophy of Buddhism*, Y.M.B.A. Press, Colombo, Ceylon, 1963.
Nanamoli Thera, *Loving Kindness* (Metta), Wheel Publication, Kandy, Ceylon.
Nanamoli Thera, *Three Cardinal Discourses of the Buddha*, Wheel Publication, Kandy, Ceylon, 1960.
Nimalasuriya, Ananda, ed., *The Buddha as a Healer*, Wheel Publication, Kandy, Ceylon, 1960.
Nyanaponika Thera, *Anatta and Nibbana*, Wheel Publication, Kandy, Ceylon, 1959.
Nyanaponika Thera, *Buddhist Dictionary: Manual of Terms and Doctrines*, Fewin, Columbo, 1956.
Nyanatiloka Thera, *Guide Through the Abhidhammapitaka*, revised edition Nyanaponika Thera, *Bauddha Sahitya Sabha*, Colombo, Ceylon, 1957.
Rhys Davids, C.A.F., *Buddhist Psychology*, London, 1924.
Sarachchandra, E.R., *Buddhist Psychology of Perception*, Ceylon University Press, Colombo, Ceylon, 1958.
Sayadaw, Ledi, *The Manual of Insight*, Wheel Publication, Kandy, Ceylon, 1961.
Smart, Ninian, *Doctrine and Argument in Indian Philosophy*, Allen and Unwin, 1964.
Soma Thera, *Kalama Sutta*, Wheel Publication, Kandy, Ceylon, 1959.
Suzuki, D.T., *Studies in the Lankāvatāra Sutra*, G. Routledge and Sons Ltd., London, 1930.
Tachibana, S., *Ethics of Buddhism*, London, 1926.

Vajiranana Thera, P., *Buddhist Meditation*, M.D. Gunasena and Co. Ltd., Colombo, 1962.
Wijesekera, O.H. 'The Concept of Vinnana in Theravada Buddhism,' *Journal of the American Oriental Society*, 1964.
Wijesekera, O.H. *The Three Signata*, Wheel Publication, Ceylon, 1960.

WORKS ON FREUD AND PSYCHOANALYSIS

Ames, Roger T., Dissanayake, Wimal., Kasulis, Thomas P. eds. *Self as Person in Asian Theory and Practice*, State University of New York Press, Albany, 1994.
Aronson, Harvey. *Buddhist Practice on Western Grounds; Reconciling Eastern Ideals and Western Psychology*, Shambhala, Boston, 2004.
Atkinson, J.W. *An Introduction to Motivation*, Princeton, Van Nostrand, 1964.
Badget, Richard, ed. *Subconscious Phenomena*, Gotham Press, Boston, 1910.
Bien, Thomas. *Mindful Therapy*, Wisdom Publishers, Boston, 2006.
Broad, C. D. *Mind and its Place in Nature*, K. Paul, Trench, Trubner and Co. Ltd., London, Harcourt, Brace and Company, New York, 1929.
Claxton, Guy. *Beyond Therapy: The Impact of Eastern Religions on Psychological Theory and Practice*, Unity Press, Woollahra, 1996.
Crane, Rebecca. *Mindfulness-Based Cognitive Therapy*, Routledge, New York, 2009.
de Silva, Padmasiri. 'The Buddha and Krishnamurti', in de Silva, Padmasiri. *Explorers of Inner Space: The Buddha, Krishnamurti and Kierkegaard*, Sarvodaya-Vishvalekha, Ratmalana, 2007.
de Silva, Padmasiri. 'Buddhism and the Tragic Sense of Life,' *University of Ceylon Review*, Vol 25, 1965.
de Silva, Padmasiri. 'Emotion Profiles: The Self and the Emotion of Pride', in Ames, Roger., Dissanayake, Wimal., Kasulis, Thomas eds. *Self As Person In Asian Theory and Practice*, State University of Newyork Press, Albany, 1994.
de Silva, Padmasiri. *An Analysis of some Psychological Concepts in Buddhism and Freud*, M.A. Thesis, Hawaii, 1965.
de Silva, Padmasiri. *An Introduction to Buddhist Psychology*, 4th edition, Macmillan-Palgrave, Hampshire and New York, 2005.

de Silva, Padmasiri. *An Introduction to Mindfulness-Based Counselling*, Sarvodaya Vishvalekha, Ratmalana, 2008.

de Silva, Padmasiri. *Twin Peaks: Compassion and Insight: Emotions and the Self in Buddhist and Western Thought*, Buddhist Research Society, Singapore, 1992.

Ekman, Paul. *Emotions Revealed*, Widenfeld and Nicolson, London, 2003.

Engler, Jack. 'Being Somebody and Being Nobody: A re-examination of the understanding of self in psychoanalysis and Buddhism', in Saffran, Jeremy ed. *Psychoanalysis and Buddhism: An Unfolding Dialogue*, Eisdom, Boston, 2003.

Engler, Jack. 'Promises and Perils of the Spiritual Path', Unno, Mark ed. *Buddhism and Psychotherapy: Across Cultures*, Wisdom Publications, Boston, 2006.

Epstein, Mark, *Thoughts Without a Thinker: Psychotherapy From A Buddhist Perspective*, Basic Books, New York, 1995.

Epstein, Mark. 'Psychotherapy Without the Self: A Buddhist Perspective,' Safran, Jeremy ed, *Psychoanalysis and Buddhism: An Unfolding Dialogue*, New Haven and London, 2007.

Epstein, Mark. *Going On Being*, Continuum, London & New York, 2001.

Epstein, Mark. *Going to Pieces Without Falling Apart*, Broadway Books, New York, 1998.

Epstein, Mark. *Psychotherapy without the Self: A Buddhist Perspective*, Yale University Press, New Haven, 2007.

Epstein, Mark. *Thoughts Without A Thinker: Psychotherapy From A Buddhist Perspective*, Basic Books, New York, 1995.

Fine, Reuben. *A Critical Re-Valuation of His Theories—Freud*, New York, 1962.

Flugel, G.C. *Studies in Feeling and Desire*, Duckworth, London, 1955.

Flugel, J.C. *Man, Morals and Society*, Pelican Books, London, 1955.

Fromm, Erich, *Psychoanalysis and Religion*, Yale University Press, New Haven, 1961.

Fromm, Erich, Suzuki D, Martino, R.D. *Zen Buddhism and Psychoanalysis*, Harper, New York, 1960.

Fromm, Erich. *Art of Loving*, Unwin Books, London, 1962.

Fromm, Erich. *Beyond the Chains of Illusion, My Encounter with Marx and Freud*, Simon and Schuster, New York, 1962.

Fromm, Erich. *The Art of Being*, Continuum, New York, 1992.

Fromm, Erich. *The Art of Listening*, Constable, London, 1994.

Fromm, Erich. *The Heart of Man*, New York 1964.

Fromm, Erich. *To Have Or To Be?* Abacus, London, 2001.

Germer, Christopher Kiegel., Ronald D, Fulton, Paul, R. eds. *Mindfulness and Psychotherapy*, Guildford Press, London, New York, 2005.

Goldstein, Joseph. *Insight Meditation: The Practice of Freedom*, Shambhala, Boston, 1993.

Goleman, Daniel, ed. *Destructive Emotions: How Can We Overcome Them?* Bantam Dell, New York, 2003.

Goleman, Daniel, ed. *Healing Emotions*, Shambhala, Boston, London, 2004.

Greenspan, Miriam. *Healing Through Dark Emotions*, Shambhala, Boston, London, 2003.

Gunaratana, Bhante, Henepola. *Eight Mindful Steps to Happiness*, Wisdom, Boston, 2001.

Hayes, Steven C., Strosahl, Wilson., Kelly G. *Acceptance and Commitment Therapy*, Guilford Press, New York, 1999.

Hook, Sidney. ed. *Psychoanalysis, Scientific Method and Philosophy*, University Press, New York, 1959.

Jahoda, *Current Concepts of Mental Health*, New York, 1959.

James, William. *Principles of Psychology*, Dover Publications, New York, 1918.

Johanson, Rune. 'Defense Mechanisms According to Psychoanalysis and the Pali Nikayas,' in, Katz, Nathan, ed. *Buddhist and Western Psychology*, Prajna Press, Boulder, 1983.

Jones, Ernest. *The Life and Work of Sigmund Freud. Three volumes*, London, Hogarth Press; Basic Books, New York, 1953-1957.

Jung, Carl. *Two Essays in Analytic Psychology*, Meridian Books, New York, 1965.

Kabat-Zinn, Jon. *Coming To Our Senses: Healing Ourselves and the World Through Mindfulness*, Hyperion, New York, 2003.

Kabat-Zinn, Jon. *Full Catastrophe Living: Using the Wisdom of Your Body and Mind to Face Stress, Pain and Illness*, Dell, New York, 1990.

Kenny, A. *Action, Emotion and Will*, London, 1963.

Krishnamurti, J. *Reflections on the Self*, ed. Martin, Raymond, Open Court, Chicago, 1997.

Kumar, Sameet. *Grieving Mindfully*, Oakland, Ca, 2005.

Kwee, Maurits G.T. Gergen, Kenneth, J. Koshikawa eds. *Horizons in Buddhist Psychology: Practice, Research and Theory*, Taos Institute Publication, Ohio, 2006.

Ladner, Lorne, *The Lost Art of Compassion*, Harper Collins, New York, 2006.

Ledoux, Joseph. *The Emotional Brain*, Widenfeld and Nicholson, London, 1988.

Leighton, Alexander H. Clausen John A. and Wilson, Robert N. *Explorations in Social Psychiatry*, Tavistock Publication, London, 1957.

Levine, Michael, P. 2000, *The Analytic Freud: Philosophy and Psychoanalysis*, Routledge, London, 2000 (One of the best studies on Freud in the tradition of analytic philosophy, going beyond the early writings of Alasdair McIntyre on the unconscious and R.S. Peters on motivation).

Levitt, Morton, ed. *Readings in Psychoanalytic Psychology*, Appleton-Century-Crofts, New York, 1959.

Lutz, Catherine. 'Need, Nurturance and Emotions on a Pacific Atoll', In Marks, Joel and Ames Roger T. eds. *Emotions in Asian Though*t, State University of New York, Albany, 1995.

Maclntyre, A.C. *The Unconscious: A Conceptual Analysis*, Routledge and Kegan Paul, London; Humanities Press, New York, 1958.

Manstead, Anthony, S.R., Frijda, Nico., Fischer, Agneta, eds. *Feelings and Emotions: The Amsterdam Symposium*, Cambridge University Press, Cambridge, 2004.

Martin, Raymond. *Self-Concern*, Cambridge Studies in Philosophy, Cambridge, 1988.

Miller, J.G. *Unconsciousness*, J. Wiley and Sons, New York, 1942.

Nyanaponika Thera. *The Heart of Buddhist Meditation*, Rider, London, 1975.

Oatley, Keith. *Emotions: A Brief History*, Blackwell, Malden, Ma, 2004.

Offer, Daniel, Sabshin, Melvin, *Normality*, Basic Books, New York, 1966.

Panditha, Sayadaw U. *In This Very Life*, Wisdom, Boston, 1993.

Peters, R.S. *The Concept of Motivation*, Routledge and Kegan Paul, London; Humanities Press, New York, 1958.

Pickering, John. *The Authority of Experience: Essays on Buddhism and Psychology*, Curzon, Richmond, Surrey, 1997.

Raymond, M. *On Krishnamurti*, Thomson-Wadsworth, Melbourne, 2003.

Reik, Theodore. *Masochism in Modern Man*, New York, 1941.
Reik, Theodore. *Of Love and Lust*, Grove Press, New York, 1959.
Rickman, ed. *A General Selection from the Works of Sigmund Freud*, Hogarth Press, London, 1953.
Rieff, *Freud: The Mind of the Moralist*, Viking Press, New York, 1959.
Rorty, Amelie, Oksenberg. 'The Coordination of the Self and the Passions', in Ames, Roger, Dissanayake, Kasulis, eds. *Self As Person in Asian Theory and Practice*, State University of New York Press, Albany, 1994.
Roubiczek, Paul. *Thinking in Opposites*, Kegan Paul, London, 1952.
Rubin, J. *Psychoanalytic and the Buddhist Conceptions of Self*, Plenum Press, New York, 1996.
Siegel, Daniel J. *The Mindful Brain : Reflection and Attunement in the Cultivation of Well-Being*, W.W.Norton & Co, New York, 2007.
Suttie, I.D. *Origins of Love and Hate*, Kegan Paul, London, 1953.
Taylor, Gabriele. *Dynamic and Abnormal Psychology*, American Book Company, New York, 1954.
Taylor, Gabriele. *Pride, Shame and Guilt: Emotions of Self-Assessment*, Clarendon Press, Oxford, 1985.
The Dalai Lama and Ekman, Paul. *A Conversation on Emotional Awareness*, Henry Holt Company, New York, 2008.
Unamuno, Miguel de. *The Tragic Sense of Life*, Dover, United States, 1921.
Unno, Mark, ed. *Buddhism and Psychoanalysis: Across Cultures*, Wisdom Publications, Boston, 2006.
Williams, Mark. Teasdale, John., Segal, Zindel., Kabbat-Zinn. *The Mindful Way Through Depression*, Guilford Press, New York, London, 2007.
Wyss, *Depth Psychology: A Critical History*, Allen & Unwin, London, 1966.

INDEX

abbocchinna, 54–55
alayavijnana, 65–68
anusaya, xxiii, 56–61
anxiety, 117–118
alienation, 165
Asampajana, 56
asceticism, 156–158
Aung, S.Z., 52–53

Beck L.W., 48, 72
bhavanga theory, 41, 49–53
bhava-taṇhā, see craving
Broad, C.D., 11, 47–48

Chandavimala, R., 33, 62–64
Conze, E., 61, 65, 163–4
consciousness (*viññāṇa*), 6–7, 9–15
  stream of, 11, 14, 54–56
conscious, the, 22–24
craving (*taṇhā*), 20–21, 57–59, 79–81
  for self-annihilation (*vibhavana-taṇhā*), 139-152.
  for self-preservation (*bhava-taṇhā*), 119-132, 140–41, 191–92
  for sense gratification (*kama-taṇhā*), 95-110.

death instinct, 133–140, 149–151, 200–03
desire in disguise (*vañchaka dhamma*), 62–64
directed disposition (*saṅkhāra*), 6–7, 15–18, 56–57, 71–73
dreams, 35–39, 70–71

ego, 27–28, 59–60, 110-119
Epstein, M., xxiii–xxvi, xxxii
feeling (*vedanā*), 18–20
Fine, R., 152
Flugel, J.C., 7, 18, 20, 133, 137, 149, 154, 201
Fromm, E., 2–4, 68, 104, 111, 118, 125, 154, 163, 164, 180–86

guilt, xii, 159–163, 215

Hartmann, H., xi, 23, 189
hiri-ottappa, 158–60, 215
Horner, I.B., 11–12, 15, 62
humanism, 1–3

id, 23–28, 62
inferiority complex, 60, 125, 192
instincts, 24–28, 77–79, 108–09, 136–38, 187–92

Jahoda, M., 174
Jayasuriya, W.F., 21, 30, 61
Jayatilleke, K.N., 8, 12, 50, 54–56, 80
Jones, E., 32, 35, 83, 131, 137, 194, 201
Jung, C., 25, 65, 202–09, 217–18

kāma-taṇhā, see craving

Levin, D., 180, 184
libido, 82–92, 107–110, 114–18

love, 63, 83–86, 91–94, 103–106, 117

MacIntyre, A.C., 3, 45–47, 172, 177
meditation, 54–55, 163, 167–69
Miller, J.G., 42–44, 72
motivation, 20–21, 76–82
theory of, 1, 9, 14–15, 23, 29–33
unconscious, 45–49, 51–56, 192–93

nāma-rūpa, 5–10
narcissism, 94, 111–119, 127–132, 181
Nyanamoli, 53, 151
Nyanaponika, xxiii, 120, 121
Nyanatiloka, 15, 16, 53, 97

Oedipus-complex, 80, 90–91, 104–5

Pap, A., 45.
paṭicca-samuppāda, 5–7, 79
Paṭṭhāna, 5–6, 79–82
perception (*saññā*), 6–7, 13–15, 21–22
Peters, R.S., 26, 35, 77, 203
preconscious, 2211, 14, 54–56
24, 189

Rahula, W., 66
Rapaport, D., 77, 78
Reik, T., 92, 104, 129–30
Rhys Davids, Mrs., xi, 18, 21, 62, 141, 158
Rieff, P., 28, 31–32, 74, 93–94, 176, 195, 201
rites and rituals, 156, 215
Roubiczek, P., 144
Rycroft, C., 178

saṅkhāra, see directed disposition
saññā, see perception
Sarachchandra, 9, 11–13, 41, 49–54, 67, 70
Sayadaw, L., 60
Schopenhauer, xi, 93, 108, 151, 181–203
sexuality, 82–84, 86–94, 198–203
Smart, N., 65
Storr, A., 176
super-ego, 23–24, 110, 161–163
Suttie, I.D., 92, 104
Suzuki, D.T., xxiii, 68

therapy, 31, 74–75, 152, 166–86
cognitive behavioural, xxviii, xxxi
mindfulness-based, xxiv, xxx, xxxii

Unamuno, M., 121
unconscious, 23–27
collective unconscious, 25, 65, 208–09
early Buddhist concept of, 8–9, 49–75, 194
Freudian concept of, 34–49, 169–172, 189

vañchaka dhamma, see desire
viññāṇa, see consciousness
viññāṇa-sota, see stream of consciousness
vedanā, see feeling
vibhava-taṇhā, see craving

Wijesekera, O.H., 10–11, 14, 107
Whyte L.L., 196

ABOUT THE AUTHOR

Dr. M.W. Padmasiri de Silva is currently an Adjunct Research Associate in the Centre for Studies in Religion, School of Historical Studies, at Monash University in Victoria, Australia. He received his BA (hons.) in philosophy in Ceylon and his MA and PhD in East-West Comparative Philosophy at the University of Hawaii. Dr. de Silva also completed a Diploma and Advanced Diploma in Buddhist Psychotherapy at Sophia College in Perth and practised as a counsellor and therapist at Springvale Community Centre from 2004 to 2007. He is currently affiliate member of CAPAV.

Prior to taking up his position at Monash University, Dr. de Silva held the positions of Professor and Head, Philosophy and Psychology Department, University of Peradeniya, Sri Lanka (1980-89); Visiting Fulbright Professor, University of Pittsburgh and ISLE Program, USA; Senior Teaching Fellow, NUS Singapore; Visiting Lecturer, University of Waikato, New Zealand and Coordinator IRC 'Environmental Education Program' in Singapore.

Dr. de Silva was awarded the best East-West Centre student in Hawaii, the UNESCO Grant for Environmental Ethics, the Asia Foundation Award for Research, and the Fulbright Award for teaching. He was also nominated for the Greenleaf Award.

His publications include *An Introduction to Buddhist Psychology*, 4th edition, Macmillan-Palgrave, Hampshire & New York, 2005; *Buddhist and Freudian Psychology*, NUS Press, Singapore, 1992; *Buddhism, Ethics & Society*, Monash University, 1992; *Twin Peaks: Compassion & Insight*, Singapore Research Society, 1992; *Explorers of Inner Space*, Sarvodaya Vishvalekha, 2007; and *An Introduction to Mindfulness-Based Counselling*, Sarvodaya Vishvalekha, 2008. He also has fifty published papers in anthologies and journals.

Dr. de Silva's most recent presentations and articles include 'Buddhist Resources for Managing Addiction', and keynote address, 'New Vistas for M.B.C.T: Emotion-Focused Therapy in Buddhism' at the 2nd Asian Cognitive Therapy Conference in Thailand, Oct 2008. 'De-pathologising Negative Emotions', at the Buddhism and Psychotherapy Conference at E-Vam Institute, Healesville, Australia, Oct 2009 (forthcoming). 'Theravada Buddhist Tradition in Sri Lanka & Thailand: Philosophical Foundations, Social Activism, Contemplative Buddhism and Issues of Human Well-Being', in Routledge History of Indian Philosophy, ed. Purushottama Billimoria (forthcoming); and a panel on 'Strangers in a Strange Land' and 'Ecology in South-eastern Asia' at the Parliament of World Religions, Melbourne, Dec 2009 (forthcoming).